?

Whatever Happened to

SHERLOCK HOLMES

*Detective Fiction, Popular
Theology, and Society*

Robert S. Paul

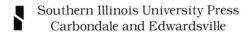

Southern Illinois University Press
Carbondale and Edwardsville

Library of Congress Cataloging-in-Publication Data

Paul, Robert S.

Whatever happened to Sherlock Holmes? detective fiction, popular theology, and society / Robert S. Paul.

p. cm.

Includes bibliographical references and index.

1. Detective and mystery stories, English—History and criticism.
2. Detective and mystery stories, American—History and criticism.
3. Christianity and literature. 4. Literature and society.
5. Theology in literature. I. Title.

PR830.D4P38 1991

823'.087209—dc20 90-23719

ISBN 0-8093-1722-2 CIP

The paper used in this publication meets the minimum requirements of American National Standard for Information Sciences —Permanence of Paper for Printed Library Materials, ANSI Z39.48-1984. ∞

To *Eunice Mary Paul*

who introduced me to the subject

and

Erik Reginald Routley

who pioneered the way

There is no need to bore ourselves with this rubbish.

—Edmund Wilson, "Who Cares Who Killed Roger Ackroyd," in
*Classics and Commercials: A Literary Chronicle of the
Forties.*

*The real connoisseurs, who avowedly prefer this type of fic-
tion to all others, and who read it with close and critical attention, are to be found among men of the definitely
intellectual class: theologians, scholars, lawyers, and to a
less extent, perhaps, doctors and men of science. Judging
by the letters, which I have received from time to time, the
enthusiast* par excellence *is the clergyman of a studious and
scholarly habit.*

—R. Austin Freeman, "The Art of the Detective Story"

The detective-story is the normal recreation of noble minds.

—Philip Guedalla, quoted approvingly by Dorothy L. Sayers

*The most curious fact about the detective story is that it
makes its greatest appeal to those classes of people who are
most immune to other forms of daydream literature. The typical detective story addict is a doctor or clergyman or scientist or artist, i.e. a fairly successful professional man with
intellectual interests and well-read in his own field, who
could never stomach the* Saturday Evening Post *or* True Confessions *or movie magazines or comics.*

—W. H. Auden, "The Guilty Vicarage," in *The Dyer's Hand
and Other Essays*

*The detective story reader is not a lover of violence but a
lover of order.*

—Erik R. Routley, in *The Puritan Pleasures of the Detective
Story*

Detective fiction . . . becomes the mirror of society.
—Robin W. Winks, in *Detective Fiction*

Contents

Preface

This preface has but one necessary, though pleasurable, purpose—to express thanks to those whose work and interest have made the appearance of this book possible.

My thanks are due to former colleagues in Austin, Texas; to my secretary, Mrs. Dorothy Andrews, who translated my original manuscript into legible form, and to Professor Prescott Williams, Jr., who not only kept me informed about recent articles on the subject in America but who also agreed to give the manuscript the benefit of his editing expertise.

But my deepest thanks must go to three special people with whom the project has been especially associated. My wife has already received a merited accolade in my dedication, but so much more is due to her, because she, with help from my daughter, Lydia (Mrs. Dean Tapley), transferred the text to our current word processor. What they have given to me in inspiration, encouragement, and practical help, only they and I could know. Special gratitude is also due to an old friend, Alison Bond, who volunteered to handle the manuscript, and who sustained my own faith in the work when the prospect of publication seemed very remote. To them all and many more, I offer heartfelt thanks.

I have tried to acknowledge wherever I have consciously used the work of others, but if I have committed any sins of omission in that respect, I hope the subject itself and the seriousness of our purpose will make amends.

Whatever Happened to Sherlock Holmes?

Introduction

The "Wrights" and "Wrongs" of Detective Fiction

I

Writing this in Texas with the mercury hovering around one hundred degrees on the weekend before July 4, one is reminded of all the enthusiastic sun worshippers who are busy packing their bags for vacations in Colorado or elsewhere—a seasonal exodus to points north and east or west, but, for me, if the budget would allow, certainly north.

And into those bags will go the holiday reading, which, despite the patriotic flavor of the season, is more likely to deal with the careers of Travis McGee or Archie Goodwin than that of George Washington, and is less likely to be written by one of the great names in English letters than by a favorite detective-story writer.

That is where we have to start, with the immense popularity of the detective story since Edgar Allan Poe sired the popular genre in 1841, and particularly since World War I. In 1963, for example, Margery Allingham guessed that mystery fiction accounted for something like 60 percent of all the books borrowed from British public libraries,[1] and although I know of no way of verifying that figure, I see little reason to question it or suggest that the percentage would be very different in the United States or anywhere in the Western world. It is this unprecedented popularity that forces us to consider the "Wright" and "Wrong" of detective fiction.

More precisely, consider the work of E. M. Wrong, who in 1926 wrote "the earliest attempt at a purposive historical and analytical survey and summation of the medium."[2] And there was Willard Huntington Wright (known to aficionados by his pseudonym, "S.S. Van Dine"), who followed a year later with his perceptive introduction to *The Great Detective Stories.*[3] The work of these two men simply underscores the point that by the 1920s, detective fiction was attracting not only amazing popularity but also intelligent appraisal and critical review.[4]

The reader may be tempted to ask rudely, "Who cares?" for in any field of academic endeavor the layperson "often finds the higher criticism wearisome";[5] but for all their seemingly esoteric erudition and pedantry, critics do occasionally unearth facts that the general public cannot afford to ignore. I maintain that this is true in the present case, for it is out of this unwonted popularity and critical appraisal that our own detective enterprise arises: *apologia pro libro meo.*

By the end of World War II, a curious fact had emerged. It was expressed very pointedly by Harrison R. Steeves, a distinguished professor emeritus of English at Columbia University. Despite detective fiction's preoccupation with crime of the most gruesome and absolute sort—murder—it was the most law-abiding and consciously moral segment of the population that had become most clearly addicted.[6] As Professor Steeves observed, "Such stories have had good readers. We are told that bishops and Supreme Court justices have shared the weakness for them. That doesn't sanctify the weakness or give it more than a fictitious dignity, but it helps to make it critically intelligible."[7]

But one was still left with a question that begged to be answered. Dr. Steeves asked that pertinent question, "Why do you and I read these things?"[8] While confessing that he read detective stories, he even admitted that he enjoyed reading good ones and countered the charge that it was an idle waste of time on the ground that some hours in our lives ought to be wasted. "I am intellectually interested, however, in my tolerance," he went on to say. "And I should like to account for it in some reasonable way, and with a less glib explanation than 'escape,' which explains nothing."[9]

But the answers he and others have given remain singularly unconvincing. It is not sufficient to suggest that people like the serious Roman Catholic churchman Msgr. Ronald Knox, the Reformed theologian Karl Barth, the biblical scholars James Moffatt and H. Wheeler Robinson (one Presbyterian and the other Baptist), essentially serious-minded statesmen like Abraham Lincoln and Woodrow Wilson, or the agnostic philosopher Bertrand Russell became involved with detective stories simply when their minds were unable or unwilling to grapple with more serious work.

What is even more to the point, this answer does not begin to explain why millions of academically trained, intellectually inclined, and professionally engaged people (Protestant, Catholic, and Jewish, besides many other kinds of believers or skeptics known only to God and the Census Bureau) have sent the sales of authors like S. S. Van Dine, Dorothy L. Sayers, Agatha Christie, Erle Stanley Gardner, Ellery Queen, Rex Stout, and many others into the stratosphere.

There are other things that Professor Steeves suggested with which I cannot agree, such as his pronouncement that reading detective stories was a peculiarly masculine occupation or his opinion that even in the early 1940s the form was showing signs of decay. But although Professor Steeves found some support for those views at the time,[10] I cannot accept them, particularly because it was a passionate female devotee—my wife—who introduced me to this vice (if that is what it is) and what should be interpreted as "decay" is really a matter for debate.

So we are left with the issues raised earlier—the continued popularity of detective stories and the curious fact that in some of its forms this fiction exerts an inexplicable attraction for people we assume to have least interest in violent crime; so again we are forced to ask the question, Why do you and I—and so many of our most exemplary colleagues and relatively innocent neighbors—read these things? At least we can give the literary critic credit for raising such a provocative question.

II

We have to return constantly to the indisputable popularity of the detective story in the twentieth century and to the detective-story writer's vested interest in maintaining its popular appeal. So the epigraph page of a detective novel that appeared in 1980 bore a single quotation from the Apocalypse: "Blessed is he that readeth" (Rev. 1.3). Blessed indeed!—writers wish to sell as many of their books as possible.

Certainly the author of the novel in question, publicized as "America's 'Mr. Best-seller,' " had no cause to be ungrateful to the American reading public.[11] The detective-story writer naturally wishes to sell stories to all who can be persuaded to put up the price of a hardback or inveigled into picking up a paperback or, if all else fails, jockeyed into creating a run on the title at the local public library. That elementary fact of literary existence with its motivational cupidity has to be kept in the forefront of this study.

Yet it may be conceded that there are considerable differences in the motivation of writers—for example, as between a person whose tome is entitled "Sixteenth-century Cranial Artifacts" and the one who writes it up as "Yorick's Revenge—A Tale of Skullduggery" or, to make the point more specific, between the archaeological monographs of Sir Max Mallowan and the popular detective fiction written by his wife, Agatha Christie.

The subject matter of a book obviously has a great deal to do with the kind of readership and presumably the royalties a writer can expect. Choose a subject that intrigues people and perhaps many will read the book; choose one of esoteric interest and one can be sure they will not. Authors are sensitive about such matters. This popularity suggests that there must be something about detective fiction in our century that produces a sympathetic response within a significant part of the reading public.

Hang on to that simple fact because of the investigative enterprise in which I invite you to join—to ask why you and many people whom you respect continue to read detective fiction. In this, the extent of the genre's appeal represents a primary clue. Apparently it is traceable to something at a deeper level than the interest in crime itself or a sordid desire to wallow vicariously in sin and gore.

The fascination with the detective story held by intelligent and otherwise blameless people has always intrigued critics. Some enthusiasts have concentrated on the inner logic of the problem of "whodunit," its "puzzle" quality, and its possible function as a kind of latter-day riddle. R. Austin Freeman described it in 1924 as "an argument conducted under the guise of fiction," while Willard Huntington Wright in 1927 actually declared that it is not fiction in the ordinary sense but "belongs rather in the category of riddles."[12]

Let us admit that at least for the "classic" form that became popular in Britain in the first half of this century—which Haycraft called *genus Brittannicum*[13] —the puzzle element is very important. Reasoning is at its center, and no doubt the challenge of joining wits with the author on an intellectual problem does provide some of the attraction for serious-minded readers.

But if that were all, the need would be more easily met, without all the attendant violence and criminality, by books of logic or crossword puzzles. Why is it that, despite the availability of puzzle books, many readers, who are pillars of respectability and morality, still turn to the detective story?

We might approach the answer by reflecting on what was written about the popular literature of a very different age: "The written word not only influences popular opinion but reflects it as well."[14] We are concerned with this latter aspect of detective fiction—with what it tells us as it becomes, in the phrase of critic and historian Robin Winks, "the mirror of society."[15]

This must be true for all writing aimed at entertainment: it *must* largely reflect public opinion. A popular novelist, newspaper cartoonist, or comedian may occasionally satirize the prevailing culture—although I am convinced that satire holds little attraction for the majority of Americans (apart from those addicted to Mark Russell)—but even the satirist will be advised not to attack too many issues which the public reveres. Persist, and the royalties will disappear and the contracts abort.

The wider the appeal, the broader and more general the presuppositions about society reflected in the book will have to be. A prophetic novel may occasionally express genius, flout the rules, and create its own following, but detective fiction does not claim to fall into that prophetic category: as Edmund Crispin remarked, "Detective stories are not concerned to preach. Their first and foremost aim is entertainment."[16]

It is the very innocence of this primary aim that makes them such significant testimonies to the prejudices and presuppositions of the society out of which they spring. When Conan Doyle set his stories in London at the turn of the century, he did not *intend* to present us with clues about the nature of English society at that time, but he did just that.

It is this significance that may have caused a later respected practitioner of the craft, Anthony Boucher, to describe such stories in Hamlet's words about the players as "the abstracts and brief chronicles of the time, ever valuable in retrospect as indirect but vivid pictures of the society from which they spring."[17] The late Erik Routley, who probably wrote more perceptively than any previous writer on the meaning of the detective story, was never more perceptive than when he quoted Ian Rodger on the epigraph page of his book: "Novelists are unpaid sociologists who make up for their lack of statistical evidence with inspired guesses."[18]

Belaboring the point? Perhaps, but here is a progression of logic for the armchair detective to follow, which will also provide us with a working hypothesis.

Detective novels reflect the society to which they are addressed, and in a way that the public must generally approve as a true picture of that society, its ethics, its values, and its basic rationality. But crime in its social context and the puzzle it presents force detective fiction, albeit in a relatively painless way, to reflect on such heavy assumptions as an ordered universe, the nature of truth, the difference between good and evil, right and wrong, and the importance of justice for a civilized society. All these ideas are ultimately grounded in theology, or in what serves as theology in a professedly secular society.

This theological connection will be something of which readers and almost all writers of the genre will be totally unaware. But in the necessity of presenting the story of a crime and its solution, the writer will have to presuppose a rational structure to our world, a world in which the laws of evidence allow the possibility of arriving at truth, in which a distinction between right and wrong is assumed, and where the attainment of justice becomes the warrant for the whole exercise.

That provides us with our working hypothesis: the writer of detective fiction, without conscious intent, appeals directly to those moral and spiritual roots of society unconsciously affirmed and endorsed by the readers. And because of his or her dependence on popular taste in order to sell books, the writer will be particularly sensitive to changes that occur in these basic attitudes of the public. If detective fiction, therefore, reveals radical changes in the theological presuppositions of society, it may help us to see the way society is going. That is the point to be argued, but before we do that, we ought to look briefly at this basic claim that detective fiction is forced to concern itself with the moral, and hence theological, basis of a society.

III

Gorky Park is a fascinating fictional account of detection in the pre-*perestroika* USSR.[19] As such, we could hardly expect it to reflect theology in any traditional sense of the term, but a reviewer of another book set in Moscow at the same period astutely observed that detective fiction is not about crime but "about setting things right, and about those special people who feel they should and can set them right."[20] Precisely. A little reflection should convince us that in order to do that, one has to have a clear conviction of the distinction between right and wrong and believe that it matters. One would also have to have some deeply rooted convictions about how rightness and wrongness in society are to be determined, and of the laws or principles that govern acceptable and unacceptable conduct in that regard. Martin Cruz Smith's Russian detective, Arkady Renko, has intensely personal principles that bring him into conflict with legal systems in both Russia and America. The reader recognizes the validity of Renko's position. The fictional national societies described in this book, whether Russian or American, are less important to us than the appeal which the author is making to his readership through Renko's personal decisions and concern for justice: he expects readers to approve. I will be arguing that during a large part of its history, the detective story reflected assumptions about the world and about human conduct that were grounded in theology, and I will argue further that if important changes occur in those assumptions, the changes will be quickly reflected in detective fiction because it touches that most sensitive area—the author's pocket.

That is the context in which the reader should understand the title of this work. The book is not specifically about Sherlock Holmes, but it is about the significance of the whole body of detective literature, because its subject matter is concerned with "setting things right." It is about characters like Conan Doyle's sage of Baker Street who were convinced that they had a vocation to engage in this enterprise, and who perhaps in later times would have put it less pretentiously, but who involved themselves in detection because it was their job or because of an accident or even because they needed a worthwhile hobby. However, our own little piece of detection is to discern that, behind all this juggling with facts to bring villains to justice, there is a society or culture that approved the detectives' exploits by avidly buying and reading these books. Crime is a fact, but civilized cultures want to be assured that matters can be "set right" and that it can be done by achieving justice against the wrongdoer.

This is recognized by those who have rightly protested that the violence of detective fiction is not to be interpreted as evidence of degeneracy in society and is not its most important characteristic but that the detective story is an affirmation of basic morality. Routley maintained that it is "the most moral kind of literature there is" precisely because it "doesn't commend a society in which crime gets more compassion than suffering."[21]

Several years earlier Margery Allingham had voiced her own protest that the genre arose not from the love of violence but as "a sign of a popular instinct for order and form in a period of sudden and chaotic change."[22] As Alexander Pope asserted over a hundred years before there was any demand for detective fiction, "Order is heaven's first law."[23]

We start then from the premise that for the greater part of the time since detective fiction began to be popular, it has owned moral assumptions that were grounded in the theologies of Western Christendom, for "no literary genre, however much it may be devoted to pure entertainment, can grow and develop for nearly 150 years unless it's rooted in the most universal human concerns."[24] However, it is certainly not traditional theology as it is expressed in ecclesiastical dogma, but as it was refined in the crucible of the Enlightenment.

IV

That is an all-important qualification. At first sight, theology and detective fiction seem to be incompatible not only because of the blood and crime involved but also because detection could not flourish until it had been freed from the bondage of dogmatic theology. The skills of detection have been used throughout recorded history, and we can find examples from very early times in both sacred and profane literature, but it has been shown that the detective story could not develop as a distinct form until the trial of criminal acts by ordeal and torture had given place to the rational consideration of objective facts. That is why Ellis Peters' delightful stories of Brother Cadfael, the twelfth-century monk of Shrewsbury, for all their cleverness in detection and the authenticity of locale and period, will always be closer in spirit to our own time than to the time about which she was writing.[25] As E. M. Wrong observed, detection could not flourish before the Enlightenment, and "a faulty law of evidence was to blame, for detectives cannot flourish until the public has an idea of what constitutes proof, and while a common criminal procedure is arrest, torture, confession, and death."[26] In judging the "Case of the False Mother" (1 Kings 3), Solomon used a psychological method worthy of Agatha Christie's Hercule Poirot, but it is nonetheless true that such methods could not become the general rule or popular with the public until most people were ready to accept scientific investigation as more efficient and more likely to establish guilt or innocence than torture on the rack or ordeal by fire. Hence, whatever examples of detection we meet in earlier literature, there could be no general acceptance of detective methods, let alone any popular call for detective fiction, until superstition was on its way out. It is no accident that we usually trace the genesis of the detective story to the adventures of a Frenchman, Eugène François Vidocq (1775–1859), and in the writings of an American, Edgar Allan Poe (1809–49).[27] The Enlightenment had done its work, and when Britain established the Metropolitan Police Force in 1829, it was clear that the discovery and restraint of criminals was beginning to be recognized as a scientific matter for professionals.

Erik Routley made some interesting observations about the significance of professional police. He suggested that there may have been a sound psychological reason for writers such as Conan Doyle representing their fictional policemen as honest but bumbling foils to their less official counterparts, since a public still scared of a professional standing army might well be unwilling to have the police represented as superhumans in control of the new arcane art of detective science. Certainly England has always had a healthy fear of anything approaching a police state. More importantly, Routley reminded us that the police were essentially created to be the public defenders of private property, in a society where the defense of the person and private property was being taken with a new seriousness: "The whole point of a police force was to make the world safe for the kind of society that England was nourishing—a bourgeois society."[28] It might be suggested that on the Western shores of the Atlantic, and indeed, everywhere in America but on the extreme frontier, industrialization and urbanization were producing the same kind of society and causing similar values to develop. It was a culture that had traveled a long way from the intensities of the Reformation but that still revered the "Protestant ethic" in its more secular guises and was committed to the morality of that ethic insofar as it was amenable to the logic of the Enlightenment and respected the rights of individual effort and private enterprise.

That should remind us that if we are to speak of a relationship between detective fiction and theology, we had better be clear about our terms.

We must first distinguish between the detective story and stories about spies, adventure, mystery, or horror with which it is often confused. John Wiley Nelson tried to establish a distinction within the genre by reserving the term *detective fiction* for the more hard-boiled type produced by Raymond Chandler and Dashiell Hammett and described the intellectual exercise of classic detection (Sherlock Holmes, Hercule Poirot, Nero Wolfe, et al.) as "detecting fiction."[29] My own inclination would be very different. Of course, there is the "rational process of discovering who did it, and how," which Nelson regarded as the characteristic, almost as the idiosyncrasy, of the older classic form of the story. This *was* their most distinctive feature. And there is, too, the simple whodunit that can sometimes descend rather prissily into a "by-whom-was-it-perpetrated."

On the other hand, *detection* was the reason why the literature became popular in the first place: "Detection is par excellence the romance of reason."[30] In the older works, there is just as much accent on the detective himself as in the later stories, but in the older works it is on the detective as a thinking machine. If more recent writers have added fresh dimensions by introducing us to agents who are tougher, more vulnerable, and more realistically human, that may well indicate significant changes in public taste and public mores; but if the detecting element is missing or totally submerged, the story has become something else and has bowed its way out (or blasted its way out) of detective fiction. Insofar as that essential element is retained, these stories still belong there. Instead of separating the aggressive (and professional) moderns from their more cerebral counterparts, it may be more important to see them as telling variations on the classic theme. H. Douglas Thomson in 1931 may have restricted his own boundaries of the detective story too narrowly for our modern taste, but he was surely right when he said that the detective story "must be first and foremost a problem. The main ingredient must be logic. If there is sensation—and we would not for worlds banish it—it should seem rather incidental."[31] Dorothy L. Sayers implies the same in a brief but perceptive account of detective fiction.[32] Historically that is its raison d'être.

Tales of mystery or horror may try to mystify the mind or curdle the blood, adventure stories may exploit their thrills, while spy stories venture into the miasma of political intrigue and may offer their own distinctive insights into the complexities of our time, but the detective story has to show that within a given set of bewildering circumstances, there is a rational solution that explains the facts.[33] Just as any work of fiction may have a love interest without being a love story, so the detective story may contain gothic mystery, horror, adventure, romance, international intrigue, and even the toughness of Sam Spade or Travis McGee, but always at the heart of it there must be a rational solution of a puzzle originating in a crime. In line with the spirit of many modern writers, the solution of that particular crime may not resolve the basic human dilemma that is sometimes represented in the detective's private perplexities, and in our day it may not reinforce anyone's convictions about absolute truth or justice, but at least the reader understands that these issues are important: to discover how this crime happened is worth the effort and the human qualities needed to winnow truth from an irrelevant mass of falsehood and prejudice are of value to society. We have already noted Edmund Crispin's reminder that detective stories are not concerned with preaching but with entertainment. He went on to affirm, "But their reason is reason."

This leads us to urge caution in use of the term *theology*, for it must be obvious that this kind of literature can be related to theology only in a very limited way. We must be wary of claiming too much. Clearly, detective fiction bears no relationship to most of the classic doctrines of Christian revelation, or for that matter to Muslim or Jewish revelation, or to the religious principles of Buddhism or Shintoism. We cannot expect fiction of this kind to offer commentary on the doctrines of Incarnation, Atonement, the Church, or the mysteries of the Trinity. We may expect some Jewish writers like Harry Kemelman to present a Jewish viewpoint, Roman Catholic writers like G. K. Chesterton, Msgr. Ronald Knox, and Ralph McInerny to offer a Roman Catholic stance, and liberal Protestants like Charles Merrill Smith to illustrate the presuppositions of liberal Protestantism. It is to be expected: readers accept it, and if they do not like the point of view, they will avoid that author when they next visit the local library or browse around the paperbacks at the airport.

This is incidental. The points at which the detective story touches theology are those at which it shows how the writer (and presumably the readers on whom he or she depends for a living) think about the universe, the order by which it is governed, and what this means for the human condition. Whether this has anything to tell us about the doctrine of 'God' is a moot point. But I would argue that many of detection's presuppositions are fundamentally theological, such as (1) a belief that our universe is structured on the basis of rational laws; (2) the conviction that 'truth' is real and can be discovered rationally by weighing the evidence; (3) the assumption that if all the facts are known, we can discover meaning in them; (4) the perception that there is real distinction between right and wrong conduct; (5) the assumption that human life is of very great, even of supreme value; (6) the recognition that although people are always capable of goodness, there is also within them an innate capacity for evil; (7) the conviction that we must strive to achieve justice for the sake of society.

These are also concerns of theology, but of theology as it relates to the secular world, to the human condition. It made an appearance at the Renaissance, but it received tremendous new impetus in the Enlightenment of the eighteenth century. Detective fiction has been conditioned by the thinking that arose out of that movement with its fresh appeal to human reason. The Enlightenment thinkers believed that the universe was governed by fixed laws that could be discovered by reason, although men like the mathematician Laplace did not always realize the theological significance of their own beliefs.[34] Like them, unless the fictional detective happens to be a member of the clergy, (e.g., Father Brown, Rabbi Small, or the Reverend Dr. Randollph), he may not be concerned with 'God' in the

religious sense of that concept. However, whether consciously or not, he or she points to the ultimate principle
behind an ordered, rational universe that our society
presupposes—an ultimate principle that does not as-
sert dogmas against the truths of scientific enquiry but
that in the anonymous guise of a detective story may be
laying claim to be their Source.

V

We should now explore some of the theological clues
for our literary sleuth to pursue in the pages that follow,
but even more importantly, clues that should be traced
in the maze of detective fiction that graces the shelves of
our public libraries.[35] Such pursuit adds a new dimen-
sion to the hobby of armchair detection, and it is the
more important because it points to a primrose path
down which we do not follow a single psychopathic
criminal, but instead a whole culture.

The Created Order

To speak of a "created order" in a society that can
still become heated by sterile arguments between evolution and creationism may seem like loading the dice.
That is not the intention. Perhaps the emphasis should
be on "order"—that detective fiction, at least in detection of the classical model, assumes that the universe
has structure and *order:* events do not happen by chance,
things *matter*, and everything has its proper order in
nature. The traditional image of the detective searching a room with a magnifying glass for burnt matches
and traces of lipstick may be far removed from reality
during the last two decades of this twentieth century,
when probably more can be accomplished by a clerk
sitting at a computer terminal than by a whole army of
bloodhounds, human or canine. But when we get to
basics, there is enough truth in the traditional image of
the sleuth to emphasize that *things*, inanimate objects
around us, the casual items of everyday life, are signifi-

cant in explaining the truth about us and the way we live. Things matter. This refers not only to things that cost a lot of money or that immediately hold our attention but to everything, however small or apparently insignificant, because everything in this universe has its own proper form and being. And this cosmic structure is governed by laws that do not change arbitrarily.

So Rex Stout's gargantuan detective, Nero Wolfe, reminds Archie Goodwin that detectives are trained to observe and register the way things act, and that particular case turned upon their remembering accurately the kind of sound or cadence heard when certain numbers were dialed on a telephone.[36] That same curious fact, that automatic telephones have their own eccentric "tempo" was also used by Cyril Hare's solicitor-detective, Francis Pettigrew.[37] But there could be no valid detection if things—in these instances telephones—did not act in a way that is authentic and consistent with their own "nature." Hammers do not hit people of their own accord, and they do not often fall accidentally on people, according to the reasoning of Father Brown in G. K. Chesterton's "The Hammer of God," while in the logical mind of Lord Peter Wimsey, there is no possibility of clocks and cactus plants moving of their own volition.[38] Agatha Christie reminds us that even conjuring tricks are capable of rational explanation when we know everything there is to know about the things being used.[39]

This may seem too small a point to make, but it indicates the belief that our universe is not capricious. No body of popular literature is so insistent in claiming that, even when appearances seem to deny it, things act in a way which belongs to their own nature, and that when all the facts are known, this inner consistency stands clear. As Jacques Barzun observed, "What happens in modern detective fiction is that objects— and more than one in each tale—are taken literally and seriously. They are scanned for what they imply, studied as signs of past action and dark purposes. This search for history in things is anything but trivial." Later in the same article he put it more epigrammatically—"Bits of matter matter."[40]

The idea that matter matters is directly related to the way in which the writer presents our mundane environment. However complicated and inane the circumstances seem to be, there *is* order and rationality, if only we can find the clue that will unlock the mystery: given the right thread, the hopelessly tangled skein can be unraveled. There is a passage in Ngaio Marsh's *Death at the Bar* in which her very civilized detective, Roderick Alleyn, is lying on a headland by the sea, watching the intricate but random patterns woven by seaweed as it is thrust forward and pulled in by the waves. And there he muses on the apparent purposelessness of existence— he describes what he sees as "a collection of ordered inanities. Rather like police investigations."[41] But that is precisely what the writer, through the story itself, assures us that police investigations are *not*. At the center of this story and every other detective story, there is the unspoken assumption that, given the facts, meaning exists which can be understood by our reason.

The one who writes such stories does not pretend either to pose or to answer the riddle of creation or of life on this planet. That would be not only pretentious but hypocritical, for the author is concerned simply with a tiny segment of life and the complex circumstances surrounding a particular crime. But within that little segment, however complicated the circumstances, the matter is pursued in perfect confidence that there is a rational explanation. For unless the evidence means something, and unless we life in a universe where meaning is possible, the whole exercise is futile. Detective stories may be a game, but the assumption is that, like life itself, this must be a game which has meaning and in which the rules are already determined.

Providence

These rules are directly related to an underlying concept of 'Providence'. Ngaio Marsh's book just cited was first published in 1940, and the incident in question suggests that the readers for whom Ngaio Marsh was then writing believed they lived in an ordered universe. Indeed, if that had not been a general belief in the Britain of 1940, there would have been little use in what most Britons were engaged in at that time. In that period of human history, people generally believed in an overruling Providence, although there were ambiguities enough to make them question it, and it could take some fairly curious forms. There is an amusing incident in one of Dorothy L. Sayers' books, first published in 1934, when Lord Peter Wimsey and the local Rector were given some straight words on this subject by an old East Anglian woman: "'Providence?' said the old woman, 'Don't yew talk to me about Providence. I've had enough o' Providence. First he took my husband, and then he took my 'taters, but there's One above as'll teach him to mend his manners, if he don't look out.'"[42] These words seem to tell us that in 1934, when *The Nine Tailors* appeared, the platitudes of the English clergy may not have been wholly understood by their congregations, but at least the words show that the readership knew enough about the subject to be able to raise a snicker. And when you ponder "there's One above as'll teach him to mend his manners," there is a native instinct that does not fall far short of the mark theologically.

By the 1950s we find that agnosticism was coming into vogue, and our century was on its way to becoming the century of the common person. Nicholas Blake puts a spotlight on this in an ironic interlude when his detective, Nigel Strangeways, decides that the best way of getting rid of an unwelcome stranger in a London pub is to launch into a profound disquisition on the relationship of Providence to coincidence. In *End of Chapter*, Strangeways pontificates:

> In an age swamped by mechanistic physics and mechanistic psychology, the only rock left above the surface is coincidence—beautiful anarchistic coincidence. In

a society that bows down and worships at the altar of statistics, coincidence is the one manifestation of a higher
Providence.
    "Aw'm a free thinker mawself."

But ignoring the interruption, Strangeways bulldozes
on:

> You will say, perhaps, that the science, art or sullen craft
> of criminal detection should confine itself to facts which
> admit of a causal explanation. I disagree. A science which
> leaves no room for coincidence—that is to say, for two ap-
> parently related events to happen simultaneously without
> there being any actual connection between them what-
> soever—is an inadequate science, a false science. Must
> you go?

For at this point, we read, the stranger in the bar
"mumbles that he had seen a friend come in, and
removed his plate, his beer and his person, the latter
visibly sweating."[43]

Strangeways' words are an amusing tilt at the wide-
spread and newly fashionable agnosticism that was
beginning to percolate into classes of society far removed from the traditional skepticism affected by intellectuals. The older attitudes were much simpler and
grounded in convictions that we recognize as belonging
to the traditional theology of our culture. They are to be
seen in Arthur Upfield's Australian aboriginal detective, Napoleon Bonaparte, just as clearly as in any of the
detectives of the English country-house circuit. In
Death of a Swagman, Bonaparte says:

> It doesn't matter two hoots whether the form of the evil is
> a murder or an unjustly harsh act. Evil is always coun-
> tered by God, or Good, or Providence, or whatever name
> you might choose to give it. You and I know, as well as
> other sensible and experienced men, that Evil never
> blesses, and the evildoer never prospers. I recognized
> that eternal law years ago.[44]

Maud Silver provides an excellent example of the older attitude. In one of the stories about her, *The Silent Pool*, Superintendent Martin goes to visit that worthy lady in the vicarage at Ledbury, and we are allowed to share his impressions:

> He sat a little drawn back from the table where John Lenton was in the habit of writing his sermons. On the right of the blotter lay a Bible and the Book of Common Prayer. Since to Miss Silver all law and justice drew its authority from these two books, the association did not seem incongruous. That the police force was upheld by what she called Providence in exactly the same way as the ministry of the Church she regarded as axiomatic.[45]

Although this story had made its appearance only three brief years before that of Nicholas Blake, it is a reminder that, side by side with new attitudes he may have discerned, there were still many readers who cherished traditional English morality, for whom, no doubt, Lord Tennyson, Maud Silver's favorite savant, would be the perennial Poet Laureate.

Justice and Truth

Whether concepts such as 'justice' and 'truth' as eternal absolutes are grounded more in Platonic philosophy than in Western theology is a debatable point,[46] but it should be clear that such concepts cannot be relativized completely without undercutting the very basis on which detection was built. Justice and truth were concepts bigger than life, and the basic assumption of the society in which detective fiction flourished was that both concepts were eternally self-justifying.

Maud Silver provides us with a beautiful example of this traditionally English point of view in *She Came Back:*

> Miss Silver was accustomed to feel very piously and sincerely grateful, not only for the success which attended

her professional activities, but for the modest comfort which this success had brought her. Part of her gratitude arose from the fact that she regarded it as a privilege to thwart the designs of the evildoer and to serve the ends of justice, which she would certainly have spelt with a capital letter.[47]

Moreover, the priority of justice as the goal of criminal investigation persists. We cannot simply belittle the concept, as Michael Gilbert's detective, Sergeant Petrella, reminds us in *Blood and Judgment* when he is getting some Dutch courage in a London pub to protest against an unjust decision by his superior officer: " '*Fiat justitia, ruat coelum*' . . . . 'Let justice prevail though the sky fall.' "[48]

Justice, however, can too easily be mistaken for mere legality. Charles Dickens declared through one of his characters that "the law is an ass," but people in Western countries have been reluctant to dismiss law as simply the whim of those in power, and this has meant that law and justice, at least before the 1960s, were often confused. Maud Silver would certainly not have recognized any wide gap between them, nor would the majority of readers who enjoyed her adventures. With that sublime but often irritating self-assurance of the Anglo-Saxon race, they would have assumed that justice was more or less identical with the law of the land, since it would have been unthinkable that British (or American) law could be unjust. Doubts might have arisen later, but during the classic period of detective fiction, all the fictional sleuths sought to bring assorted culprits under the due process of law in the blithe but firm conviction that the ends of justice were being served. As Joseph Wood Krutch commented about the genre in 1944, "Detective stories commonly provide that particular happy sort of ending which is the most perfect of all and which may be described as 'justice triumphant.' "[49]

The confusion that can occur between law and justice can also confuse justice with retribution and punishment. The older writers obviously recognized no problem, although even as early as 1928 Dorothy L. Sayers pointed out the problems a sensitive writer might face when she had to bring even a fictional character to the gallows; but Sayers was one of a kind, and for the greater number, the problem was simply not seen, or avoided by means of a confession and convenient suicide.[50]

Justice reigned, and it was enshrined in the office and full panoply of law. When Erle Stanley Gardner's detective-attorney, Perry Mason, is reminded by a truculent client that he pays the bills, Mason declares, "I am working for a blind woman. They carve her image on court-houses. She has a pair of scales in one hand and a sword in the other. They call her Justice, and she's the one I'm working for, right at the moment." And then we read, "He swung down the left corridor, leaving Witherspoon to stand, muzzled, and more than a little angry."[51]

It was a lovely exit line. And if you belong to the right generation, you can still visualize the broad back of actor Raymond Burr—TV's Perry Mason—disappearing down the passage on the television screen. But is this simply to be dismissed as flamboyant writing, or does it contain the hint that, at least at the time that story was written, most people believed in a justice that was not relative but, for all practical purposes, absolute?

Something similar might be asked about the concept of truth as it appears in detective fiction. Lesley Egan's attorney-detective, Jesse Falkenstein, reminds his brother-in-law, Andrew Clock, that "the truth always matters," and Ruth Rendell's Chief Inspector Wexford ponders the similarities between criminal detection and the work of a historian, and asks if it is simply "the curiosity that wants to see everything, know everything, be in the swim, that when made scholarly, is the prerogative of the historian and the archaeologist?"[52] The historian Robin Winks makes that connection even more explicit; for although historians may know that they can never be absolutely sure about the truth of any historical problem, they still continue like detectives to scratch at the evidence.[53] Somewhere in those facts and yet always beyond them, the truth exists.

The Value of Human Life

The detective story seems to have risen in popularity at a time when human life began to receive new value. This is obviously related to the earlier discussion about justice, because it is clear that detective fiction is not likely to be popular in societies where an individual's rights under the law are not recognized or where they are flagrantly repressed.

The value of the individual appears in almost all the stories. It does not matter if the victim is an unknown tramp, an escaped convict, a cabinet minister, a noble peer, or a string of social nonentities,[54] the detective assumes the same painstaking effort to reach a solution, and the same wheels of justice are set in motion: when a human life has been taken in peace time, the law (ideally understood) takes no account of the social standing of the victim or the culprit.

In judicial terms this is a general endorsement of the Judeo-Christian affirmation that the author of justice, God, is no respecter of persons. At the entrance to the little graveyard at Céligny near Geneva, where Richard Burton is buried, it is represented very graphically: *Ici Egalité.* Death brings us all to the same level and every person is equal in the sight of God.

Justice must therefore be done whether or not the victim is a likable or worthy person. In Agatha Christie's *Appointment with Death*, the victim was a thoroughly detestable old woman who made everyone's life a misery and who was not much loss to society. Several people including Hercule Poirot, Agatha Christie's little Belgian detective, and Dr. Gerard, a young French medical man, were discussing the woman's death, and Poirot asked Gerard whether he was satisfied with what had happened. Gerard replied emphatically that he was not, because his instinct as a doctor was to preserve life and not to hasten death. "Therefore," he continued, "though my conscious mind may repeat that this woman's death was a good thing, my unconscious mind rebels against it! It is not well, gentlemen, that a human being should die before her time has come."[55]

Agatha Christie made the same ethical point in another of her novels, *One, Two, Buckle My Shoe*, where several unimportant people are killed. One of the suspects is a man of high position and national influence who may have murdered them for motives of public safety. When Poirot tackles him, the suspect expostulates, "Don't you realise, Poirot, that the safety and happiness of the whole nation depends on me?" Poirot replies, "I am not concerned with nations, Monsieur. I am concerned with the lives of private individuals who have the right not to have their lives taken from them."[56] The dialogue may strike us as pretentious and out-of-date; and yet can any civilized life be sustained unless the societies in which we live share that concern? Detective fiction, despite its preoccupation with violent death, plays out its game of make-believe on the fundamental assumption that people matter. Perhaps even more importantly, we should realize that these stories would have no readers unless writers could be sure that the majority of people in the society where their wares are being offered also believe that people matter.

Fallen Nature

Christian doctrine speaks about our human nature in terms of *imago dei*, and that may be hinted at sometimes in the idealization of the detective. But Judeo-Christian tradition also recognizes that humankind is a fallen creation, and that the human heart, in the words of the prophet Jeremiah, "is deceitful above all things and desperately wicked: who can know it?" (Jer. 17.9).

Well, who *can* know it? It is this fallible aspect of human nature that the detective story is better able to explore and although we may not be too surprised to find it revealing depravity, it may be more surprising to find it insisting that the possibility of such depravity exists in every person. We will not provide many examples of this, since that might spoil too many good stories for our readers, but as one rather unlovely character says, "Everybody has secrets. . . . The most innocent-looking people have things they want to hide."[57] That is a basic premise of detection, and it is worth observing that detective fiction and the theology that stands at the base of our culture start from the same realistic view of human nature that refuses to take us at our own self-estimate. One of the older amateur detectives says that he enjoys detecting because, when crime is about, the working of people's minds gets "much more easy to trace. . . . and you can see much more how they become thieves and murderers, even if they don't."[58] There is a delightful illustration of the sinful violence that often hides behind our innocent masks in Michael Gilbert's *Close Quarters*. Sergeant Pollock has to go to a cathedral close to investigate a particularly brutal series of murders and in order to get a feel for this normally sanctified atmosphere, he decides to visit the cathedral for Evensong. He arrives just before the choir and clergy enter the building and, as he watches the procession approach, he ponders:

> How could anyone gazing on this display of composite piety entertain even for a moment the thought that they might have been mixed up in the sordid mischief of the past fortnight? How divorced they were from all notions of brutality and violence. It was only when they got closer that Pollock noted that the boy in front of the file on the left had a rich and quite unmistakable black eye.[59]

We all have it in us.

A passage in one of Agatha Christie's early World War II novels brings together many of the themes we have considered in this introductory chapter. It points to the theological presuppositions behind ideas of jus-

tice, human dignity, and culpability which were accepted in our Western society at the time she wrote. It is
a story cited earlier in which a man of great influence
and power misuses his power and causes the death of
many people. A short time after Poirot solves the mystery, he is walking home when he is joined by another
character in the story, a mysterious Mr. Barnes.

> They walked on for a little way, then Barnes asked cu-
> riously:
> "What are you thinking about?"
> Hercule Poirot quoted:
> *"Because thou hast rejected the word of the Lord, he
> hath also rejected thee from being king."*
> "Hm—I see—" said Mr. Barnes.
> "Saul—after the Amalekites. Yes, you could think of it
> that way."[60]

The quotation is taken from one of the most bloody
tales of retribution in the Old Testament, but beyond
the primitive savagery, it makes the point that those of
great natural ability could forfeit the positions of influence and trust in which Providence placed them by
ignoring "the word of the Lord."[61] Something similar
should be said as we look beyond the violence of the
crime with which practically every detective story begins; but the most significant thing about that quotation from our perspective is that Agatha Christie could
assume it would be recognized, understood, and approved by her readers. In the year that book appeared,
the first full year of World War II, the British people had
good cause to acknowledge that Providence might call a
person of special ability to save a nation, for on May 13,
1940, Winston Churchill became prime minister and
challenged his people by telling them that he had nothing to offer "but blood, toil, tears and sweat." It was also
clear that at no period of their history were the British
people more ready to believe that the struggle in which
they were engaged was essentially moral and spiritual.
Whether they owned religious feelings or not, Agatha

Christie's readers were prepared to endorse the sentiment that if there is a Providence, it must be moral: justice and truth are at the heart of it.

One of the earlier literary critics of the detective story, Marjorie Nicolson, may have appreciated the significance of the point I have been trying to make when she observed that, "the most persistent readers of detective literature today [1929] are the philosophers and the scientists who were bred under an older system of belief," and she suggested that this interest might represent a revolt "from a changing universe, without standard and without order" and therefore may represent their attempt to return to "a simpler causality under which they are more at home." She went on to observe that when the professorial reader turned to detective fiction he or she simply carried over into a different medium the fun of the chase and the ardor of pursuit that provides much of the zest to life.[62] Even if the assumptions behind Nicolson's observations only approximate to the truth about the theological bases of Western culture, that is still sufficiently significant to warrant a serious study of detective fiction from a theological perspective.

What I therefore invite you, the reader, to do, is not to give up reading detective fiction but to engage in the game of detection at a different level. By all means read your favorite authors to discover the culprit in violent crime and the motives behind it. But at the same time, I suggest you look for clues about the society in which we live, and ask yourself if—or how far—it has shifted from the ethical presuppositions which the detective story during the classical period tried to reinforce—those principles on which Western civilization was founded.

A pretentious enterprise? Perhaps. But in view of the rapidity with which our world has been changing in the last half of the twentieth century, who can doubt that such an inquiry is viable and possibly even useful. In any case, at the lowest level, it may provide a handy and plausible excuse for continuing to read the stuff.

Part 1

The Classical Period

In praise of ladies dead and lovely knights
—William Shakespeare

1

Those Eminent
Victorians

The Victorian era brought the detective story its
great popularity: it rose to that recognition during a
time that, more than any other, deserves to be regarded
as the British Century.

That is not to suggest that all or even most of the
writers were British. There were other pivotal figures,
such as Edgar Allan Poe and Eugène François Vidocq,
Émile Gaboriau, Fortuné du Boisgobey and Maurice
Leblanc, all of whom certainly owed no allegiance to
Victoria Regina but who, during these years, set the
detective story firmly on the path it was to follow. However, it was not the writers who were altogether responsible for catapulting the detective story into popularity
but the society of fogbound London. Gilbert Keith Chesterton, himself an eminent Victorian, recognized the
genre as one that particularly celebrated urban civilization.[1]

It was a civilization dominated by the regal figure of
the dumpy little Queen, whose influence extended to
every continent, whose sovereignty covered a quarter of
the world's land surface and even more of its oceans,
and whose understanding of culture was measured less
in terms of elegance and aesthetics than in terms of
integrity and law. It was a society which, like its sover-

eign, was liable to be "not amused," and in which the forces of "secular puritanism" were in the ascendant. That is the background against which this chapter should be read.

I

The last thing we should attempt is a history of the detective story's development, primarily because it has been covered adequately elsewhere but also because such a history concerns us only in a limited sense.[2] However, we should note that all historical surveys follow much the same route. After tipping their hats to the ways in which perceptive predecessors brought primitive culprits to account, they note the fascination of the seventeenth and eighteenth centuries with true crime stories and then trace the first hazy lineaments of the detective story in accounts of the Bow Street Runners and police spies who had often been recruited from the ranks of the criminals on whom they legally preyed.

By this route we arrive at Eugène François Vidocq, the most celebrated of the legitimized turncoats, and the founder in 1811 of the French Sûreté. Through his autobiographical *Mémoires*, Vidocq's influence on later crime writers was admittedly significant, but as Julian Symons observes, that influence "did not rest on his skill in analytical analysis, for he had none."[3] We cannot at that date speak of a genre of detective fiction as we now recognize it.

There is general agreement that "detective fiction as we know it begins with Poe."[4] Edgar Allan Poe, particularly in his three most famous stories about the private investigator, the Chevalier C. Auguste Dupin— "The Murders in the Rue Morgue," "The Mystery of Marie Rogêt," and "The Purloined Letter"— produced a whole new movement in popular literature that we have come to know as detective fiction. There seems to be some uncertainty among the critics as to whether or not we should include "The Gold-Bug" as part of this seminal Poe corpus, but I would argue that it deserves a place as the first of the stories concerned with the solution of a cipher. But however large or small we make the generic corpus of Edgar Allan Poe, there is no doubt of the debt that detective fiction owes to his work.

At a dinner celebrating the centennial of the American writer's birth, Sir Arthur Conan Doyle said of Poe's stories that "each is a root from which a whole literature has developed." And he asked, "Where was the detective story until Poe breathed the breath of life into it?"[5]

That is a basic question. What was the distinctive character of Poe's stories that made later crime fiction different from all the writing about crime that had gone before? One can make the obvious point that Poe's stories were fictional whereas most of the earlier efforts purported to be based on fact, although that generalization must not be pushed too far because William Godwin's *Adventures of Caleb Williams* (1794)—to which we must return—was fictional and had preceded Poe's stories by several decades, and Poe's story, "The Mystery of Marie Rogêt" presented a very thin French veneer over a rough case of American fact.[6] Clearly the unique contribution Poe made in the development of the detective story does not lie simply in the fictional characteristics of his stories.

There were several aspects of Poe's portrayal of his detective-genius, Dupin, that were persistently copied by later writers. These include Dupin's eccentric and slightly misogynic character, the originality of his reasoning, his rivalry with the regular police, and sensational success. Poe added to this the literary gimmick of a loyal but rather pedestrian associate to chronicle the successes of the brilliant sleuth with suitable accuracy and awe. But these traits do not constitute the real center from which detective fiction was to take its distinctive character. For that we must look to the methods employed by Dupin.

Henry Douglas Thomson clarified the situation when he pointed out that, although the Dupin stories are dissimilar in structure, in each of them "the problem is the thing," and Dupin "is the personification of analysis, the mouthpiece of the logical activity."[7] It is the use of rational analysis in a new and creative manner that distinguishes Poe's stories and sets the pattern of all that was to follow—a fusion of the creative insights of the new romanticism with the logical analysis that had dominated the Age of Reason. This heady nineteenth-century mixture of romantic humanism and analytic rationality is illustrated in a significant passage in which Poe introduces his readers to his new-style detective-hero, Dupin:

> As the strong man exults in his physical ability, delighting in such exercises as call his muscles into action, so glories the analyst in that moral activity which *disentangles*. He drives [*sic*] pleasure from even the most trivial occupations bringing his talent into play. He is fond of enigmas, of conundrums, hieroglyphics; exhibiting in his solutions of each a degree of *acumen* which appears to the ordinary apprehension praeternatural. His results, brought about by the very soul and essence of method, have, in truth, the whole air of intuition.[8]

This emphasis on analysis inspired later writers who found in the *art* (some say *science*) of detection a perfect medium. A modern literary critic has suggested that this enabled Poe, through the character of Dupin, to avoid preconceptions and see the world in a new way: it combined "the best features of an orderly Rationalism and a creative Romanticism while avoiding the pitfalls of each."[9] And we would add, it did so in order to reach a more rational solution to the problem presented by crime.

Poe's inheritance from the Enlightenment is clear. He observed both of himself (the chronicler) and Dupin in "The Murders in the Rue Morgue," "Neither of us believe[s] in praeternatural events. Madame and Mademoiselle L'Espanaye were not destroyed by spirits."[10] At the end of "The Mystery of Marie Rogêt," he even added an instructive paragraph on the relationship between coincidence and divine Providence:

In my own heart there dwells no faith in praeter-nature. That Nature and its God are two, no man who thinks will deny. That the latter, creating the former, can, at will, control or modify it, is also unquestionable. I say "at will"; for the question is of will, and not, as the insanity of logic has assumed, of power. It is not that the Deity *cannot* modify His laws, but that we insult Him in imagining a possibility for modification. In their origin these laws were fashioned to embrace *all* contingencies which *could* lie in the Future. With God all is *Now*.[11]

This illustrates the theological and intellectual climate of the Eastern Seaboard society in which Poe lived and worked. It was a climate deeply imbued with the rational ideals of the Enlightenment but increasingly inspired by a new romantic belief in the capacity of the human spirit. Poe was born in Boston in 1809, and moved to Richmond, Virginia, at an early age and then schooled in England between the ages of six and eleven (1815–20). His return to America was at a time when the transcendentalist controversy reigned as one of the major topics of conversation in the more sophisticated circles of England's former colonies. In 1819 William Ellery Channing delivered his famous Baltimore sermon in which he declared that the 'truth' or 'revelation' "is left by God to be decided at the bar of reason."[12] Channing continued his influential ministry in Boston until his death in 1842, and although he backed away from the romantic ideas of younger transcendentalists like Ralph Waldo Emerson, he was still regarded by them as "our bishop." The Transcendental Club was founded in 1836, and two years later Emerson produced his manifesto of the new movement in his address to the graduating class at Harvard.[13] Almost at the same time Poe was producing "The Murders in the Rue Morgue" (1841), another young radical, Theodore Parker, was raising a furor with his sermon, "The Transient and Permanent in Christianity."[14]

These events are not cited because Poe belonged to the movement — indeed, he "made enormous fun" of one of the younger and more pretentious transcendentalist poets[15]—but because they indicate some of the prevailing ideas of the society in which the detective story was born. It was an intellectual climate well suited to producing, as has been said of Poe's fiction, "a type of story which proclaims, in Hegel's words, that 'Pure reason, incapable of any limitation, is the deity itself.' "[16] Decidedly this was not in the America of Joseph Smith and his Mormon pioneers, nor yet of the enthusiastic camp meetings and frontier revivals. It was generated in that part of America which still looked to Europe for inspiration and approval, and the popularity with which such stories were received suggests that in the reading public there was plenty of resonance to the new beat.

From Edgar Allan Poe there is a direct rationalist (or analytic) line to Conan Doyle and the detective fiction that has dominated the popular literature of our civilization through much of this century. Whether one turns to the French writers like Gaboriau, du Boisgobey, Leroux, Leblanc, and later the *romans policiers* of the Belgian Georges Simenon, or to the English works of Wilkie Collins and the detective motifs in Charles Dickens, the pattern had been set.[17] Gaboriau's detective Monsieur Lecoq in *Le Crime d'Orcival* (1867) declares that the investigation of a crime is "nothing more than the solution of a problem. Given the crime, established and obvious, we begin by investigating all the circumstances, serious or trivial, all the details, all the particular characteristics. When these have been carefully collected, they are sorted and organized by date. In this way we know the victim, the crime and the circumstances and we need to find the third term of the problem, the X, the unknown factor—in other words, the guilty party."[18] Although we find obvious national differences in the detective fiction of France, Britain, and America arising from different national histories or from variations in judicial and police procedure, fundamentally "a detective story, whether written in French or English, may be defined

as a tale in which the primary interest lies in meth-
odological discovery, by rational means, of the exact
circumstances of a mysterious event or series of events.
The story is designed to arouse the reader's curiosity by
a puzzling problem which usually, though not always,
concerns a crime."[19] From the time of Poe, the rational basis was assumed and took precedence over any sensationalism
that might be involved, but the detective story was a
puzzle in which logic was applied not only to an intractable mass of circumstantial detail, but also to the
characters involved as suspects. That insight was perhaps the major contribution of romanticism.

Gaboriau's first detective, the amateur Père Tabaret
in *L'Affaire Lerouge* (1866), describes how he became
fascinated with detection through reading police reports and memoirs about crime:

> So that little by little my interest was drawn to that mys-
> terious power, buried deep in the Rue de Jérusalem,
> which keeps a watchful and protective eye on society,
> misses nothing, lifts the most impervious veils, sees
> through every plot, guesses what is not openly revealed,
> knows exactly the worth of a man and the price of his
> conscience, and collects in its green folders the most dan-
> gerous as well as the most shameful secrets.[20]

Who or what was the "mysterious power" on which
Gaboriau bestows such a personalized character here?
Perhaps he was thinking of no more than the pervasive
influences of police intelligence and of the agencies of
law and order that spread out from the Sûreté Générale.
Probably so, but he speaks of it almost in terms of
divinity. In any case he recognizes in this power the
primary agent watching over society and protecting it
from the chaos caused by crime. That is an important
clue for us because it suggests that as this kind of
literature grew in popularity, there was an increasing
number of readers who had a vested interest in that
society and who would echo Père Tabaret's concern.

So we arrive in Victorian England, a society in which the ground was already cleared and prepared—or, if you prefer a biblical image, a house "empty, swept, and garnished" (compare Matt. 12.43–44 and Luke 11.24–25) ready for possession by detective fiction. It was a society which, beneath all the formal choral beauty of its religious establishment and the pious intensity of its religious Nonconformists, was thoroughly pragmatic in everything that touched day-to-day living. Britain was enthusiastically turning the discoveries of science to industrial use and was creating a national philosophy out of utilitarianism: it was a nation in which the secularized Protestant ethic was being quickly marshaled into wealth and possessions.

Erik Routley's major contribution to our study is his insight that Sherlock Holmes ministered to the prevailing mood of "secular puritanism" in Victorian England. He describes the "secular puritan" ethos in this way:

> The positive principle in the English puritan tradition (which is, as I believe, not wholly or even primarily a religious movement) has three basic constituents: intellectualism, moralism, and the acceptance of the values of the city. The weighty religious associations of puritanism are the result of its having manifested itself at a time when religion was in any case the chief talking-point of every articulate Englishman—the sixteenth century. But you can be, and by Holmes's time people of several generations had been, committed to the values of secular puritanism without holding dissenting religious views, or indeed any religious views at all. Most puritans today are humanists.[21]

II

The character Routley describes as "the secular puritan" is closer to Mr. Worldly Wiseman than to Bunyan's Pilgrim; but Puritanism under any name has always had a bad press: intellectualism can become a "prosy, unimaginative outlook" or one that despises manual labor; moralism can be "stuffy, bigoted and pharisaical"; and industrial cities can produce unsavory ghettos. On the other hand, Routley affirms, Puritan values could be presented positively "as a love of just and rational conversation, a passion for social justice which leaves room for individual development and distinction, and a denial that in order to live the good life you must live in the English countryside." In these less pejorative senses, even "secular puritanism" "is rational, wary against hypocrisy and self-deception, often of limited imagination, but always of unlimited optimism about the possibilities of achievement by the human mind."[22]

This was precisely the kind of society within which Arthur Conan Doyle's stories about Sherlock Holmes received immediate acclaim, but its distinctive features had been building up for many years, and *mutatis mutandis*, could have been found in other countries that had nothing to do with historic Puritanism: the pragmatism that developed out of the Enlightenment's emphasis on reason could make us all kin. So in a book published in 1888, *The Passenger from Scotland Yard,* it is a French hotel manager who expresses the growing fear of any politics or behavior that threatened "the rights of property,"[23] while the French police followed similar practices to the British in the pursuit of crime. Indeed, France had led the way in the Enlightenment, and if the Anglo-Saxons were about to win preeminence in writing about detection, it was perhaps only because those countries possessed a Puritan cultural substratum which was congenial soil for this seed; and also because there were those in British society at least who were quick to see how it could be applied to practical and eminently lucrative ends.

It is important to recognize that "secular puritanism" rarely acknowledged its religious ancestry. More often than not it treated the pieties of Victorian religion with amusement or barely concealed contempt, and although there may be an intimate and direct relationship between the secular hedonism of the *fin de siècle* and the popular evangelicalism of that time, it was a relationship that neither side was anxious to admit.

We see something of this in Wilkie Collins' classic story *The Moonstone*.[24] Collins detested the conventional morality affected by Evangelicals: he made acid comments about the restrictions imposed by "the established Sunday tyranny" in Britain.[25] Throughout the story he tilted at the hypocrisy that sometimes hid beneath the charitable endeavors of people like Godfrey Ablewhite, and delivered a cruel caricature of their gullible female supporters—the nineteenth-century groupies—in the character of Drusilla Clark. But he slipped the knife in even more deftly in his description of Gabriel Betteredge, the Verinders' elderly butler. Betteredge declares that he is not superstitious, but he has implicit faith in the supernatural power of "the book" as the supreme guide for his life. His conviction is that such a book "never was written, and never will be written again."[26] But this book was not the Bible, it was *Robinson Crusoe*!

Apart from the evidence it provides about the growing mood of secularity in some sections of Victorian society, what place does *The Moonstone* occupy in the development of the detective story? Collins simply called his story "a romance," but T. S. Eliot described it as "the first, the longest and the best of the modern English detective novels," and Dorothy Sayers regarded it as "probably the very finest detective story ever written."[27]

Such impeccable character witnesses can hardly be ignored: *The Moonstone* cannot be dismissed as a minor essay that happens to have been written sometime between Edgar Allan Poe and Sir Arthur Conan Doyle; yet it does not present many of the conventions that were later to become popular in detective fiction. First, it contains more than one story; it is three separate stories that are woven into a single narrative which concerns the loss and recovery of a large yellow diamond—the Moonstone.[28] Again, murder is committed, but it occurs comparatively late in the account and is almost incidental to the real story concerning the Moonstone. When the murder occurs, there is some initial doubt about the victim, but none at all about those who perpetrated the crime. Furthermore, for all the author's insistence on the "fame of the great Cuff," it is difficult to represent Sergeant Cuff as a forerunner of the great detective.

Sergeant Cuff is certainly the most important agent of detection in the earlier part of the book and he becomes significant again at the end, but for the most part, he is entirely mistaken and is absent from the central part of the story. Perhaps we should consider him more as a prototype of efficient police work of the kind that would later give us Commander Gideon of Scotland Yard or Lieutenant Mendoza of the L.A.P.D., while on the reverse side of the coin, Superintendent Seegrave personifies bumbling inefficiency and uniformed officiousness.

I suggest that the significance of *The Moonstone* is that detection is carried out by many different characters in the book, even to some extent by old Gabriel Betteredge, although he seems to have functioned better as a Watson than as a Sherlock Holmes. We reach the solution to the mystery because several characters become involved in the detection, and with the advantage of historical hindsight, we see that each of them could be regarded as a prototype for styles of detection that have waxed and waned in the thriving detective fiction industry. Collins show us how broad the possibilities are.

Lady Verinder's solicitor, Matthew Bruff, for example, exhibits not only a vintage taste in cynicism but also a practical understanding of the law and of human nature that qualifies him, at least in some sense, as the literary ancestor of all future lawyer-detectives from Perry Mason to Antony Maitland and Jesse Falkenstein; Ezra Jennings, the unpopular doctor with keen insights into paranormal behavior, discovers the essential clue in the disappearance of the Moonstone and sets the stage for the solution of the mystery. He is therefore an unlikely forerunner to medical detectives such as Dr. Thorndyke. Similarly, Franklin Blake, the victimized "hero," is himself an example of every innocent amateur in later fiction who finds himself (or herself) forced into detection by an unkindly and ironic fate, while even Octavius Guy ("Gooseberry"), the London urchin, offers a characterization repeated in the Baker Street Irregulars.

There is no great detective in the story, but there is one character that suggests some original traits for the great detectives in later books. Mr. Murthwaite occupies a relatively modest, though crucial, place in *The Moonstone;* he is introduced to us as "a long, lean, wiry, brown, silent man," an explorer and an expert on the East, who is full of mystery and arcane knowledge.[29] It is he who immediately recognizes the danger associated with possession of the Moonstone, who is able to subdue the Indian jugglers by speaking to them in their own language, and who finally witnesses the reinstatement of the diamond. For the greater part of the story, Murthwaite seems to be an incidental character, but he contributes insights that are vital to the eventual resolution of the mystery.[30] On the one occasion when the astute but practical Matthew Bruff interviews him at length about the relationship of the Indians to the stone, Murthwaite's attitude reminds us somewhat of Sherlock Holmes lecturing a dim-witted Watson.[31] Yet although he gives full weight to the fanaticism and occult nature of Indian religion, he is totally unwilling to explain events supernaturally:

> We have nothing whatever to do with clairvoyance, or with mesmerism, or with anything else that is hard of belief to a practical man, in the inquiry that we are now pursuing. My object in following the Indian plot, step by step, is to trace results back, by rational means, to natural causes. Have I succeeded to your satisfaction so far?[32]

It is indeed very much to Matthew Bruff's satisfaction and fully in line with the pragmatism and rational science of that time.

The Moonstone reflects and reinforces the analytical spirit of the age, which had already been appropriated in the detective fiction of Edgar Allan Poe. The significance of Collins' book was in the catholicity of its approach to detection. It does not develop the idea of the great detective that had been started by Poe and that would be taken up by Doyle, but some of the characteristics of that development are visible in the figure of Mr. Murthwaite. More importantly, however, the book shows us how many different kinds of people can be involved in solving a mystery. It also suggests a variety of ways in which future writers might develop the detective story.

It has been said that only two detective novels written between The Moonstone (1868) and The Hound of the Baskervilles (1902) were memorable—Israel Zangwill's Big Bow Mystery in 1895 and H. F. Wood's Passenger from Scotland Yard, which had been published in 1888.[33] Zangwill's story is a classic example of the "locked-room mystery."[34] But it is H. F. Wood's Passenger from Scotland Yard that carries our work forward at this point because it provides us with some significant clues about what was happening in Victorian society. Wood's hero, Inspector Byde, shows us how far down the social scale the official police officer was in Britain, but also he shows how the profession was able to rise so rapidly in status and esteem. Byde is a Londoner, who, "to please Mrs. Byde," has rented sittings at the local Wesleyan chapel without apparently engaging himself to attend, and despite his persistent antipathy to Total Abstinence reformers.[35] The ground of his prejudice against such people is that they are always claiming "the monopoly of the Christian virtues."[36]

Inspector Byde has little formal education, but he is determined that his son, Edgar, shall have the start in life that he lacks himself. However, the inspector is not a person simply to sit back and bemoan his own inadequacies. He improves himself by attending evening classes at an institute in Camberwell and by taking the opportunity to learn French; but his greatest enjoyment during odd leisure moments is to puzzle through the propositions of Euclid which he has copied from his son's school textbook! Byde is fascinated by mathematical symbols and uses them freely in analyzing his cases:

> How they cleared the mind, these formulas and symbols, meditated Mr. Byde. He would not deny that his colleagues who never used a single symbol, or any formula, could not have arrived at exactly the same result with a lapse of time precisely commensurate. But their methods were impressionist, not scientific.[37]

That is the point—the method has to be scientific: everything should be subjected to analysis through the cool rational process . That is where so many of his colleagues could go wrong:

> Give them something to do outside the common run of criminal cases! Give them a problem to solve in the regions of pure reason—["regions of pure reason—regions of pure reason," muttered the inspector, with great gusto—"one of the boy's phrases, I think; ah, if I had had the education which that boy has had!"]—take them out of the routine where their experience of the criminal classes was backed up by the "from information I received," and how many successes would be scored by the majority of his colleagues?

Byde recognizes that impressions—the romantic and subjective judgments of the individual—have their own proper place and might even be correct. But they would convince nobody else, "whereas a scientific method cleared the head and shaped the judgment; imparted confidence to the inquirer, and wrung acquiescence from the most unwilling of lookers-on; climbing to an irrefragable conclusion through irrefutable steps."[38] So Inspector Byde, complacently full of his night-school learning, soliloquized.

It all came together for Inspector Byde in the logic of pure reason, experienced in its highest form in mathematics. That was where his colleagues throughout the British police force were defective:

> None of them appeared to divine that in their business lay vast possibilities of scientific method. It was his misfortune to be incapable, educationally, of exploring, defining, and expounding those methods proper to the domain of pure reason, as his son would say; but at any rate the conception was his own—the conception of a scientifically-trained detective force applying mathematics to their regular work, reasoning on infallible processes, with symbols and by formulas. *He* might be incapable of realizing the conception, but there was his son Edgar![39]

Wood's delightful portrayal of this able and ambitious officer is a fascinating illustration of how the Enlightenment and the pragmatism that followed were changing Victorian society. There was no limit to what a hard-working man like Inspector Byde (or even more, young Edgar) might achieve in the new world that was opening up to reasoning and science, if only such a person was prepared to apply the new methods to practical goals. By this time, the world was ready-made for Sherlock Holmes.

It has always been said that Puritans take their pleasures sadly, and I suspect that "secular puritanism," lacking the hopes and ecstasies of faith, probably takes them most sadly of all: there seems to be so much more to be gained by staying on the job. Erik Routley argues plausibly that detective stories provided the secular puritan of Victorian England with the justification he or she needed to take time off for fiction: they satisfied the demand for rational solutions, they upheld the moral values of the society in which the reader had such a high stake, and—especially in Sherlock Holmes—they emphasized the concerns of urban society against the semifeudal qualities of the landed gentry. On this last point, Dr. Watson wrote about Holmes:

> Neither the country nor the sea presented the slightest attraction to him. He loved to lie in the very centre of five millions of people, with his filaments stretching out and running through them, responsive to every little rumour or suspicion of unsolved crime. Appreciation of nature found no place among his many gifts, and his only change was when he turned his mind from the evil-doer of the town to track down his brother of the country.[40]

Sherlock Holmes may be known by his deerstalker cap, but the public transport he favored was the railway carriage and the hansom cab, and he was very much a man of the city: he reflected a society that was rapidly becoming urbanized. The significant decisions in Victorian Britain were no longer being made by those who had lived for generations on country estates, but by the industrialists of Birmingham, Manchester, and Bradford. Perhaps this is partly why it has been observed that "it was hardly Doyle himself but his readers who were the architect of his success."[41]

III

Speculations about Sherlock Holmes' religious beliefs belong to mythology rather than to serious research. It has been variously suggested that he was a spiritualist like his creator (although Conan Doyle did not publicly espouse that cause until 1917), that he was an adherent of Tibetan Buddhism, that he was a Roman Catholic, that he was a liberal humanist or freethinker, or that he was a born-again Christian out of Evangelical Protestantism.[42] The evidence for most of these theories rests on very flimsy grounds, and we are obviously in the shadowy sphere of Holmesian myth—which may say something about our interest today in consistent mythologies,[43] but does not offer us many clues about the religious presuppositions of either the central character in the stories or the readership. Perhaps the very number of different suggestions testifies more to growing pluralism — note the interest at the end of the 1880s in comparative religion — among Victorian readers, than to the spiritual stance of the fictional Holmes.

We may be skeptical about the suggestion that Holmes was converted by the great Baptist preacher Charles Haddon Spurgeon or unable to agree that because he believed in divine forgiveness and that our lives are not our own, he accepted an Evangelical doctrine of salvation.[44] Still there is a good deal in the Holmes corpus that suggests that he (or rather, Conan Doyle) endorsed many of the views found in the popular Protestant theology of that time.

In common with the greater number of Victorians, and despite the fervent oratory of the professional atheist Charles Bradlaugh and the publications of agnostic George Jacob Holyoake, Holmes thought the idea that our universe had been produced by chance "unthinkable."[45] One may assume that he believed in God as the Creator of an ordered universe, although most of the other references to Providence and the Deity in the stories come through other characters or may be regarded as the conventional kind of speech that hovers between sincere piety and plain blasphemy. So when Jefferson Hope challenges the Mormon, Enoch Drebber, Hope cries out, "Let the high God judge between us." And in the confrontation with Stangerson, Hope declares, "Providence would never have allowed his guilty hand to pick out anything but the poison." Later Jefferson Hope dies of a stroke in prison while awaiting his trial, and it is Watson who observes, "A higher Judge had taken the matter in hand, and Jefferson Hope had been summoned before a tribunal where strict justice would be meted out to him."[46]

In this there is nothing of Holmes although he seems to have held similar views. "Well, it is not for me to judge you," he tells John Turner after receiving his confession, and reminds his visitor that, because of age and diabetes, he would soon have to answer for his crime "at a higher court than the Assizes." Then when the old man leaves,

> "God help us!" said Holmes after a long silence. "Why does fate play such tricks with poor, helpless worms? I never hear of such a case as this that I do not think of Baxter's words, and say, 'There, but for the grace of God, goes Sherlock Holmes.' "[47]

Was it fate or divine Providence? Holmes was extremely sensitive to the problem of human suffering. To a woman who had been badly scarred by life he exclaimed, "The ways of fate are indeed hard to understand. If there is not some compensation hereafter, then the world is a cruel jest."[48] It has been suggested that this indicates Holmes believed in divine justice and retribution hereafter, but it ought to be clear that he left that matter open: there *should* be such a compensation hereafter if life was to make rational sense.[49] Similar sentiments can be seen in "The Adventure of the Illustrious Client," which is a story about retribution, but retribution in *this* life. It is Kitty Winter who introduces the note of eternal judgment when she says of the culprit that he "ought to be down in a lower hell than we if there was any justice in the world!"[50] It is the punishment that she inflicts on the villain in the present that causes Holmes to exclaim, "The wages of sin, Watson — the wages of sin!" and then to add, "Sooner or later it will always come. God knows, there was sin enough."[51]

From all this we gather that although Sherlock Holmes would like to be assured of future compensations for the inequities of this life, he is much more concerned with inequities experienced here and now by those who appear to have little defense against them. Holmes believes in the Creator of an ordered universe but also recognizes that the evidence about Providence is paradoxical, if not contradictory. Like all who have been forced to acknowledge the authority that reason imposes, he sees the ambiguity of life and the seeming contradictions of an existence that challenges every attempt to make rational sense of it. The paradox is presented most poignantly in human suffering, as Holmes indicates to Watson after being visited by old Josiah Amberley:

> "Did you see him?" he asked.
> "You mean the old fellow who has just gone out?"
> "Precisely."
> "Yes, I met him at the door."
> "What did you think of him?"
> "A pathetic, futile, broken creature."
> "Exactly, Watson. Pathetic and futile. But is not all life pathetic and futile? Is not his story a microcosm of the whole? We reach. We grasp. And what is left in our hands at the end? A shadow. Or worse than a shadow—misery."[52]

Holmes, like most people of that time, was a theist, but again, like most of his contemporaries, he recognized that at the heart of the doctrine of Providence, the problem of suffering is not wholly amenable to logic. After he has received an honest and moving confession at the end of "The Adventure of the Cardboard Box," we read:

> "What is the meaning of it, Watson?" said Holmes solemnly as he laid down the paper. "What object is served by this circle of misery and violence and fear? It must tend to some end, or else our universe is ruled by chance, which is unthinkable. But what end? There is the great standing perennial problem to which human reason is as far from an answer as ever."[53]

The evidence is ambivalent. All the logic is not on one side. There is, for example, a well-known passage in "The Naval Treaty" that not only contradicts Watson's claim that his friend is indifferent to the country but also shows that Holmes was fully aware of arguments that could be presented for the essential goodness of Creation:

> He walked past the couch to the open window and held up the drooping stalk of a moss-rose, looking down at the dainty blend of crimson and green. It was a new phase of his character to me, for I had never before seen him show any keen interest in natural objects.
>
> "There is nothing in which deduction is so necessary as in religion," said he, leaning with his back against the shutters. "It can be built up as an exact science by the reasoner. Our highest assurance of the goodness of Providence seems to me to rest in the flowers. All other things, our powers, our desires, our food, are all really necessary for our existence in the first instance. But this rose is an extra. Its smell and its colour are an embellishment of life, not a condition of it. It is only goodness which gives extras, and so I say again that we have much to hope from the flowers."[54]

The comment has nothing to do with the matter in hand, and we wonder why it is introduced, but it shows that Conan Doyle himself was very conscious of the paradox which the doctrine of Providence presented. This passage probably represents the prevailing view among intelligent people at that time—a belief in God which was ultimately based on natural theology. The rapid growth of theological liberalism at the end of the nineteenth and beginning of the twentieth centuries is an important clue to the kind of society in which the Sherlock Holmes stories became so popular.

IV

In a world which has become so used to rapid change, it is difficult for us to realize the traumatic effect of the nineteenth-century scientific revolutions upon the faith of thinking people. In 1880 Dr. Robert Dale, the distinguished minister at Carrs Lane, Birmingham, addressed some theological students. "A hundred years ago, fifty years ago, thirty years ago," he said, "our fathers were in possession of exact definitions of all the great truths of the Christian faith. Immense provinces of Christian doctrine were laid down in their theological schemes with all the definiteness and clearness of an Ordnance Survey." But at the time he was speaking, Dale asserted, "all this has passed away. The power of the theological tradition is decaying. . . . The substance of the ancient faith remains, but people find it hard to give their faith a definite expression; and on many questions which seem remote from the central truths of the Christian revelation there is the greatest indecision and uncertainty."[55] In 1889 a group of Oxford High Anglican scholars attempted "to put the Catholic faith into its right relation to modern intellectual and moral problems" in *Lux Mundi*.[56] The need for such a restatement was dictated by the remarkable series of scientific revolutions that had affected chemistry, physics, astronomy, geography, geology, and biology in the first half of that century.

In 1870 Charles Darwin himself admitted that his faith had been knocked topsy-turvy by his own discoveries. "My theology is a simple muddle," he said. And he added this comment, which reveals virtually the same perplexity that Sherlock Holmes expressed: "I cannot look at the universe as the result of blind chance, yet I can see no evidence of beneficent design, or indeed of design of any kind, in the details."[57] Holmes made an exception of the flowers, but if he had been more of a countryman and a naturalist, he might have reflected on the carnivorous habits and floral arrangement of the sundew! Apparently this was a gap in a science in which his knowledge was, according to Watson, "variable," although Holmes seems to have known of Darwin's theory of the survival of the fittest and probably accepted it.[58] On one occasion Holmes spoke of the danger that would arise for humanity in the survival of those who were morally "the least fit."[59]

The explosion in scientific knowledge inevitably caused the questioning of traditional religious orthodoxies. One of Alfred Lord Tennyson's best-known poems refers wistfully to the time when there had been no divorce between the truths of science and the truths of religion, and the poet longs for a time in the future when the unity of all truth will be manifested once again:

> We have but faith: we cannot know;
>> For knowledge is of things we see;
>> And yet we trust it comes from Thee,
> A beam in darkness: let it grow.
>
> Let knowledge grow from more to more,
>> But more of reverence in us dwell;
>> That mind and soul, according well,
> May make one music as before.[60]

Tennyson's words are revealing. Knowledge would "grow from more to more," of that there could be little doubt, but all he can do is to plead that scientific studies should be conducted with reverence for the Ultimate Mystery. The substance of ancient faith might still live on in the hearts of many, but the future seems to be in the hands of rational science.

Sherlock Holmes was the exemplar of that rational science as he used its logic and methods in defense of the things the Victorian age valued most. It is a scientist-turned-writer who, through one of his characters, makes the comment, "Sherlock Holmes performed the remarkable feat of being the first human being, either real or fictional, ever to become a world idol entirely because of his character as a reasoning being. It is not his military victories, his political charisma, his spiritual leadership—but simply his cold brain power. There is nothing mystical about Holmes. He gathered facts and deduced from them."[61] Throughout the stories Watson was at pains to show Holmes' complete dedication to the scientific and rational pursuit of crime, his total indifference to anything that did not serve that end, and his rejection of any emotion that might hinder his objectives. "If I claim full justice for my art," Sherlock chided Watson, "it is because it is an impersonal thing—a thing beyond myself. Crime is common. Logic is rare. Therefore it is upon the logic rather than upon the crime that you should dwell. You have degraded what should have been a course of lectures into a series of tales."[62]

We can appreciate, although Holmes might not, that it was precisely because Watson gave us a series of tales rather than a course of lectures that we have heard of Sherlock Holmes. But the central theme of detection is still reason:

> "The ideal reasoner," he [Holmes] remarked, "would, when he had once been shown a single fact in all its bearings, deduce from it not only all the chain of events which led up to it but also all the results which would follow from it. As Cuvier could correctly describe a whole animal by the contemplation of a single bone, so the observer who has thoroughly understood one link in a series of incidents should be able to accurately state all the other ones, both before and after. We have not yet grasped the results which the reason alone can attain to."[63]

This undoubtedly reflects the optimistic if deterministic attitude of science at that time; and in some measure religion, if it was to retain credibility among intelligent people, would have to come to terms with it.

That is the point of the Sherlock Holmes annals: in Edmund Crispin's phrase, "the reason is reason." Holmes may have flouted convention by his addiction to cocaine and he may have agreed with Watson's possibly unpopular view that war is a very silly way of settling disputes, but in the main he endorsed the views held by most of his fellow citizens.[64] He held the accepted views regarding crime and punishment, retribution and the need for law and order; he shared the horror of suicide and sexual vice, and he had just enough eccentricity in his own life-style to make his personality real in an age that valued individualists.

But in all cases where the supernatural was in question, the evidence turns out to be entirely factual and the agencies material. For example, in *The Hound Of the Baskervilles,* there seems to be a good deal to suggest a supernatural agency at work, "I have hitherto confined my investigations to this world," Holmes said. "In a modest way I have combated evil, but to take on the Father of Evil himself would, perhaps, be too ambitious a task."[65] It has been argued that this proves that Holmes believed in a personal Devil.[66] However, to most people, Holmes' statement will sound like irony, particularly since the whole thrust of that story is to show that, despite all appearances, the events near Baskerville Hall were susceptible to rational explanation. After all, as Holmes observes a little later in the story (perhaps with similar irony), "The devil's agents may be of flesh and blood, may they not?"[67] Holmes may have affected to despise Gaboriau and disparage Poe, but Conan Doyle followed the patterns they had established and Holmes' reputation was built on the methods Lecoq and Dupin had initiated.

There is not much more we can say about Sherlock Holmes' religious assumptions. On occasion he speaks of saving souls, but his intent is to save lives.[68] He voices the conventional pieties in the way they have always been voiced by civilized people in periods when they are respected, and he accepts the theological conventions of a society in which "secular puritanism" had established the conventions. Two portraits were to be found at 221B Baker Street that reinforce this. The unframed portrait of the American Congregational divine Henry Ward Beecher was to be found on the top of Watson's books and a portrait of General Charles George Gordon hung on the wall.[69] Watson particularly admired Beecher, who had been a leader in the antislavery cause, as well as Gordon—an Evangelical soldier who had died in 1885 at the hands of the Mahdi's followers at Khartoum. Such men were popular heroes in Britain at that time, especially among the increasingly influential Nonconformists and their secular anti-Corn Law Liberal supporters.[70] They represented what appeared to be the wave of the future.

Holmes was in sympathy with this wave and accepted at least those parts of popular theology that did no violence to the scientific method. He was clearly a theist insofar as theism gave the only rational explanation of goodness in creation; he accepted contemporary views of justice and of crime and punishment, and regarded suicide with great horror. He also regarded a system of rewards and punishments beyond this life as the only means by which human mortality could be considered rational. If a modern skeptic finds it difficult to reconcile this with Holmes' empirical rationalism on other matters, these beliefs were accepted by all but the most blatant skeptics of that era. About the same time that Conan Doyle began to write his stories, the author of a book on a relatively secular branch of history affirmed that a "fundamental, and as many believe, the most essential part of Christianity, is its doctrine of reward and punishment in the world beyond; and a religion which has nothing to say about this great enigma we should hardly feel to be a religion at all."[71] Sherlock Holmes expressed the spirit of his age and, as H. Douglas Thomson remarked, "Although Sherlock Holmes lived through the war [i.e., World War I] his period must remain Victorian."[72]

V

Sherlock Holmes contributed at least two things to the future development of detective fiction. He gave us the image of "the great detective," and Holmes' success established the "classical" tradition in which crimes were solved essentially through the detective's superior reasoning. These contributions are very closely related.

Sherlock Holmes has become the prototype of the great detective. True, both the image and the distinctive method of reasoning go back to Poe's enigmatic character, Auguste Dupin, but it was Sherlock Holmes who established in the public mind the image of what a great detective should be. With enough idiosyncrasies to keep him interesting, he marked out the path that would be followed by a series of supremely rational detectives, who like him, would be single-minded in their pursuit of justice, eschew romance, and build their success on what they deduced. Side by side with this, as a minor motif, Dr. Watson quietly established the tradition of the relatively dull but loyal associate who doubles as the great detective's chronicler and foil; Sherlock Holmes, Hercule Poirot, and Nero Wolfe always get the kudos, but Watson, Hastings, and Archie Goodwin usually get the girls, and at least fictionally, the royalties!

Although the success of the great detective was immediate, the image itself was not as absolute as it often appears to be in the fictional detectives who followed Holmes. Sherlock Holmes was not omniscient and he was not infallible. Soon after his appearance before the reading public, Watson listed areas in which Holmes was completely devoid of knowledge and others, such as botany, in which his knowledge was at best "variable."[73] Watson also noted that "The Musgrave Ritual" was one of perhaps half a dozen cases in which the mystery was solved though Holmes had actually erred.[74] And although it might be somewhat ungallant to suggest that Irene Adler represents a stalemate, that little episode certainly produced a draw.[75] Holmes himself, for all his superb self-confidence, did not regard himself as infallible. After one frustrating case he charged Watson, "If it should ever strike you that I am getting a little over-confident in my powers, or giving less pains to a case than it deserves, kindly whisper 'Norbury' in my ear, and I shall be infinitely obliged to you."[76]

Yet Holmes always gives the *impression* of omniscience and infallibility, and that is what he handed on to his successors. In spite of having listed the areas in which Holmes was ignorant, Watson invariably spoke of his friend's abilities in terms of amazement mingled with awe: "There was something in his masterly grasp of a situation, and his keen, incisive reasoning, which made it a pleasure to me to study his system of work, and to follow the quick, subtle methods by which he disentangled the most inextricable mysteries. So accustomed was I to his invariable success that the very possibility of his failing had ceased to enter my head." And in those rare cases when Holmes did fail, "it happened too often that no one else succeeded."[77]

The great detective was essentially the supreme reasoner in the classical tradition of detective fiction, but Holmes handed on the legacy in another distinctive way; it was not only in the logical faculty, but in the extent to which he had it. There is something awesomely godlike in the character of the central figure that is conveyed to the readers. The character of Sherlock Holmes seems to be too intense, too committed, too unfailingly correct in his reasoning to be described as a personality—or even to be regarded as human in any of the ways lesser mortals recognize humanity in themselves or in others. Conan Doyle may have regarded him as a supreme example of homo sapiens, but what happens to *homo* when *sapientia* crowds him out to the point where we seem to have a walking intelligence? We are given the impression of *uncanny* ability. Watson found no keener pleasure than in following Holmes during an investigation, "and in admiring the rapid deductions, as swift as intuitions, and yet always founded on a logical basis, with which he unravelled the problems which were submitted to him."[78] We are also told of Holmes' comprehensive filing system which made it difficult "to name a subject or a person on which he could not at once furnish information," and Watson says that instead of going on holiday, Holmes preferred to stay in the center of London.[79] Surely the image we have here is that which we had as children of that divine eye (or today a celestial computer terminal) brooding over every bedroom and piercing the innermost recesses of our naughty little hearts!

Perhaps this suggestion of divinity in the great detective is not accidental. It must have been unconsciously comforting for those who believed in the continuance and stability of society to think that crime never goes undiscovered, that justice is always triumphant, and that there is One (or Those) whose universal surveillance and unfailing rightness ensure that all will be well in this best of all possible worlds! The vicarious assurance that later generations might get from Spiderman and Superman were here to be found in the great detective. It was fiction, and the public knew it, but it could still be comforting. In this way the classic tradition of the great detective, whose omniscience was revealed in the discovery of sin, and whose infallible rationality ensured that it would be punished, was born, baptized, and flourished.

Look at that society. The scientific methods of detection were coming into stride at a time when Europe in general and Britain in particular were promoting the practical results of Enlightenment reasoning further and more lucratively than before. Later, America would push them still further. But in such prosperous societies, many people who found the leisure to read were increasingly conscious of how much they had to lose as they enjoyed ever-rising standards of wealth, comfort, and luxury. They had a vested interest not only in society, but in the ethics of that society, because only an accepted standard of morality could guarantee stability. H. Douglas Thomson saw the relevance of this to detective fiction when he observed, "If the interest [in detective fiction] were solely or even largely an interest in crime, the ethics that form the basis of the detective story's setting would be pointless. In the detective story, alone probably of all fiction, moral standards are not examined or questioned."[80] The basic question is not *whether* ethics are involved, but who determines what the ethics are. For the moment, we would note that at the heart of the new and phenomenal success of the detective story ushered in by Sherlock Holmes, the ethical interests were those of the people who wished to sustain the society they enjoyed. In promoting the great detective, omniscient (possibly) and infallible (usually), society produced a god made in its own image.

VI

This classical tradition in detective fiction is real, and it has dominated the genre for much of this century, but its popularity over the past eight decades may hinder us from recognizing that it was not the only way the detection of crime might be handled fictionally. The Victorians did not leave us with the classic tradition alone. At the beginning of the nineteenth century, there were two directions in which crime writing might develop, and the classic pattern won its predominance at least in part because it caught up and endorsed many of the things that the dominant culture wanted to believe about itself. In the figure of the great detective who defended that society and upheld its moral code, society discovered a myth of what it most truly worshiped. So the great detective prevailed.

But a radically different strain of detective writing had appeared unexpectedly in 1794 with the publication of *Caleb Williams*, by William Godwin, a Calvinist Nonconformist minister, who had apostatized from his faith to support the French Revolution.[81] The original title of this work was *Things as they are; or, the adventures of Caleb Williams*. The title is significant because it suggests that Godwin intended to write about society as it was, and not as it was usually represented in fiction. As Julian Symons observed, "The particular importance of *Caleb Williams* is that it denies all the assertions to be made later through the detective story. In the detective story, the rule of law is justified as an absolute good; in Godwin's book, it is seen as wholly evil."[82] This radical recasting of cultural values, represented in *Caleb Williams*, could be traced later through Maurice Leblanc's prince of thieves, Arsène Lupin; in the amateur cracksman Raffles, created by Conan Doyle's-brother-in-law, E. W. Hornung, and there are later hints of it in the shadowy early career of Margery Allingham's Albert Campion. More to the point, Julian Symons has pointed out that, by raising the possibility of official corruption or a close alliance between the forces of law and order and the criminal elements in society, *Caleb Williams* started a tradition that was eventually caught up in the work of American writers like Dashiell Hammett and Raymond Chandler.[83]

This radically critical approach to society has become more pronounced in the last half of our present century, and it underscores the question in this book's title. Meanwhile we are concerned with the classical tradition which tended to affirm the values of Western society, and if we are to understand why the line represented by *Caleb Williams* remained largely submerged, we must recognize what such writing implied about society and the threat it held for those who felt defensive about the status quo. As E. M. Wrong remarked about Leblanc's Arsene Lupin; "To make a hero of the criminal is to reverse the moral law, which is after all based on common sense, for crime is not in fact generous, but mean."[84]

There is truth in that statement although it may sound a little stuffy. But it underlines the point that, for the greater part of this century in the West, most people who read the literature supported the societies in which they lived and hence endorsed not only the prevailing morality but also, whether consciously (G. K. Chesterton) or unconsciously (Rex Stout), the theological positions on which that morality and those societies were based.

We may also reflect on the fact that in pursuing the downfall of his former protector and benefactor, Caleb Williams actually brings his own career and life to ruin. He has always recognized the possible threat to himself in his course of action:

> The consequences were such as might well appal the
> stoutest heart. Either the ignominious execution of a
> man whom I had once so deeply venerated, and whom

now I sometimes suspected not to be without his claims to veneration; or a confirmation, perhaps an increase, of the calamities I had so long endured.[85]

The story of Caleb's tragic career and Falkland's fall may indeed serve as a fictional object-lesson of how the fate of society and that of its deliberate detractors are often linked. What *Caleb Williams* illustrates is the ambiguity of all human cultures. As a modern editor of Godwin's book has observed, "Only after Caleb succeeds in his 'hateful mistake' of bringing Falkland to trial at the end does he realize that the system itself abets injustice, even when a 'just' decision is reached."[86] Godwin's work represents a radical tradition in detective fiction, diametrically different from that of the mainline writers whose work we will consider in the classical period of the nineteenth and early twentieth centuries.

2

The Golden Age

I

From Sherlock Holmes through World War II, detective fiction experienced its own "golden age." Not only did we witness an incredible burgeoning of the detective story at this time, but the distinctive features of the classic form were established by a plethora of gifted writers on both sides of the Atlantic. For, in spite of Howard Haycraft's designation of the mode as *genus Britannicum*,[1] no one nation or people held a monopoly on it.

As an aside, one of the more perceptive modern commentators, Julian Symons, challenges many of the assumptions made by his predecessors. For example, he questions Dorothy Sayers' suggestion that detective fiction could not arise in any culture before the establishment of a regular police force, and he points out that the genre's legacy is not limited to a single strand that stretches from Poe through the French writers to Conan Doyle, but that there is another important line of development that originated in William Godwin's *Caleb Williams*.[2] The significance of this, as we have seen, is that far from endorsing the existing social order, these writers were critical of it, if not actively antagonistic to it. The contrast between human law and ideal justice became accented to the point where the former was interpreted as likely to destroy the latter—or at least frustrate it.

But this point will be reserved for comment later. At the moment, we are concerned with the golden age of detective fiction. And since the nineteenth century was uniquely the "British Century," there may be some justification for Howard Haycraft's term *genus Britannicum* for the classic form of the detective story that evolved during these years, because it certainly developed with an affinity to fogbound London. It is also important to recognize this British ethos and the fact that we are speaking about writers and a reading public which, in the main, felt comfortable with the status quo and supported its ethical foundations. That being so, we may expect the books to reflect the social prejudices of the national culture in which they appear, but we may also expect them to reflect some of the island qualities that so dominated that age and gave the genre its supreme exemplar in Sherlock Holmes.

What were these qualities? It was the age of the gifted virtuoso, from Dr. W. G. Grace in sport to Charles Haddon Spurgeon in the pulpit. But preeminently it was an age when the social life of Britain was dominated by the public-school (which in Britain *means* private school) ideal of educated and aristocratic leadership—values and attitudes perpetuated for future generations and extended far beyond any public-school readership by the foundation of *The Boys' Own Paper* in 1879. It was elitist and predominantly male, and the ideal was exemplified especially in sport. This was the period when Baron Pierre de Coubertin began agitation for the modern series of Olympic Games with an international conference at the Sorbonne in 1894. Also, the Oxford and Cambridge annual boat race from Putney to Mortlake on the Thames originated in 1856, and the first international cricket test match between England and Australia took place in 1877. But this athleticism gloried in its amateur status, and over a quarter of the earth's surface Britain expected to win its little Waterloos "on the playing fields of Eton."

If Rudyard Kipling was the Poet Laureate of the empire, surely Sir Henry Newbolt was the poet who linked imperial success to the public-school sporting tradition. His poem, "Vitae Lampada" (learned by heart by generations of British schoolboys), begins with the minor challenge of a school cricket match and ends on the sands of Omdurman or with Kitchener at Khartoum:

There's a breathless hush in the Close tonight—
Ten to make and the match to win—
A bumping pitch and a blinding light,
An hour to play and the last man in.
And it's not for the sake of a ribboned coat,
Or the selfish hope of a season's fame,
But his Captain's hand on his shoulder smote—
"Play up! play up! and play the game!"

The sand of the desert is sodden red—
Red with the wreck of a square that broke;
The gatling's jammed and the colonel dead,
And the regiment blind with the dust and smoke.
The river of death has brimmed his banks,
And England's far and honour a name,
But the voice of a schoolboy rallies the ranks:
"Play up! play up! and play the game!"

Many of these admired qualities reappeared in the concept of the educated, gifted amateur detective, and the challenge of the detective's mental gymnastics became the intellectual counterpart of physical contests on the sports field. Detective fiction of this period assimilated the sporting instinct of fair play: the author was expected to play fair with his or her readers by providing them with all the clues that would give them an equal opportunity with the great detective to reach a correct solution to the mystery. The amateur status was particularly admired as central to this public-school tradition. So wrote A. A. Milne in *The Red House Mystery:*

For the detective himself I demand first that he be an amateur. In real life, no doubt, the best detectives are the professional police, but then in real life the best criminals are professional criminals. In the best detective stories the villain is an amateur, one of ourselves: we rub shoulders with him in the murdered man's drawing room; and no *dossier* nor code-index nor finger-print system is of avail against him. It is the amateur detective who alone can expose the guilty man, by the light of cool inductive reasoning and the logic of stern remorseless facts. Indeed, this light and this logic is all which I will allow him. Away with the scientific detective, the man with the microscope! What satisfaction is it to you or me when the famous Professor examines the small particle of dust which the murderer has left behind him, and infers that he lives between a brewery and a flour-mill? What thrill do we get when the blood-spot on the missing man's handkerchief proves that he was recently bitten by a camel? Speaking for myself, none. The thing is so much too easy for the author, so much too difficult for his readers.

For this is really what we come to: that the detective must have no more special knowledge than the average reader. The reader must be made to feel that, if he too had used the light of cool inductive reasoning and the logic of stern remorseless facts (as, Heaven bless us, we are quite capable of doing) then he too would have fixed the guilt.[3]

Although this passage is overstated, the amateur sporting tradition stands clear and the last paragraph expresses the ideal in the classic detective story very succinctly. It was a game, an intellectual contest between the author's great detective and the reader, and clearly both parties must be given equal opportunity to reach the correct solution.

However, it is also apparent that detective fiction could not remain at this ideal but elementary level. Sooner or later it would have to come to grips with the new techniques and possibilities opened up by science. The amateur ideal and the sporting aspect of the form is emphasized, however, when we reflect that during the

last half of the nineteenth century most of the popular
sports in Europe and America were defining their rules
and establishing their boundaries.

In the oath tendered to prospective members of the
(British) Detection Club, also in Msgr. Ronald Knox's
"Detective Story Decalogue" and in S. S. Van Dine's
"Twenty Rules for Writing Detective Stories," detective
fiction followed the same pattern.[4] All of these attempts
to regulate the medium emphasize (1) the reader's right
to have equal opportunity with the detective to solve the
puzzle; (2) no deception must be practiced on the reader
that is not applied to the detective himself; and (3) the
motives should be personal and not part of an international plot. Some of the proposed rules exclude any love
interest or sensationalism and insist that the central
crime must be murder. As Van Dine remarked at the
beginning of his "Twenty Rules," "The detective story is
a kind of intellectual game. It is more—it is a sporting
event. And for the writing of detective stories there are
very definite laws."[5]

II

Julian Symons was one among few modern critics
to recognize the social and philosophical implications
of detective fiction, for he noted the generally conservative stance that most of the writers took, concerning
social and political issues during this period, answer-
ing the demand of the people for "books that would
reinforce their own view of the world and society."[6] In
addition, he said of the writers that "the interest of
their work lies in the ingenuity with which problems
are propounded and solved, rather than in the ability to
create credible characters or to write stories interesting
as tales rather than as puzzles."[7]

A further contribution of Julian Symons to our
understanding of the development of detective fiction is
his recognition that the whole period covered by the
golden age may be divided into two distinct stages of
development: (1) the earlier period from the time of

Conan Doyle, which was dominated by the short story; and (2) the period that begins in the 1920s, when writers began to experiment with the book-length novel. A moment's reflection should convince us that the genre could not remain at the level of the short story because of the place occupied by human character in crime and detection and also because of the consequent frustration at the limitations imposed by a short-story format.

Within these limitations, however, the major detective figures amply illustrate characteristics that would become typical of the whole genre during the classical period. The collections or series of detective stories that deserve some notice are: G. K. Chesterton's "Father Brown" stories; Melville Davisson Post's tales of his rural sleuth of the American Virginian frontier, Uncle Abner; and *The Man in the Corner*, Baroness Orczy's strange stories of an elderly man who practiced his detection while sitting in the corner of a London A.B.C. teashop.[8]

Of these, probably the Father Brown stories achieved the greatest popularity and are most significant for the present study. In many ways Chesterton, an established writer who delighted in paradox, was his own greatest paradox. He was both a Roman Catholic apologist and a patriotic—even, at times, chauvinistic—Englishman. He was an apologist for Roman Catholicism several years before he became an official convert. But this gives to the Father Brown series the ambivalence of papal allegiance within a society which was decidedly and, at times even aggressively, Protestant in its public profession. As Father Brown declares about his native England, "I come from there. And the funniest thing of all is that even if you love it and belong to it, you still can't make head or tail of it."[9]

The ambivalence is seen in many different forms within the stories: as a Roman Catholic priest Father Brown is both the defender of traditional order and critical of the prevailing social establishment in the name of that traditional order. So he believes in the cosmology of faith and the theological assumptions on which it was founded, but he is critical of those features of British society or of British imperialism due to religious or philosophical influences outside Catholicism. He maintains reason and justice to be at the moral heart of the universe: "Reason and justice grip the remotest and the loneliest star. Look at those stars. Don't they look as if they were single diamonds and sapphires? Well, you can imagine any mad botany or geology you please. Think of a forest of adamant with leaves of brilliants. Think the moon is a blue moon, a single elephantine sapphire. But don't fancy that all that frantic astronomy would make the smallest difference to the reason and justice of conduct. On plains of opal, under cliffs cut out of pearl, you would still find a notice-board, 'Thou shalt not steal.'"[10] This was the cosmology of faith that was shared by the society in which Chesterton lived. On the other hand, he tilted at all forms of Calvinism and Puritanism (particularly that of the Scots), he questioned French rationalism and therefore opposed rationalistic atheism. But, despite England's racial and national prejudices, some of which he shared, he was also extremely critical of the British establishment.[11]

Indeed, the paradox of Chesterton himself goes further, for although as a Roman Catholic apologist he was a supporter of the post-Tridentine Catholicism of Vatican I, politically he was a radical and closely attached to the Liberal Party. For many years he contributed to Liberal daily papers, such as the *Daily News.* This means that, although his stories exhibit a hierarchical and traditionalist view of nature, they endorse a democratic view of society.

Critic Erik Routley was an ordained minister in a church with Calvinist roots, but he probably used a more perceptive lens on the Father Brown stories than any other commentator.[12] He noted that Chesterton, the apologist, presented the Roman Catholic church "as the church of the common man," and Chesterton himself describes it as "wedded to common sense."[13]

This is another place where the curious contradictions of Father Brown are seen. Chesterton opposed rationalism as a form of pseudoreligion,[14] but as a Thomist he insisted on the proper place of reason in theology. In "The Blue Cross," Father Brown discusses theology with another "priest" (a French thief, Flambeau), while Valentin, the head of the French police force, listens from his hiding place behind a tree on Hampstead Heath:

> The taller priest [Flambeau in disguise] nodded his bowed head and said:
>
> "Ah, yes, these modern infidels appeal to their reason; but who can look at those millions of worlds and not feel that there may well be wonderful universes above us where reason is utterly unreasonable?"
>
> "No," said the other priest; "reason is always reasonable, even in the last limbo, in the lost borderland of things. I know that people charge the Church with lowering reason, but it is just the other way. Alone on earth, the Church makes reason really supreme. Alone on earth, the Church affirms that God Himself is bound by reason."[15]

A short time later, when Flambeau's disguise has been stripped away, Father Brown remarks that he became convinced that Flambeau was a false priest because he had attacked reason—and *that* is "bad theology."[16]

For all his support of the Vatican I papacy, Chesterton anticipated some of the insights of modern liberation theologians. Father Brown is, in some ways, representative of "the common man." Routley noted that Chesterton repeatedly described Father Brown as "commonplace."[17] The priest persistently sets himself against wealthy industrialists and recognizes the legitimate claims of the poor, notably in South America.[18] In the name of Christianity, Chesterton was even prepared to say kind things about the socialism that was appearing in Europe. There are some significant allusions to this in "The Flying Stars," a story that led to Flambeau's conversion. When Mr. Crook—a young man in a red tie—is discovered standing on a wall, Ruby Adams warns him not to jump:

> He took no notice of the girl's alarmed adjuration, but leapt like a grasshopper to the ground beside her, where he might very well have broken his legs.
>
> "I think I was meant to be a burglar," he said placidly, "and I have no doubt I should have been if I hadn't happened to be born in that nice house next door. I can't see any harm in it, anyhow."
>
> "How can you say such things?" she remonstrated.
>
> "Well," said the young man, "if you're born on the wrong side of the wall, I can't see that it's wrong to climb over."
>
> "I never know what you will say or do next," she said. [19]

A little later the sight of the magnificent diamonds given to Ruby by her godfather, Sir Leopold Fischer, causes Mr. Crook, of the red tie, to observe that it would have been natural for some attempt to have been made to steal them en route to the Adams house;

> "Quite natural, I should say," growled the man in the red tie. "I shouldn't blame 'em if they had taken 'em. When they ask for bread, and you don't even give them a stone, I think they might take the stone for themselves."
>
> "I won't have you talking like that," cried the girl, who was in a curious glow. "You've only talked like that since you became a horrid what's-his-name. You know what I mean. What do you call a man who wants to embrace the chimney- sweeps?"
>
> "A saint," said Father Brown.
>
> "I think," said Sir Leopold, with a supercilious smile, "that Ruby means a Socialist."
>
> "A Radical does not mean a man who lives on radishes," remarked Crook, with some impatience; "and a Conservative does not mean a man who preserves jam. Neither, I assure you, does a Socialist mean a man who desires a social evening with the chimney-sweep. A So-

cialist means a man who wants all the chimneys swept and all the chimney-sweeps paid for it."[20]

In most of the stories, as Routley observed, "You, the reader, are being gently accused of being over-sophisticated, wrong about the demands of being a gentleman," and wrong about the demands of being a servant.[21]

Father Brown is the antithesis of the great detective who endorses the status quo. He is insignificant, fallible, commonplace, and he expresses a healthy skepticism about society.

Erik Routley's insight into the Father Brown stories goes deeper than the recognition that they gave Chesterton an opportunity to make social comment or to offer a major departure from the superhuman type of the great detective.[22] Routley recognizes that these stories arose directly out of Chesterton's commitment to faith and were not simply incidental to it. The stories about Father Brown "are almost all moral theology presented as detection. It is, therefore, impossible in writing about him to avoid a certain amount of language that recalls moral theology in its popular form. Detective literature is seventy-five percent moralism anyhow; but here it is entirely moralism."[23]

Perhaps deeper still there is the insight into the *way* Father Brown investigates crime. At one level his method is common to all detection in its frank use of reason, but unlike many private detectives, Father Brown does not engage in detection "by making himself larger than the criminal, nor confound the established police force by demonstrating greater skill or education than its members have."[24] Basically his personal method is his ability to identify himself with the thought processes that make a criminal perform a criminal action:

> "You see, I had murdered them all myself," explained Father Brown patiently. "So, of course, I knew how it was done." . . .
> "I had planned out each of the crimes very carefully,"

went on Father Brown. "I had thought out exactly how a thing like that could be done, and in what style or state of mind a man could really do it. And when I was quite sure that I felt exactly like the murderer myself, of course I knew who he was."[25]

This means that Father Brown, unlike other amateur detectives, engages in detection not in spite of being a priest but while fulfilling his pastoral vocation; he is a detective *because* he is a priest. So his concern for justice and truth is no less clear for him than it is for the police, but it is different. Where the latter look for conviction, Father Brown looks for confession and conversion; while the police are concerned about crime, Father Brown is concerned about sin. It has been pointed out that in all the stories about him there is only one account of an actual arrest.[26] Father Brown pursues his objective, "by making himself less, not greater, than the criminal, by 'getting inside him,' as he puts it; by never allowing himself to say, 'That's a thing I could never have done.' "[27]

III

Almost at the opposite wing of the ecclesiastical scene is Melville Davisson Post's investigator of mysteries, Uncle Abner. We do not know his surname but he is "Uncle" Abner to his young amanuensis and nephew, Martin—the son of Abner's brother Rufus. Abner's investigations are closely associated with the work of Squire Randolph, a perceptive magistrate who must account for any unexplained deaths on the early nineteenth-century Virginian frontier. The events in the stories seem to have taken place just before the outbreak of the Civil War, possibly during the presidency of Millard Fillmore (1850–53).[28]

Abner is not only a convinced Christian, he is also a Calvinist and a committed Puritan:

> I ought to say a word about my Uncle Abner. He was one
> of those austere, deeply religious men who were the prod-
> uct of the Reformation. He always carried a Bible in his
> pocket and he read it where he pleased. Once the crowd at
> Roy's Tavern tried to make sport of him when he got his
> book out by the fire; but they never tried it again. When
> the fight was over Abner paid Roy eighteen silver dollars
> for the broken chairs and the table—and he was the only
> man in the tavern who could ride a horse. Abner belonged
> to the church militant, and his God was a war Lord.[29]

In a later story, Abner is likened to Oliver Cromwell, and
he is obviously the kind of character who in an earlier
century might have recrossed the Atlantic to join Cromwell's Ironsides. We read that he has, "the frame of the
empire builder on the frontier of the empire. The face
reminded one of Cromwell, the craggy features in re-
pose seemed molded over iron, but the fine gray eyes
had a calm serenity, like remote spaces in the summer
sky. The man's clothes were plain and somber. And he
gave one the impression of things big and vast."[30]

But although Abner appears to be the epitome of
the Calvinism that existed like New England bedrock
beneath the Puritanism of early America, he is not to be
confused with the puritanical stereotypes that have
become popular. An unshakable belief in divine Providence was central to his thinking, but he refused to
reduce predestination either to fatalism or to chance or
to concede that God could have anything to do with the
infliction of human tragedy and disaster.[31] So in "The
Adopted Daughter," he refuses to engage in a duel
because he cannot believe that God would direct an
assassin's bullet.[32]

His unwillingness to saddle Providence with the
responsibility for human tragedy is particularly illustrated in "The Doomdorf Mystery" which is perhaps his
most ingenious piece of detection.[33] It centers in a
closed-room mystery where there could have been no
possibility of an intruder having shot the old man,
Doomdorf, at the time he died; and yet it happened.

Abner refuses to accept the most obvious answers, even when supported by plausible but false confessions. The solution satisfies not only his reason's demand for a logical answer in accordance with the factual evidence, but also his theological requirement that justice should be done and be seen to have been done.

Abner's professed Protestant theology raises some interesting points of comparison with Chesterton's Roman Catholic Father Brown. These go beyond the obvious contrast between the nineteenth-century frontier in Virginia and the society of nineteenth-century England where the industrial revolution was in full spate.

1. Unlike Father Brown, Abner has no particular *modus operandi* for detection. He tries to convince suspects of their theological shortcomings and particularly of the inevitability of God's justice, but his primary concern is not—like Father Brown's motive—pastoral, but admittedly retributive. Indeed, in that regard, he considers justice more important to society than charity: "I am persuaded that there exists a greater thing than charity—a thing of more value to the human family. Like charity, it rejoiceth not in iniquity, but it does not bear all things or believe all things, or endure all things; and, unlike charity, it seeketh its own. . . . Do you know what thing I mean, Smallwood? I will tell you. It is Justice."[34]

Uncle Abner's method is founded upon native common sense combined with a wide knowledge of human nature, particularly a knowledge of the perverse ways in which mortals can sin, but it is centered in his fundamental belief in the activity of a divine Providence in human affairs. And justice is at the center of his Calvinist theology because it is at the heart of the doctrine of Providence. However, this justice is not to be equated with human justice, even with the laws of Virginia. "The law," he observes in an argument with a suspect, "is not always justice."[35] Indeed there are occasions on which he is prepared to disregard legality in order to achieve justice.[36] In response to the claim that, in order to be free of subjectivism, our ideas of justice must be determined by civil laws, Abner claims that what is just and right has already been placed in the heart of the individual, presumably the conscience.[37]

But if true justice could not be equated with human laws, much less could it be equated with the law that a lynch mob might try to take into its own hands.[38] Melville Davisson Post gave us a clue to its nature and its relation to his own religious convictions when he dedicated the Abner stories to his father "whose unfailing faith in an ultimate justice behind the moving of events has been to the writer a wonder and an inspiration." That statement illustrates the spirit in which the character of Uncle Abner was conceived and suggests the relationship of the religion it represents to the society of post-Jeffersonian America. "It is a world," declares Abner to Squire Randolph, "filled with the mysterious justice of God."[39]

2. In contrast to Father Brown's occasional endorsement of sentiments that come close to socialism, Uncle Abner endorses the Protestant work ethic. He discusses this with the hunchback Gaul in one of the earlier stories, when Gaul curses the problems of getting good workers:

> Labor was a lost art and the breed of men run out. This new set were worthless—they had hours—and his oaths filled all the rafters. Hours! Why, under his father men worked from dawn until dark and cleaned their horses by a lantern. . . . These were decadent times that we were on. In the good days one bought a man for two hundred eagles; but now the creature was a citizen and voted at the polls—and could not be kicked. And if one took his cane and drubbed him he was straightway sued at law, in an action of trespass on the case, for damages. . . . Men had gone mad with these new-fangled notions, and the earth was likely to grow up with weeds!
>
> Abner said there was a certain truth in this—and that truth was that men were idler than their fathers. Certain preachers preached that labor was a curse and back it up with Scripture; but he had read the Scriptures for him-

self and the curse was idleness. Labor and God's Book
would save the world; they were two wings that a man
could get his soul to Heaven on.[40]

In the opinions of Gaul, we see the Protestant work
ethic being pressed into the support of slavery, but in
the Virginia of the 1850s that would hardly be regarded
as surprising. However, what is surprising is to see the
way in which Abner modifies his theology to presage
future sentiments rather than to reflect contemporary
popular prejudices. So he intervened to prevent a slave
woman being wrongly accused of theft, helped poor
immigrants to escape accusations of murder, and for all
his support of the Protestant work ethic, insisted that
all our possessions are no more than held on a lease
from God.[41] We are hardly surprised to find Abner
citing Old Testament examples, but we may be surprised to find his protest against the vindictive slaughter of Indians.[42]

3. We can expect Abner, as a post-Jeffersonian
American, to express a proper respect for human reason. He discounts supernatural phenomena almost as
firmly as Auguste Dupin or Sherlock Holmes, but his
faith in the God of the Bible will not allow him to
disregard the possibility of God intervening in a miracu-
lous way through human agents.[43] On the other hand,
he holds that even our subconscious presentiments of
truth must have a rational basis. However, we must
never allow ourselves to confuse God's knowledge of the
truth with human reason.[44] Indeed, he is scathing
against the agnosticism of postrevolutionary humanism for, "the fear of God is the beginning of wisdom."[45]
In some ways, that persistent stance against contemporary unbelief makes the stories of Uncle Abner as much
an essay in Christian apologetic as are Chesterton's
tales of Father Brown.

But no less than the Father Brown stories, Uncle
Abner's exploits are important for us because they reveal the relationship of justice to civilized society in the
making and recognize the essential place that religion

has in that aspect of societal evolution. Perhaps at this point, Melville Davisson Post goes even further than G. K. Chesterton by recognizing that this essential function of religion belongs not to one established church but to all churches.

In the story "Naboth's Vineyard," reflecting on the incident in the Book of Kings, there is a point where Abner calls on the citizens in a courtroom to stand up and take the responsibility of placing a judge under the obligations of the law:

> It was a strange and instructive thing to see. The loud-mouthed and the reckless were in that courtroom, men who would have shouted in a political convention, or run howling with a mob, but they were not the persons who stood up when Abner called upon the authority of the people to appear. Men rose whom one would not have looked to see—the blacksmith, the saddler, and old Asa Divers. And I saw that law and order and all the structure that civilization had builded up, rested on the sense of justice that certain men carried in their breasts, and that those who possessed it not, in the crisis of necessity, did not count.
>
> Father Donovan stood up; he had a little flock beyond the valley river, and he was as poor, and almost as humble as his Master, but he was not afraid; and Bronson, who preached Calvin, and Adam Rider, who traveled a Methodist circuit. No one of them believed in what the other taught; but they all believed in justice, and when the line was drawn, there was but one side for them all.[46]

IV

Other short-story writers of the golden age do not always provide us with that kind of clear-cut testimony. Perhaps the nearest example may be the anonymous "man in the corner," created by Emma (Emmuska Magdalena Rosalia Marie Joseph Barbara), Baroness Orczy, of the Hungarian nobility. After sojourns in Brussels, Monte Carlo, and Paris, the Baroness eventually settled in London and established herself through the French Revolutionary exploits of another of her fictional creations, the Scarlet Pimpernel. The appearance of "the man in the corner" tales spans almost the whole of the first decade of the present century; they began to appear in magazines in 1901 and finally received publication in book form in 1909.[47]

Despite the author's marriage to Montagu Barstow, the son of a Yorkshire Nonconformist minister, we cannot invest the revelations of the man in the corner with any obvious theological meaning.[48] He speaks of Providence, but it is at best providence of a casual, indiscriminate kind, and at worst punitive.[49] The Baroness was at least aware enough religiously to recognize in England the existence of churches other than the established Church of England, and in Scotland the distinctions between Presbyterians and Roman Catholics, but she does not make any theological capital out of these religious resources.[50]

Because of this, the man in the corner is much further from Father Brown and Uncle Abner than either of them are from each other. He probably deserves to be regarded as representative of the mundane and commonplace in human nature even more than the nondescript figure of Chesterton's Father Brown. Certainly the Baroness' character is the antithesis of all the bright and socially acceptable young scions of the British gentry who were later to carry the detective torch from Dupin and Sherlock Holmes into our own time. His chosen confidante is Polly Burton, a struggling young London journalist, who runs across him from time to time while taking her meager lunch in a London A.B.C. cafe. At the time of their first encounter,

> Polly thought to herself that she had never seen anyone so pale, so thin, with such funny light- coloured hair, brushed very smoothly across the top of a very obviously bald crown. He looked so timid and nervous as he fidgeted incessantly with a piece of string; his long, lean, and

trembling fingers tying and untying it into knots of wonderful and complicated proportions.[51]

Those persistent and omnipresent Gordian knots must never be cut but always patiently unraveled, whether the problem was presented in string or in criminology. That is the measure of the difference between the man in the corner, as the first of the truly "armchair detectives," and those we have considered to this point. The other detectives never reduced detection wholly to an exercise in ratiocination, and at least identified themselves with their suspects to the point of physically examining the scene of the crimes and gathering material evidence. The man in the corner brushes most of that aside and considers crime simply as a chess problem: "Crime interests me only when it resembles a clever game of chess, with many intricate moves which all tend to one solution, the checkmating of the antagonist—the detective force of the country. Now, confess that, in the Dublin mystery, the clever police there were absolutely checkmated."[52]

There is not a great deal more that need detain us. Occasionally, the stories reveal perceptive social comment, as in the recognition that during the first years of this century, England entertained considerable prejudice against Germans.[53] The stories remain curiously amoral, however, partly because the man in the corner scorns the police and also because he appears to be completely indifferent to the apprehension of those who disrupt society by crime. Also, there is a twist at the end (certainly not to be spoiled for any subsequent readers by giving inadvertent clues) which would be entertaining, if it did not concern a particularly gruesome and reprehensible crime.[54]

V

The other short-story writers of this period add little to our purpose. Detective fiction was surveying the landscape to find the natural line of its own advancement, and writers concentrated more on exploiting the idiosyncrasies of their own detectives than on the development of detection as such.

Perhaps in protest against overspecialization and the employment of esoteric knowledge, Arthur Morrison's Martin Hewitt stressed detection through plain common sense and observation, rather in the spirit of "Kim's game" so beloved of the early Boy Scout movement. "I can't say I have a system. I call it nothing but common-sense and a sharp pair of eyes."[55]

At the same time, since the nineteenth century had become supremely the century of science and technology, the appearance of the scientific detective could not be long delayed. He was provided in R. Austin Freeman's creation, Dr. John Evelyn Thorndyke, who in many ways reflected the scientific interests of his creator.[56] Freeman also experimented with what has been described as the "inverted detective story," in which the reader is first presented with the complete account of a crime and then carried through a meticulous survey of its discovery and the way in which evidence leads to the solution. Thorndyke emphasizes, "the necessity of pursuing the most trivial clue to an absolute finish," and "the urgent need of a trained scientist to aid the police."[57]

Within this same category of the detective with a special emphasis or gift, we may count the many female detectives who begin to appear. By the turn of the century, attempts had already been made to introduce women detectives who challenged the male athleticism presumed to be necessary for an essentially masculine occupation. And very soon the twentieth century was to become the century of female achievement in this regard with the appearance of Anna Katharine Green's the *Leavenworth Case* (1878), Matthias McDonnell Bodkin's *Dora Myrl: The Lady Detective* (1900), Reginald Wright Kauffman's *Miss Frances Baird, Detective: A Passage from her Memoirs* (1906) and Baroness Orczy's *Lady Molly of Scotland Yard* (1910).[58]

But this emphasis on idiosyncrasy in detection

probably achieved its *ne plus ultra* in Ernest Bramah's stories of Max Carrados, an amateur who practiced detection although totally blind.[59] Most of the stories emphasizing physical limitations are so obviously preoccupied with the intellectual superiority of the detective and the mental gymnastics necessary to overcome whatever obstacles the writer has set for his or her leading character, that they do not offer much scope for profound reflection. Of their kind, the Carrados stories are a tour de force and are not without commentary on English society at that time. Bramah considered the period of his writing (the first third of this century) as one of irresponsibility, when people had become slack about fulfilling their contracts—the kind of society that might engender vigilantes or the "private retributionist."[60] He pokes fun at the curious little snobberies we practice, such as a claim to be too discriminating about the coffee we drink, and he was well aware of the prejudices and problems caused by Britain's colonial empire.[61] Although one story ends with the rather unsatisfying conversion of its chief culprit by the Salvation Army, no attempt is made to relate this religious and ethical change to any implications for society.[62] He was also critical of sensationalism in the press, Christian Science, and capital punishment.[63] In "The Ingenious Mr. Spinola" he forecast our computer age.[64] And in "The Disappearance of Marie Severe," he gave attention to the problem of the child molester.[65] But perhaps he is most important in linking the earlier period of detective fiction to the longer novels that were to follow. Because of his disability, Max Carrados was forced to identify himself with the criminal mind. Regarding the solution of one problem, he remarked to his friend, the private investigator Carlyle, "To me it seems absolutely simple and inevitable. Perhaps that is because I should have done it—fundamentally, that is—just the same way myself."[66] In identifying themselves with the thought processes that produce crime, detectives such as Max

Carrados and Father Brown were pointing to the new form that detective fiction would take, in which the clues would be observed not only at the scene of the crime, but much more importantly, in defects of character.

3

The Gilded Cage

The English Country-House Murder

I

The importance of motive in the solution of a crime, particularly a crime of murder, has always been recognized—money, social stigma, the temptation to eliminate some of life's more detested restraints are actual causes of violent crime. But behind each of these motives, there are people and the drives that come from personality—greed, pride, and lust, to recognize them in less romantic terms. This underscores the insight that human character provides the most fertile field for clues of crime, because crimes are committed by people. At some point, it must have become quite clear to writers that, in order to continue the "game" developed in detective fiction and to give the reader a fair chance of reaching an independent solution, they would need a longer format than could be provided by the short story. The evolution of the novel itself demanded the interplay of character. As J. B. Priestley, who experimented with the medium himself, wrote: "The novelist, whatever else he does, should be able to show us people who by some means or other, through delighted fascination, repulsion, or mere conviction that in their own world they exist, catch and hold our imagination. If his characters fail to do this, then the novelist has failed."[1] His must have been a general realization that "clues of character" more often than not provide the most important evidence for crime which caused detective fiction to move rapidly out of the short-story form into the novel. In the years during and immediately following World War I, this realization was exploited by some remarkable British women writers, including Dorothy Sayers and the most prolific of them all—Agatha Christie. Later they were joined by the likes of Margery Allingham, Georgette Heyer, Gladys Mitchell, Josephine Tey, and New Zealander Ngaio Marsh. It was not quite a British or feminine monopoly, but there is no doubt that the "league of British women" led the way and developed the characteristics of what we may call the English country-house murder.

II

The basic elements of this style rapidly developed in the years immediately after World War I. In many ways the style itself may have been an exercise in nostalgia—an attempt to return to the best of prewar Britain and to the ordered society where all social classes worked harmoniously and in which everyone knew his or her "place."

One of the most vivid memories of my first year at Oxford in 1939 was that of being present as an undergraduate at the Encaenia when P. G. Wodehouse was awarded his honorary degree as Doctor of Letters. In thinking of the light literature of the twenties and thirties, we should remember the influence of Wodehouse's creations—particularly the image of that supercilious, deceptively effete-looking, but remarkably resilient representative of the "British upper class," Bertie Wooster, as well as Wooster's loyal servant, the dependable, seemingly obtuse, but very capable man, Jeeves. So, Death Bredon (Lord Peter Wimsey) in Dorothy Sayers' *Murder Must Advertise* is described as a "cross between Ralph Lynn and Bertie Wooster," and as testimony to the popularity of Wooster's type, we read that the main office of Pym's advertising agency has in it, "a dark youth in spectacles, immersed in a novel by P. G. Wodehouse."[2] The public-school types had done well in the bloodbaths of Ypres and Passchendale, where the peculiar qualities of feudal loyalty, ingenious improvisation, and the ability to play a game of rugby in a bog and a snowstorm came into their own. After the war this lighthearted approach had not served them so well in the bloodless efficiency of "Civvy Street."[3]

But that is morbid, and the British public likes to treat its pets with affection and not dwell too long on the number of beagle pups that find their way into the vivisectionist's laboratory. So let us recognize the pet and put him in a setting where his lovable gifts can again be given full play and where he can once again evoke all the nostalgic feelings of youth. In the world of adventure heroes and Bertie Wooster escapades, the new-style detectives took to the format like ducks to water or seagulls foraging inland after a storm.

And so the Wooster pattern became the fashion. Like the amusingly irresponsible Bertie, the detective hero was essentially an amateur from the upper classes. Dorothy Sayers' Lord Peter Wimsey, Margery Allingham's Albert Campion, Nicholas Blake's Nigel Strangeways, and H. C. Bailey's Reggie Fortune may not have all been born to the purple, but they were certainly born to a delicate shade of puce. And as if to emphasize the wartime social unity of the English class system, just as Wooster has his Jeeves, Campion has his Magersfontein Lugg (his former batman) and Wimsey his Bunter. (Bunter had also served as batman for Wimsey during World War I.)[4] A similar figure appears in the character of Nicholas Blake's ex-prize fighter factotum Bellamy.[5]

Hence the popular literature of the period features a number of unemployed, and perhaps largely unemployable, gentlemen who delve into intrigue and adventure just for the fun of it. Sapper's Bulldog Drummond is a prime example in the adventure story of the time. But to him we must add the new-style heroes of detection. Society after World War I rapidly became a scene where adventure could be played out and where life and death issues might be pursued with characteristic élan by the unemployed young representatives of the English upper class who, a few years earlier, had dived out of the sun at Fokkers or thoughtlessly launched themselves over the top of the trenches in Flanders. They had all the heroic and intellectual equipment to become the ideal amateurs for a new fashion in detective fiction.

The realities and loyalties of the Great War were often deliberately evoked. Wimsey still lived with the trauma of the fighting; the loyalties of the struggle are reflected in the special relationship of the officer to his "man"; and Agatha Christie's Tommy and Tuppence Beresford shared the problem experienced by many of being out of work. Later, when postwar society had become more settled and showed signs of breaking out of its social restrictions, Dame Ngaio Marsh made the successful experiment of transferring her young aristocrat (Roderick Alleyn) to the ranks of the professional police, but usually the amateur status was jealously preserved.

The only notable exception to the hero model was Agatha Christie's even bolder break with the public-school tradition in making her detective hero, Hercule Poirot, a former member of the Belgian police force who had been brought to England as a refugee by the exigencies of the German invasion of his country. He was acceptable to the English of that time as a representative of "brave little Belgium," but his entrée into the English class structure was underwritten by his friend and collaborator, Captain Hastings. In her first detective novel, *The Mysterious Affair at Styles,* which appeared in 1920 and was obviously written in the last days of the war, Poirot is staying in the village as a Belgian refugee and becomes involved in the events at Styles Court, a house where Hastings is a guest while convalescing from a war wound.

III

The English country house provided an ideal setting for the young heroes to show their skills. It became
a favorite context for the detective fiction of the 1920s
and 1930s. Nancy Blue Wynne writes of Agatha Christie's first foray into the field, "A traditional Christie
device first encountered in this novel and successfully
repeated many times is the setting of a crime in a large
upper-class household." Wynne also notes that in this
book, Agatha Christie intended to make the delineation
of character, "a more important part of the detective
story than any author before her."[6] This would demand
a longer format than the short story.

Ideally, the English country-house murder, as the
phrase suggests, takes place in the countryseat of English nobility—in a manor house belonging to a member of the gentry, with a full complement of servants to
act as witnesses and to complicate the suspicions. In
this setting a number of guests may be brought together for a weekend party and this means that most of the
suspects, together with the detective and the culprit,
belong to the same social class and similar educational
background. Occasionally, the group of suspects is aug-
mented by characters from the village, county guests,
the doctor, or the parson. It is important, however, that
there should be a closed circle of suspects and an
amateur detective drawn from the same class. This
evens the odds in the battle of wits. It is a "gilded
cage."

Later writing was to push this self-contained aspect of the country-house murder even further by trap-
ping the houseparty for a week or so by means of a
blizzard, flood, or other natural disaster. This meant
that the relatively small group of suspects and victims
was effectively cut off from the outside world, enabling
the tension to mount and providing a time limit for the
amateur detective to solve the problem before the arrival of the police and the reduction of the puzzle to a
matter of police routine. One of the best examples of

this closed context is Agatha Christie's novelette *Three Blind Mice*, which has become a living piece of social history in the long-running play *The Mousetrap*.[7] True, the country house is not owned by semifeudal gentry, but it is "Monkswell Manor: Guest House," owned by a young couple, Molly and Giles Davis, who are trying to make a living from it. Otherwise the conditions are much the same as in other country-house murder tales.

In this kind of detective fiction, the circumstances are so arranged that all the characters have motives for the crime, all have alibis or not, and therefore all come under scrutiny and suspicion as culprits. The cleverness of the author is shown by the skill with which he or she manages to hide the real culprit until the very end of the story and the skill with which suspicion is shifted from one suspect to the next.

All these conditions are illustrated in Agatha Christie's tour de force of 1939, which appeared originally under the title, *Ten Little Niggers*.[8] In this story the closed context is provided by "Nigger Island" ("Indian Island" in the American version) off the Devonshire coast. All the participants could be suspected of having committed murder previously and they may therefore, on this occasion, each be suspected of being the culprit. Each in turn becomes the victim and finally the police are presented with what appears to be a completely insoluble mystery, for, in the words of the true culprit, "It was my ambition to *invent* a murder mystery that no one could solve."[9] However, the ethical concern of the time appeared in the culprit's confession to having a strong sense of justice:

> It is abhorrent to me that an innocent person or creature should suffer or die by any act of mine. I have always felt strongly that right should prevail.
>
> It may be understood—I think a psychologist would understand—that with my mental make-up being what it was, I adopted the law as a profession. The legal profession satisfied nearly all my instincts.
>
> Crime and its punishment has always fascinated me.[10]

Often, the solution of the English country-house murder is presented in a denouement when the detective brings all the suspects together and reviews the evidence against each. This maintains the character of the English country-house murder as an intellectual puzzle in spite of all suggestions of adventure, chase, or international intrigue in earlier chapters.

Although this represents the ideal form, the essential characteristics may be repeated in an infinite number of variations—an isolated island, a railway carriage, a river boat, a trans-Atlantic liner, or any social context where the number of suspects can be limited and the action contained within strictly controlled limits.

IV

The significance of the changes that may be traced in Agatha Christie's work demands a chapter of its own.[11] Clearly she was the supreme exemplar of this kind of mystery; "queen" of crime not only because of her incredible productivity as a writer, but even more because of her unsurpassed skill in beating the reader to a solution. Her culprits cover the whole spectrum from the detective's trusty helper to the "victim." But it would be unkind to future readers to say much more in the way of elucidation.

Christie's books repeatedly use the country-house format. To cite a few examples: *The Murder of Roger Ackroyd* (1926), regarded by some as her greatest detective story and by others as the great betrayal, takes place in Roger Ackroyd's countryseat, King's Paddock; *The Secret of Chimneys* (1925) may begin in Bulawayo, Africa, but the action centers in the home of the Brents, which is described as one of the stately homes of England; *The Sittaford Mystery* (1931)[12] concerns a murder perpetrated while a number of local people are engaged in a séance at Sittaford House; *Peril at End House* (1932) tells of a series of murder attempts that culminate in a death at the former home of Sir Nicholas

Buckley, situated on a rocky promontory near the fictional St. Loo on the Cornish Riviera.

The gilded cage was peculiarly adapted for the mysteries featuring Miss Jane Marple, because she operated most effectively in the relatively confined setting of the fictional English village, St. Mary Mead. *Murder at the Vicarage* (1930) is the first of the Miss Marple series; its solution is reminiscent of those grade-school problems which ask us to think of a number, add three, multiply by five, and take away the number we first thought of. The story also reflects the social and ethical presuppositions of Britain just before World War II. It was an extremely prejudiced (artists were expected to be people of loose morals) and class-conscious society, but the Church of England was still at the center of that society. We meet Miss Marple as a pillar of the church of St. Mary Mead and the vicar, the Reverend Leonard Clement, who not only discovers a body in his own study, but is closely associated with Miss Marple in reaching a solution.

The influence of the Church is seen in the vicar's observation to Colonel Protheroe that justice must be maintained, but that it should be tempered with mercy.[13] Miss Marple has no hesitation in regarding certain events that saved the life of the curate, the Reverend Mr. Hawes, as "providential."[14] In some ways it is still a relaxed society; one of the residents of St. Mary Mead confesses that he did not lock the door of his cottage because "no one does lock his house up round here."[15] But there are signs of a changing mood in Christie's novel. A period of increasing social liberalism is personified in the ideas of Dr. Haycock and his opposition to capital punishment, expressed in this conversation with the vicar:

> He [the doctor] was silent for a moment or two and then said, "We think with horror now of the days when we burned witches. I believe the day will come when we will shudder to think that we ever hanged criminals."
> "You don't believe in capital punishment?"

"It's not so much that." He paused. "You know," he said slowly, "I'd rather have my job than yours."

"Why?"

"Because your job deals very largely with what we call right and wrong—and I'm not at all sure that there's any such thing. Suppose it's all a question of glandular secretion. Too much of one gland, too little of another—and you get your murderer, your thief, your habitual criminal. Clement, I believe the time will come when we'll be horrified to think of the long centuries in which we've indulged in what you may call moral reprobation, to think how we've punished people for disease—which they can't help, poor devils. You don't hang a man for having tuberculosis."

"He isn't dangerous to the community."

"In a sense he is. He infects other people. Or take a man who fancies he's the Emperor of China. You don't say 'how wicked of him.' I take your point about the community. The community must be protected. Shut up these people where they can't do any harm—even put them peacefully out of the way—yes, I'd go as far as that. But don't call it punishment. Don't bring shame on them and their innocent families."

I looked at him curiously.

"I've never heard you speak like this before."

"I don't usually air my theories abroad. Today I'm riding my hobby. You're an intelligent man, Clement, which is more than some parsons are. You won't admit, I daresay, that there's no such thing as what is technically termed 'sin,' but you're broad-minded enough to consider the possibility of such a thing."[16]

The reaction of the conservative English of the time to such liberal ideas is seen in the protest of the Chief Constable, Colonel Melchett at "all this namby-pamby-ism."[17]

In some ways Miss Jane Marple reveals her closer relationship with the earlier classical detectives than with those who were to follow. Her detective method was that of finding simple parallels to the existing situation within the normal peccadilloes and petty tensions of village life. In a conversation with the vicar, she says:

> "But, after all, that is a very sound way of arriving at the truth. It's really what people call intuition and make such a fuss about. Intuition is like reading a word without having to spell it out. A child can't do that, because it has had so little experience. But a grown-up person knows the word because he's seen it often before. You catch my meaning, Vicar?"
>
> "Yes," I said slowly. "I think I do. You mean that if a thing reminds you of something else—well, it's probably the same kind of thing."
>
> "Exactly."
>
> "And what precisely does the murder of Colonel Protheroe remind you of?"
>
> Miss Marple sighed.
>
> "That is just the difficulty. So many parallels come to the mind. For instance, there was Major Hargraves, a churchwarden and a man highly respected in every way. And all the time he was keeping a separate second establishment—a former housemaid, just think of it! And five children—actually five children—a terrible shock to his wife and daughter."
>
> I tried hard to visualize Colonel Protheroe in the role of secret sinner, and failed.
>
> "And then there was that laundry business," went on Miss Marple. "Miss Hartnell's opal pin—left most imprudently in a frilled blouse and sent to the laundry. And the woman who took it didn't want it in the least, and wasn't by any means a thief. She simply hid it in another woman's house and told the police she'd seen this other woman take it. Spite, you know, sheer spite. It's an astonishing motive—spite. A man in it, of course. There always is."[18]

This is very close to Father Brown's method of identifying himself with the suspects by trying to think his way into a criminal's mind when plotting the crime. And we read that from the pastoral perspective of her vicar,

Miss Marple had "an uncanny knack of being always right."[19]

A reflection of these older values is to be seen in the words of Maud Silver, Patricia Wentworth's counterpart to Jane Marple, to a prospective client: "I must ask you to think clearly about this. I can take no case with any other object than that of discovering the truth. I cannot undertake to prove anyone innocent, any more than I would undertake to prove anyone guilty. I feel obliged to make this perfectly clear to an intending client. Perhaps you would like a little more time to think it over."[20]

V

The English country-house mystery does not depend for its popularity on any one writer, even one as prolific and creative as Agatha Christie. Margery Allingham uses it extensively. One of her best-known novels, *The Black Dudley Murder*, takes Albert Campion to a gothic situation in the gloomy manor house of Black Dudley, to solve the mystery caused by the death of its owner, Colonel Coombe.[21] *A Cargo of Eagles* concerns Doctor Jones' inheritance in a sinister house in the village of Salty.[22] Allingham's *Mystery Mile* tells of the search by an American, Judge Crowdy Lobbett, for the leader of a dangerous gang in the village of Mystery Mile in the Suffolk marshes, where he and his children have rented the manor house.[23] A later novel, *Black Plumes*, repeats the gothic atmosphere, in a house in Hampstead belonging to an art critic, involving the murder of his partner.[24] The format is repeated in such stories as Catherine Aird's *Stately Home Murder*.[25]

It would be possible, but not strictly germane to our present interest, to present an exhaustive survey of this format, even in terms of English titles. However, perhaps the best way to deal with the country-house murder is to take one or two of the most important novels as representative of the whole genre.

The Red House Mystery

Since A. A. Milne's the *Red House Mystery* has been described as "one of the three best mystery stories of all time,"[26] we might suppose that it would provide the ideal example of the post–World War I English country-house mystery.

It is set in the Red House, country residence of the rich and eligible young bachelor Mark Ablett, and a murder takes place during one of his weekend house parties. The story does not altogether fulfill its promise, however, because very soon after the crime is committed, most of those who are staying in the house are proved innocent and are permitted to return to their respective homes. The crucial problem is not the identity of the culprit. This seems to be clear to amateur sleuth Antony Gillingham, his faithful "Watson"—Bill Beverley—and presumably, most of the readers fairly soon in the course of events. The problem is the identity of the victim. The mystery may fulfill Milne's own basic requirements for amateur detection, but it does not help in our theological quest. Presumably Gillingham pursues his project because he believes in justice being done, although whether justice is ultimately achieved is a moot point. The story is more explicit if the whole enterprise is regarded as a sporting event in which the sleuth is able to use his remarkably retentive mind and ability to excel at "Kim's game."[27] In response to Gillingham's determination to discover the truth, Bill Beverley can be relied upon to exclaim, "By Jove! That's it!" at all the appropriate places, and he reflects on their enterprise as, "a jolly kind of detective game that he and Antony were playing." In keeping with this sporting spirit, he anticipates an exciting nocturnal excursion as "rather fun."[28]

As a reflection of the views of English people about justice or retribution, *The Red House Mystery* does not provide much clear evidence, and one might just as well examine the theology implicit in the author's better known hero, Winnie the Pooh.

Trent's Last Case

E. C. Bentley's chef-d'oeuvre was also a tour de force. *Trent's Last Case* made a great impression when it first appeared, and a contemporary reviewer regarded it as a "detective story of unusual originality and ingenuity."[29] Most of the other reviewers who have commented since have been lavish in their praise. Willard Huntington Wright and Dorothy L. Sayers both regarded it as a "masterpiece," while Lee Wright regarded it as "outstanding," and John Carter thought it was "sufficient for immortality."[30] A few, including Ronald Knox and Raymond Chandler, were more critical, and I agree with H. Douglas Thomson's opinion that the last thirty or forty pages are wearisome and redundant.[31]

Perhaps the most important feature of the book was noted by Erik Routley and Julian Symons when they cited E. C. Bentley's own complaint, "It does not seem to have been generally noticed that *Trent's Last Case* is not so much a detective story as an exposure of detective stories."[32] This insight is probably the most valuable in discussing *Trent's Last Case.*

From the position taken by Philip Trent, artist, journalist, and amateur crime investigator, the detection follows naturally in the style of the gilded cage. The story concerns the death of Sigsbee Manderson, an immensely wealthy American industrialist and financier who owns White Gables. The number of suspects is virtually restricted to those living or visiting in the house or those staying at the nearby hotel in Marlstone. Trent's detection naturally reflects the society and assumptions of the time. Although the victim, Manderson, is described as being not in the slightest bit religious, the issue was real enough to evoke comment, and he is supposed to have had some of the least popular virtues of residual Puritanism.[33] Although Trent confesses that in some things he declines to help the police, assisting the cause of justice appears to be one of his major objectives, and this naturally involves him in the pursuit of truth.[34] At the same time, in his relationship with Scotland Yard's Inspector Murch, he has no difficulty in defining the principles of his own investigations as "detective sportsmanship." Bentley goes on to observe that, "Mr. Murch, who loved a contest, and who only stood to gain by his association with the keen intelligence of the other, entered very heartily into the 'game.'"[35] It is also interesting to note that Marlowe, who became a leading suspect, is described as giving out "that air of clean living and inward health that is the peculiar glory of his social type at his years."[36] Marlowe is a young man in his twenties, recently graduated from Oxford! Very much the public-school type.

When we consider the thrust of the book in broader context, it points to conclusions that are more ambiguous. Bentley dedicated it to his friend G. K. Chesterton, the litterateur convert to Catholicism. Perhaps as an overture to Chesterton, one of Bentley's characters, although an avowed atheist, complains that because he favors abstinence from meat on one day of the week, he has the reputation of being a Roman Catholic.[37] Similarly we get a persistent impression that Bentley shares some of Chesterton's prejudices, such as his dislike of Puritanism and its work ethic. So he expresses his disgust at Manderson's puritanical nature and his hatred of what he perceives as American plutocracy. One of the characters says of the victim, "Such men as he were unfit to live," while Trent himself, on hearing of Manderson's death, declares, "I wouldn't have a hand in hanging a poor devil who had let daylight into a man like Sig Manderson."[38] However, we have the impression that, despite these radical sentiments, Trent generally supports the society existing in Britain and the forces of law and order that sustain it.

The situation is rather different when we look at the story from the perspective of Marlowe, the leading suspect, or even Trent's elderly friend, Mr. Nathaniel Burton Cupples, described as a "man of unusually conscientious, industrious, and orderly mind," and "a highly regarded member of the London Positivist Society."[39] It seems evident that Cupples represents Bentley's own liberal political views, which would certainly have been shared by Chesterton, and which were fashionable in British intellectual circles during the period just after World War I. Cupples was deeply critical of the direction Western society was taking: "This is a terrible time in which we live, my dear boy. There is none recorded in history, I think, in which the disproportion between the material and the moral constituents of society has been so great or so menacing to the permanence of the fabric. But nowhere, in my judgment, is the prospect so dark as it is in the United States."[40] Along the same lines, Bentley has some pungent comments on the way industry treated labor, was properly critical of American lynch law, thought that being descended from the American Indians should be a matter of pride, and considered how a servant might reflect on what it would like to be a billionaire.[41] Some of this may be put down to anti-American prejudice, but the mood was reflected in other writers of the time. For example, Dorothy Sayers has a trenchant criticism of capitalistic advertising in *Murder Must Advertise.*[42]

Bentley's empathy for Chesterton's political radicalism may best be seen in the comment of the perceptive Mr. Cupples that "as a rule it is in the task of penetrating to the spiritual truth that the administration of justice breaks down."[43] Father Brown would have agreed, and the truth behind that agreement may indicate how far this book was, as its author suggested, an exposure of the detective stories in the golden age. Change was imperatively needed, and it was imminent.

VI

Detective fiction, even with the classic British accent, could not remain within the conventional confines of the gilded cage or even within the social limitations of the golden age period. That was far too constricting for a literary form that would be forced, in the period after 1918, into realism. Perhaps Dorothy Sayers illustrates that sea change. Her Lord Peter Wimsey corpus begins at

the family seat, Riddlesdale in Yorkshire, and illustrates
Wimsey's detective agility in saving his brother, the Duke
of Denver, from the charge of having murdered his sister's
fiancé.[44] But Wimsey could not be kept in such a rarefied
atmosphere. Soon after the appearance of *Clouds of Witness* (1926), his interest shifts from the artificiality of a
countryseat to real life, as Sayers explores the emotions
and reactions of her detective when he becomes involved
with a woman accused of murder in *Strong Poison* (1930),
and in the long saga of his wooing that carries us through
Gaudy Night (1935) and *Busman's Honeymoon* (1940).
In *The Documents in the Case* (1937), with Robert Eustace, Sayers turned to a crime based upon a piece of
scientific esoterica.

These stories suggest that Sayers could not restrict
her genius to the limitations of a gilded cage or to the
conventions that had been followed during the golden
age period.

The British golden age of detective fiction was to
have plenty of imitators and examplars on both sides of
the Atlantic, because it supported the prevailing cultures and a view of justice that undergirded traditional
values within Anglo-Saxon societies. It is to be seen just
as clearly in Arthur Upfield's mysteries among the
sheep stations of the Australian outback and in his
half-caste detective, Inspector Napoleon Bonaparte, as
it is in Lord Peter Wimsey among the teacups of rural
England or in the apple pie and clam chowder of Phoebe
Taylor's Asey Mayo on Cape Cod.

But detective fiction could not be contained by such
limitations, either in terms of context (the English
countryseat) or in respect to an unnaturally successful
detective. Leo Bruce's story of Sergeant Beef in the *Case
for Three Detectives*, first published in 1936, becomes
a parody of the whole genre.[45]

The murder takes place in the country house of Dr.
Thurston in rural Sussex, in a setting that is described
as "very English."[46] The situation is equipped with a
sinister butler, Stall, and a chauffeur too true to be
good, Fellowes, together with a normal complement of

house guests of suspicious backgrounds and dubious motives. We are also introduced to a fanatical local vicar, Rider, a pragmatic local doctor, Tate, and a skeptical local lawyer, Williams.

The caricature of the golden age is pushed further by the parody of the three most popular amateur detectives of that period. Lord Simon Plimsoll (like Sayers' Lord Peter Wimsey) is described as arriving in an entourage of three Rolls Royces and with his "man," Butterfield. The house guest who purports to write the story is reminded by Lord Simon's speech "of a dialogue I had heard in a cabaret between two entertainers whose name I believe was Western."[47] Plimsoll also, like Wimsey, is a collector of incunabula and a connoisseur of fine food and wines. Monsieur Amer Picon is a parody of Hercule Poirot and interjects French phrases when English thought becomes too profound or the situation too tense. So too, Monsignor Smith is the counterpart of Chesterton's Father Brown; he is a Roman Catholic prelate interested in ecclesiastical minutiae and theology and given to Chestertonian paradoxes. He carries an umbrella, is described as "vague and ineffectual" and, we read, "Mgr. Smith blinked in the blank and innocent way which I knew concealed his most intelligent discoveries."[48]

In contrast Sergeant Beef, the local policeman, is described as having a "raw red face and thirsty moustache" and "looked as though he would have been happier in the local public bar."[49] This brings us to the amanuensis, Townsend, the teller of the story, cast as Agatha Christie's Captain Hastings to the trio of famous criminological prestidigitators. He very soon recognizes that he is "expected to be something of a fool" and finds himself "plunged into this role of enquiring and credulous fool."[50]

A neat twist to the parody is that the true solution of the murder of Mary Thurston is reached by Beef rather than by any of the three brilliant amateurs. Leo Bruce puts his finger on the basic flaw of the peculiar form that had developed detection as a game; it was "a mere game like chess," or an entertaining game of hide-and-seek.[51] As Townsend observes:

> Thurston still had not appeared, but I understood that
> he was to be present at the enquiry that evening. I was
> thankful that he had kept out of the way all day. My
> knowledge of these situations, gathered from some study
> of them, taught me that we were all behaving according
> to the very best precedents, but I could not help feeling
> that a man who had just lost his wife might not see it
> that way. I had learnt that after a murder it is quite prop-
> er and conventional for everyone in the house to join the
> investigators in this entertaining game of hide-and-seek
> which seemed wholly to absorb us. It was not extraordin-
> ary for there to be three total strangers questioning the
> servants, or for the police to be treated with smiling pa-
> tronage, or for the corpse to be pulled about by anyone
> who was curious to know how it had become a corpse.
> But when I thought of the man to whom the tragedy
> would be something more than an entrancing problem
> for talented investigators, I really wondered how these
> queer customs had arisen.[52]

In some ways the book is an indictment of those
who read detective fiction for one suspects that, like the
residents in Dr. Thurston's house, the general reader,
after sufficient time has been given to the natural feelings of the wife or husband of a fictional victim, is apt to
reflect that "bereavement, on these occasions . . . is a
bore; detection is what matters."[53] The detective fiction
of the gilded cage was in many ways wholly unrealistic
and took totally outrageous liberties with life. So when
Lord Plimsoll telephones the local hotel manager to ask
him some rather impertinent questions about the night
off that his porter enjoyed each week, we read, "The
manager appeared to feel no astonishment at this sudden
query from a stranger."[54] And later Townsend writes:

> I felt nauseated, suddenly, with the whole affair. This re-
> lentless tracking down of the criminal seemed gruesome.

Lord Simon, gently sipping his brandy, so obviously considered it all to be a most absorbing game of chess, "something to occupy a chap," that for a moment I lost all patience with him. And the brilliant little Picon, whose humanity was more evident, he too could not help enjoying his own efforts—and that disturbed me. Certainly I had never known Mgr. Smith actually hand a man over to the Law, but even that was partly because the criminals he discovered had a way of committing suicide before he revealed their identity.[55]

No wonder that Townsend feels like leaving the amateur experts to their own devices, "and going out into the air."[56]

And at the end, in proving all the experts wrong, Sergeant Beef indicates the artificiality of this kind of detection by showing that the crime could be easily solved by the routine application of simple police procedures. He insists throughout that it is far too simple a crime to exercise the creative genius of such distinguished gentlemen and such elaborate theories. Perhaps the last word may belong to Lord Plimsoll, and it may also indicate why the classic detective fiction of the golden age would have to change its format. As the noble lord observes, "I am not one to get excited about the jolly old police, but I'm climbin' down a peg. . . . Lord, what a relief it is to have been wrong for once! You don't know the monotony of infallibility!"[57] Infallibility is far too august a quality to be claimed for long by any human being, however clever or erudite, and as crime is committed by human beings, the solution in this mortal world more often than not depends on very human qualities. Sergeant Beef wonders why they *try* to make it complicated and remarks at the end that the solution of a crime is not dependent on the theories of sheer genius but just "police business."[58] This is much closer to life as we know it than the unreal contexts reflected in the golden age.

At the same time, although the form we have been discussing is too artificial to provide a permanent mold for detective fiction, it enjoys vigorous and persistent vitality. Most of the stories that were written in Britain from the 1920s to the end of World War II and even to the end of the 1960s were basically of this kind, with suitable variations of time and place; but although the detection was conducted as "a mere game like chess," one suspects this is because it unconsciously provided many of us with moral support for the things we want to believe about the society in which we live.

However, we face a problem in presenting this chapter because the finest practitioners of any art never allow themselves to become embalmed in prevailing fashions. They may conform for a time, but they will ultimately become, if not the trendsetters, then certainly the precursors of new directions. Two such writers spring immediately to mind: Dorothy L. Sayers and Agatha Christie. Chronologically they belong to this chapter, but in terms of their contribution to detective fiction, they foreshadowed change; and, in the case of Agatha Christie, the sheer length of her career meant that her writing became an encapsulated history of the detective fiction writer's art in our century.

4

Shadows of Change

Dorothy L. Sayers, among Others

I

When Dorothy Leigh Sayers (1893-1957) decided to do something, she did it one hundred percent, bringing all her considerable abilities into play, whether it was translating a poem from French or Italian, riding a motorcycle, engaging in photography, falling in love, writing a detective story, or investigating theology. Her background, education, religion, capacities, and even her prejudices gave her the equipment to provide the kind of detective story that England between the wars (i.e., 1918-39) appreciated. She hit the right note and the public responded. At home during vacations from Oxford, or during intermittent bouts of unemployment after graduation, she often immersed herself in the works of Conan Doyle, Edgar Wallace, or Leblanc's adventures of Arsène Lupin. She gave as her excuse that she was studying the genre because "that is where the money is."[1] We might be tempted to dismiss this as little more than a student's excuse for wasting time or doing what she wanted to do anyway, except that she did everything so single-mindedly, and her later success as a writer of detective fiction shows that we cannot take her reason for mastering the genre too lightly.

Her world was the world of post–World War I Britain, with its large number of romanticized but largely jobless young officers. There were even larger numbers of jobless ex-Tommies or ex-Tars, but they were not romanticized. Dorothy L. Sayers belonged to the world of classically educated amateurs, with all the prejudices and elitism that belong to the English public-school and university tradition. The men of that class were trained to believe that ability to write a good piece of Latin verse would justify their leadership in any field and would stand them in good stead whether they were commanding a cavalry troop on the Northwest frontier, administering a Crown colony, or serving on the governing board of a bank. Specialized knowledge was of limited value. So it was the *amateur* detective who caught the imagination of the detective-story reading public, because so many of these readers belonged to the same class—or if they did not belong, still admired, envied, and emulated it. It was the world of Bulldog Drummond, of Tommy and Tuppence Beresford, and Albert Campion, and when eventually Ngaio Marsh produced an acceptable professional police officer in Roderick Alleyn, we are left in no doubt that he went to the right schools and belonged to the right family. It was assumed that a good degree from one of the older universities could fit anyone for anything, just as it was assumed that belonging to the right clubs and knowing the right people was sufficient to achieve preeminence in any field of human endeavor.

Sayers herself is a good illustration of how it worked. She had been educated in the classics by her father, the Reverend Henry Sayers, who had been headmaster of the cathedral choir school at Oxford and later incumbent at Bluntisham in East Anglia. She went to Somerville College, Oxford ("first class honours," modern languages, specializing in French, 1915). She was therefore one of the first women graduates to receive the degree when in 1920 Oxford University admitted women to its degrees.

Her first publication was a book of verse (*Op. 1*) in 1919. She became successively an effective copywriter for a London advertising agency (Benson's), the remarkably popular writer of detective fiction that we know, a playwright, an influential writer of Christian apologetic, and finally the translator of Dante's *Inferno* and *Paradiso*. Even that does not exhaust her activities or her capacities. Earlier she had immersed herself in solving crossword puzzles and in photography; she played the violin and the saxophone, and we are informed that she had an excellent contralto voice. She was the twentieth-century epitome of the "Renaissance man" except—and here is the paradox—she was a twentieth-century woman. The idea of essential paradox is perhaps the insight that we should carry into our understanding of Sayers and particularly her approach to theology. We meet paradox at almost every point in her life. Brought up in the conventional piety of the established Church of England, she flouted its respectability, even to the extent of having an illegitimate child in 1923 and marrying a divorcé in a registry office two years later. Even in her Christian apologetics, she was among the first to use four-letter expletives for the sake of realism. Indeed, it was that realism which finally forced her to renounce the writing of detective fiction and to concentrate on telling the Christian story.

But it was the Christian story interpreted by the Church—the gospel not only of personal affirmation but of the creeds: for Dorothy Sayers, it was impossible to be a Christian without being a Church theologian, that is, impossible to confess Christ without also engaging in the most rigorous thinking about the relation of this historic person to what Christians understand as 'God'. As she wrote later, "If we really want a Christian society, we must teach Christianity, and it is absolutely impossible to teach Christianity without teaching Christian dogma."[2] At this point one is tempted to include a further chapter entitled "Dorothy L. Sayers, Theological Detective, or, what a strange lady discovered about the remarkable birth and horrid murder of Jesus

Bar-Joseph," but I fear that would carry us too far from our subject. However there is a sense in which the whole of Sayers' career centered in that basic paradox of Western history and society.

II

Paradox is also to be seen regarding her work in detective fiction. Most of her books appeared in the 1930s, and we would expect the work of one of her background and education to illustrate a basic affirmation of the status quo in Britain during the golden age. Her writings *do* illustrate this but they illustrate more, for side by side with those aspects of her writing that reaffirm traditional stances of Western culture, we also recognize her radical questioning about the course that it was taking. Some of the detective fiction of the 1930s was already becoming ambivalent at that point. Sayers was realistic about herself and also perhaps about the society of which she was a part. She was, for example, extremely critical about the commercialism of that time and of the advertising gimmickry that seemed to give it its base, but she had little hesitation in taking a position within an advertising agency when the opportunity presented itself. She showed a similar realism with her entry into the field of detective fiction. As one of her biographers observed, "A writer astutely casting about for best-seller income in the 1920s was bound to recognize the opportunities for detective fiction. It was the golden age of the detective novel."[3] This was the time when an interest in puzzles of all kinds engaged the literate and educated English-speaking public, and it was therefore a period when Sayers could cash in the qualities her education and temperament gave her.

However, there is a good deal of difference between promise and achievement and that is where her single-minded commitment was important. From the first, she seems to have recognized that the future lay not with writing simple detective puzzles but with the development of character demanded by classical novels. Later she wrote:

> When in a light-hearted manner I set out . . . to write the first "Lord Peter" book, it was with the avowed intention of producing something "less like a conventional detective story and more like a novel." Re-reading *Whose Body?* at this distance of time I observe, with regret, that it is conventional to the last degree, and no more like a novel than I to Hercules.[4]

Certainly *Whose Body?* does not bear comparison with her later books, but it is not to be brushed aside so casually. One of her biographers has described it as "a short, highly intelligent book," and went on to point out that the whole personal cycle and family of Wimsey appear in it.[5]

That may be not only the measure of Sayers' thoroughness and dedication, but it may also indicate her contribution to the development of the detective story and incidentally, to its significance for our subject. In this latter respect, her writings contributed first to the recognition of character in the writing of crime novels and secondly in her interest to discover the direction into which society would move.

Dorothy L. Sayers' contribution to detective fiction is the paradox of a writer who was in some ways the epitome of all that was represented by the writers of the golden age. In that sense she was strongly affirmative of the culture of which she was a part, but she also illustrates a new realism about the place of crime and justice in that society which began to send detective fiction on new and uncharted courses.

A thoroughgoing analysis of the Lord Peter Wimsey corpus could certainly show how the books reflected the Britain of that time, but in two respects we see them as precursors of new directions.

The Integrity of Character

Although the character of Lord Peter Wimsey may be less developed in *Whose Body?* than in her later books, the fact that Wimsey appears complete with a family and personal history shows that he already had his own integrity as a character. In some ways he may owe a good deal to the depictions of detectives in earlier writers. He was "a gifted amateur. He excelled in ratiocination. He was always clever about detecting the culprit and the manner [murder was accomplished]— however ingenious the crime."[6] And of course, Wimsey had all those qualities of culture, aristocracy, family, and wealth that were most envied by the middle-class British reading public and by middle-class Anglophile Americans.

But Wimsey had his own integrity as a character. For all the likeness that he and Bunter may have to Wodehouse's Bertie Wooster and Jeeves (or for that matter, to Margery Allingham's Albert Campion and Magersfontein Lugg), the relationship of Peter Wimsey to Bunter went beyond the stereotypes. Whether Sayers saw Wimsey at the end "as slightly Christ like," as one of her biographers thought, is doubtful. She insisted that, although he was "brought up religious," for he was able and willing to discuss theological matters with Inspector Parker (who made a hobby of reading New Testament commentaries), and given an ethical problem, he willingly went to the clergy, he was not religious. The integrity of her characters was very important to Sayers because it pointed to a fundamental theological insight. As she said near the beginning of *The Mind of the Maker*, "In considering the question how far the writer should permit his imagined characters to become the mouthpiece of his personality, we touched the fringe of that permanently baffling problem, the free will of the creature."[7]

Later in the same book, she illustrates this point about the integrity of character in the development of her plots. In *Gaudy Night*, for example, the person who has been tormenting Harriet Vane destroys a set of chessmen that have a special meaning to Harriet because they had been given to her by Wimsey:

> A reader afterwards said to me; "I realised, the moment they were mentioned, that those chessmen were doomed." Nothing, when one comes to think of it, could be more obvious from the point of view of plot-structure. I can only affirm (without much hope of being believed) that it was by no means obvious to *me*. The chessmen were, at first, connected with the character-development, and with that only. But when the plot demanded their destruction, there they were ready. Though I did at that moment realise that this incident clamped the two parts of the story together in a satisfactory and useful manner, it was not until my reader pointed it out to me that I understood the incident to have been, in actual fact, predestined—that is, that plot and character, each running true to its nature, had inevitably united to bring the thing about.[8]

The incident in *Gaudy Night* has theological implications far beyond the personal character of Harriet Vane's tormentor since it hints at the possibility of predestination, of special Providence and of the way in which that special Providence may be related to free will.

Concern Regarding the Course of Western Society

Dorothy L. Sayers cited a further illustration of character development in *Murder Must Advertise*, which also illustrates her concern for the way in which Western culture was moving. She intended to present in that book two worlds—the world of advertising, and the post-World War I world of "bright young things." "I mentioned this intention to a reader, who instantly replied: 'Yes; and Peter Wimsey, who represents reality, never appears in either world except in disguise.' It was perfectly true; and I never noticed it. With all its defects of realism, there had been some measure of integral truth about the book's Idea, since it issued, without my conscious connivance, in a true symbolism."[9] She was equally critical about both those trendy worlds in Western society. In some ways the book itself is an indictment of the trend to commercialism with its dubious morality.[10] In its pages we also witness Dorothy L. Sayers' disgust with the drug/drink hedonism and ill-digested socialism represented by the fashionable British society of that time. Although none of her novels explicitly dealt with the relation of the Church to society, she regarded the Church and the Christian message as the cultural focus of British society.

There is a passage in *The Nine Tailors* (1934) where Wimsey and Bunter are making their way through a night of snow and blackness to their destination in the bleak remoteness of the eastern fens of England. We then read, "The sound of a church clock, muffled by the snow, came borne upon the wind; it chimed the first quarter. 'Thank God!' said Wimsey. 'Where there is a church, there is civilisation.' "[11]

That statement represents Sayers' basic conviction about society, but it may also represent the unconscious assumption of most of the detective-story writing during the first half of this century. Sayers' books may have forecast change in the direction of realism and a more comprehensive approach to crime writing, but she had her own feet firmly planted in the older values of her native culture.

III

Although other writers of the 1930s were probably far less able or willing to offer religious answers to the societal problem than Dorothy Sayers, we can find in them hints that detective fiction was about to move in new directions. In the books about Sergeant Beef, by Leo Bruce, we have already seen signs of dissatisfaction with the aristocratic and sporting tradition of the golden age. Perhaps the eventual demise of the classic puzzler type of detective story was forecast in the incredible convolutions of plot that we find in the 1930s. They present us with a *reductio ad absurdum*. Two such books come to mind: Gladys Mitchell's *The Saltmarsh Murders* (1932) and *Death by Request* (1933), which was the single foray into detective fiction of Romilly and Katherine John. At first sight it seems as if both these books would demonstrate the close relationship between theology and detection because, in both cases, the narrator is a clergyman—in the first case the Reverend Noel Wells, the curate of Saltmarsh, and in the second case the village vicar, the Reverend Joseph Colchester.

But in both cases, that first impression is illusory and both books illustrate the rapid separation of English society from its theological roots. In *The Saltmarsh Murders*, there are several signs of a change of mood—Noel Wells himself is an ineffectual type of parson who had gone into the church under the inducement of a £30,000 legacy.[12] He speaks of keeping "the Anglican flag flying," but he expects the police to search around in order to "bolster up" their understanding of the truth.[13] Gladys Mitchell's eldritch detective, Mrs. Bradley, Wells admits, makes one think "in the words of the rather Nonconformist hymn, that she was on the Lord's side."[14] She disbelieves in hell and capital punishment, or at least wants to get the latter humanized, and therefore she may represent the trend of the new modernity.[15]

We are clearly moving out of the classical period with its old-world standards, because the "tougher element of the village" was already Americanized enough to chew gum, although Noël still regarded P. G. Wodehouse as Britain's greatest living author.[16] The fashion in British society at that period (early 1930s) to be vaguely sympathetic to left-wing causes is also indicated in the description of the financier, Bransome Burns, as one who possesses "the most completely fossilized intelligence she [Mrs. Bradley] had ever encountered."[17] Mrs. Bradley also has enlightened views about sin and sex, and the book even dares to hint at incestuous relationships.[18] Shades of the permissive society! It is also clear that whatever privileged position the Church might still occupy in British culture of the 1930s, it was not immune from serious criticism and its clergy were regarded as capable of very human passions.

Something of the same is illustrated by the Johns' *Death by Request*.[19] Here the clerical amanuensis is a perfect "Captain Hastings," the Reverend Joseph Colchester. We soon learn of his friend's skepticism in religious matters, and of the general questioning about capital punishment at that time.[20] We learn of the Reverend Mr. Colchester's sympathy with socialism, and later his resentment at the injustices and class distinctions implicit within British society.[21] Indeed, because of the readiness with which the members of the house party at Friars Cross were prepared to put all the blame on Frampton, the butler,[22] the book appears to be an exposition of the World War I song:

> *It's the same the whole world over;*
> *It's the poor what gets the blame,*
> *It's the rich that gets the pleasure,*
> *Ain't it all a bloomin' shame?*

It is recognized that Frampton's complaints regarding the upper classes were largely justified.

Despite the centrality of the Reverend Mr. Colchester in the story, it does not reinforce confidence in the Church and its ministers at that stage of English national life. Indeed, there are several aspects in which the presence of the reverend gentleman does not ring true. For instance he is forced to admit that the influence of Sunday was "little felt at Friars Cross."[23] But it is difficult to think that, as a priest of the Church of England, Mr. Colchester would not attend divine service himself, and never once in the course of the book, do we read of him retiring to read his daily offices. A further point at which this description of an Anglican clergyman of the period does not ring true is his indifference at the suggestion of divorce, which was at that time forbidden to members of the Church of England. This is not true to the character of the English clergy of that period.

In the introduction to *Death by Request*, we read, "The use of a clerical narrator has many advantages for this particular piece of fiction, not least among which is the way it enables the authors to turn out a celebration of hocus-pocus—locked rooms, sinister actions, striking disclosures and all—while remaining essentially poker-faced. *Death by Request* is a splendid example of literary puzzle-setting."[24] I am not at all sure that the use of a clerical narrator gives all the advantages that are suggested here, but certainly both *Death by Request* and *The Saltmarsh Murders* are illustrations of the classical British murder puzzle carried to the nth degree. This has resulted in extreme convolutions of plot and all in aid of a final twist that will defeat the ingenuity of the most brilliant and critical reader. My own problem with this is that, although the writers may play fair in giving the reader all the material evidence, the evidence provided through *character* is inconsistent. Obviously the time was rapidly approaching for a new format for detective fiction if the genre was to survive.

5

Acquiring an English Accent

The British Import

During the twenties and thirties of this century many American writers of detective fiction paid Britain the sincerest compliment of imitation. Although soon a homegrown American tradition in crime writing would appear that made a decisive break from the classical form, there was a persistent and even dominant strain which appropriated the values of pre–World War I Western culture for American society. The imitation of the British form was so pronounced in some writers that, apart from the necessary differences in locale and idiom, it was often unclear on which side of the Atlantic the particular writer had originated.

I

John Dickson Carr, who also wrote under the name of Carter Dickson, once took up residence in Britain for several years. And it is evident that his detective creations belong almost exclusively to United Kingdom originals. Carr's Dr. Gideon Fell could have been created by the English genius, scholar, and creator of Father Brown, Gilbert Keith Chesterton, while Carr's alter ego

Carter Dickson employed the uncouth but recognizably English gentleman, Sir Henry Merrivale. America was producing a number of writers who used the format of the classic puzzler within new-world settings and who, *mutatis mutandis*, followed the example of the British. Erle Stanley Gardner with Perry Mason, Rex Stout with Nero Wolfe, and Frederic Dannay and Manfred Lee with Ellery Queen are simply a few of those who exploited the classic format and whose work illustrated the cerebral type of detective fiction. Nor was the distaff side unrepresented: Mary Roberts Rinehart, Mignon G. Eberhart, and Phoebe Atwood Taylor continued a tradition which had been laid down at the time of Sherlock Holmes by the American writer Anna Katherine Green.

However, the genre was casting around for new ideas and because of the apparently insatiable demand for puzzles, fictional crimes appeared in increasingly bizarre circumstances. In the frantic search for newer and cleverer forms of obfuscation to maintain readers' interest, writers on both sides of the Atlantic developed their own patented style. Gardner's Perry Mason invariably solved the case by a last-minute courtroom confrontation and denouement; Rex Stout's gargantuan detective Nero Wolfe, like British sleuths of the same period, flaunted his erudition, and refused to budge from his old brownstone house in New York City; Ellery Queen, the character created by Frederic Dannay and Manfred B. Lee, played off a gentle rivalry with his father, an officer in the New York City police department, just as Richard and Frances Lockridge exploited an even gentler rivalry between their husband-and-wife detective team, Gerald and Pam North. As a result, the plots often strike us today as artificial and contrived.

John Dickson Carr made locked-room mysteries his specialization: each Carr story became a tour de force, but almost inevitably the format took the detective story further and further away from reality. In *The Mad Hatter Mystery*, the writer's English affiliation was shown by his primary setting, the Tower of London.[1]

The story begins with what appears to be a childish prank that turns sour in violent death—a murder that resolves itself in accidental death, and a suicide that should not have taken place. A further example of convoluted detection is *Dead Man's Knock*. The murder takes place on an academic campus in America, where Dr. Gideon Fell is a visiting professor. Too many incidents are left unexplained, or explained too glibly, such as, why so many people are moving around the countryside at 6:30 on a Sunday morning or why they have the unchallenged right to wander at will into each other's houses. Most strange of all, we wonder why the police almost fade from the story and the visiting English academic is allowed to take command of the investigation. However the story emphasizes the values of the golden age by distinguishing between legal guilt and moral guilt, between legal justice and ideal justice. The Anglo-Saxon claim to a unique view of justice is voiced by Lieutenant Henderson of the local police force: "We're a peculiar lot here. We believe in justice."[2]

Examples of values to which the society of the golden age adhered are to be found in the cases of Perry Mason. For example, in *The Case of the Waylaid Wolf*, Mason says to Paul Drake, regarding the leading witness and suspect, "Whenever she tells her story on the witness stand, Paul, it'll be the truth. It won't be the story that's the most expedient. I think that the truth is not only the most powerful weapon, but as far as I'm concerned it's the only weapon."[3] When Arlene Ferris is acquitted from the charge of murder, she remarks to Della Street that although it might be just another case for Perry Mason, for her it is her whole life. This immediately brings Della Street to the defense of her boss: "It's his whole life, too. . . . His life's work is to see that justice is done, not only in one case, but in *all* his cases."[4] As Julian Symons commented, with reference to Dorothy L. Sayers and others of this period, "One of the most marked features of the Anglo-American detective story is that it is strongly on the side of law and order."[5]

II

America seems to bear a love-hate relationship to Britain and nowhere is this more pronounced than in tales which have a New England setting. In Texas the cry is "Remember the Alamo!" but throughout New England it appears to be "Remember Bunker Hill!" For many patriotic Americans and for all patriotic New Englanders, England has been the traditional enemy, so if an Englishman appears in a yarn based in New England, the reader is well advised to take note and to be duly suspicious of his high-falutin' airs, his unpopular blondness, and the equivocations of speech and accent; it is no accident that American sporting idiom interprets "putting English on a ball" as giving it a bias and a sneaky tendency to do the unexpected. On the other hand, the New England attitude is sometimes ambivalent, because there is grudging recognition that its own cultural roots are to be traced to the British Isles. After all, the language did come from there, along with the common law and New England's bedrock Puritanism.

This ambivalence may be seen in Virginia Rich's *Baked Bean Supper Murders*. The reader cannot help being suspicious of young Rodney Pickett, with his spurious pretensions to British nobility. But the cultural debt to Britain is also acknowledged, so that at the height of the action, Eugenia (Genia) Potter admits her preference for tea prepared in a teapot the British way and for English muffins. Furthermore, a sympathetic Scotsman is introduced into the story, and his appearance may go to show that there is really no ill feeling toward the British per se, possibly because Scots, like Americans, have distinguishable accents. Finally, we read that Genia, while recuperating from a particularly vicious attack on her person, spends her time reading "Angela Thirkell's novels of English country life."[6] The ambivalence is less pronounced in the delightful stories of Phoebe Atwood Taylor, featuring her Cape Cod detective Asey Mayo. Written, as several of them were, during the years of World War II, they reflect the views of an Anglophile rather than an Anglophobe. There can be no doubt that Asey Mayo's support for traditional values of justice and truth in his own career, together with that of the Porter automobile company, is a tacit recognition of the Puritan work ethic. Aunt Eugenia Crane provides a further example of the Puritan work ethic in a native New Englander.[7]

The characteristics of the country-house murder could be reproduced anywhere and were not simply limited to New England, although there is something about the close-knit small Cape Cod communities of the Asey Mayo stories that makes the format particularly congenial. But the form could be adapted to any place in the United States where a limited number of closely associated characters face the intrusion of violent death and are held captive by that situation.

Lange Lewis' the *Birthday Murder* is a transatlantic version of the English classic murder transposed to California.[8] The action takes place in the Hollywood house of Victoria Jason, a successful screenwriter, who has been married for six months to Albert Hime, the more-or-less successful director of grade B films. It is a second marriage for both partners. When Albert is found poisoned after dinner and coffee with his wife in their gilded-cage setting, the only possible suspects, apart from Victoria herself, are some of the privileged people who belong to the Himes' social circle. They include Moira Hastings, a starlet who desperately wants to star in the great film based on Victoria's best-selling story, "Ina Hart" (the story of a wife who poisoned her husband), which Albert was to direct; Bernice Saxe, Victoria's best friend; Captain Sawn Harriss, Victoria's first husband; and the maid, Hazel.

In several other ways, the story reflects the gilded-cage motif. It depicts the Hollywood world of the 1930s and the liberal ideas current in film circles at that time. We are given candid criticism of American capitalism at the time when Victoria is introduced to her first husband's parents:

Once, when Victoria introduced the subject of a strike which was filling the newspapers, there was a profound silence. Then Aunt Jessie spoke for them all when she said, reasonably and gently, "These people don't know what real tragedy is. The limited scope of their lives makes them regard such matters as hours and wages as important." The butler poured the wine, the heads nodded and the light from the candles was reflected in the hanging tears of the chandelier above the long table with its damask cloth.[9]

To further illustrate the same social period with a theme that would be repeated in the sixties, there is the revolt of Sawn, a privileged middle-class son, against his wealthy parents.

Sawn, however, was of another generation. In college he learned enough to see for the first time the tragic contrasts of the system of which his family was one product and the striking miners another. He went through a period of ruthless bitterness which caused his people much suffering, and was once nearly jailed for hitting a policeman in the eye during a Communist demonstration in New York. By the time Victoria met him he was a thin young man in full swing of revolt against his people and what they stood for. He was living in a small dark apartment in lower New York. He had finished his education and was determined to make his living as a writer.[10]

Although Lieutenant Richard Tuck of the L.A.P.D. homicide squad could never be confused with the aristocratic young dilettantes of the classic period, he follows a similar method by arranging a recapitulation, with Virginia and her guests, of the events during the crucial period of the crime.[11]

Mignon G. Eberhart's *R.S.V.P. Murder* reflects the sixties in a different way.[12] This book may strike the modern reader as dated because the social scene represents the thirties and forties rather than the sixties when it appeared. The setting belongs to the same period as the old aristocratic New York City brownstone with its creaking stop-start elevator, but the story illustrates ethical concerns that were dominant later in the sixties. Richard Amberly has been the chief suspect since his wife Cecile was murdered a year before the story opens. She was an alcoholic and when drunk tended to pick up any man who happened by. An alibi has been concocted for Amberly by his lawyer, Orle Hilliard, but if everybody had told the truth, Amberly, although innocent, would almost certainly have been convicted. Sometime later Hilliard dies while on holiday in Europe with his daughter, Fran. Since he has no money to leave her, earlier he has written to five people whom the truth would hurt (including Amberly) and asks them, in exchange for his silence, to help his daughter financially. The book excuses this blackmail on the grounds that Hilliard is a sick man and desperately anxious to provide for his daughter. This is not a convincing argument, but it poses the kind of ethical dilemma that is more likely to be explored in the sixties than in the earlier period.

Hilda Lawrence's *Death of a Doll* is a further example of the English country-house murder translated into American.[13] There are no blue-blooded aristocrats, and the crime does not take place in a country house; rather, the scene is a New York City girls' hostel, Hope House, and most of the suspects are to be found among the boarders. However, the ambience, if that is not too pretentious a word, is similar to English counterparts. The hostel represents a relatively closed society and therefore a limited number of suspects. The detection is carried through by a "gentleman," Mark East, who if not exactly an aristocratic amateur, eats at the right places and knows the right people. Moreover, if there are no aristocrats in the British sense, there are those who would pass as very acceptable substitutes: Roberta Beacham Sutton and her husband Nicholas who initiate the investigation, and Nicholas's two maiden aunts, Miss Beulah and Miss Bessie Pond, not to mention Miss Monica "Monny" Brady, the head of Hope

House. The servants too are suitably respectful, loyal, and ill paid, while Dr. Martin Luther Kloppel and police officer Foy are suitable New York City counterparts to the doctor and the local detective-inspector in a country village crime.

III

All the foregoing stories illustrate a general similarity to the classic puzzler type of detective fiction that was appearing in England. Some writers went much further, though, in their imitation of the English popular style, by allowing their detectives to become almost exact replicas of the amateur detectives that were gracing the pages of writers like Margery Allingham and Dorothy L. Sayers. It has been pointed out that Ellery Queen began as "a supercilious aristocrat who condescendingly assisted his long-suffering father, Inspector Richard Queen."[14]

The works of Elizabeth Daly are set in locales strongly resembling those of the English country-house crime literature—a number of them in the residences of wealthy American families.[15] But the resemblance to the British style is most striking in the character of her bibliophile detective, Henry Gamadge, who has been described as "the American Peter Wimsey." He is "charming and genteel, dashingly attractive to women," and "makes his home on the posh East Side of New York."[16]

In S. S. Van Dine's (Willard Huntington Wright's) Philo Vance series, the imitation of the English model reaches the point of caricature. All Philo Vance's cases involve people from the top ranks of New York society—a close and almost incestuous circle of wealthy and eccentric acquaintances. Not only is Vance himself extremely wealthy and therefore able to indulge his interest in music, books, and various forms of art, but he carries Anglophilia almost to the point of absurdity: he wears a monocle and is snobbish about the tea he drinks;[17] he uses the style of affected speech to be found in Peter Wimsey; and he thinks nothing of inter-

spersing his observations with classical allusions and
quotations from foreign languages and then leaving
them untranslated. Willard Huntington Wright was
himself an academic and even introduced footnotes
into his novels — a fad that fortunately was not imitated.
Philo Vance had been educated, at least in part, at
Oxford, and he shows the typical artistic prejudices of a
European dilettante.[18] He supports the view of sportsmanship common at that time: "Not very fair-minded,
your lady of vengeance — in fact, a rather bad sport,
don't y' know, tryin' to get some one else punished for
her little flutter in crime."[19]

Vance is originally drawn into detection through
his school friendship with John F.-X. Markham, the
New York District Attorney. Markham is asked by Major
Anthony Benson to investigate the murder of his brother and business partner, Alvin Benson.[20] In true classic
fashion, the police and Markham in turn suspect Mur-
iel St. Clair, a singer who had dined with Alvin the night
he was shot; Captain Philip Leacock, her jealous fiancé;
man-about-town Leander Pfyfe, along with Colonel Bigs-
by Ostrander — both friends of Alvin; and Mrs. Anna
Platz, Alvin's housekeeper.

However, the Vance stories hint at changes in attitude that were to come later. In *The Benson Murder
Case*, Markham protests that by the time they arrive at
Benson's apartment, the evidence could have been
obliterated. Vance then presents a very "advanced" view
of cosmic reality and of the conservation of matter to
Markham:

> If anything, no matter how inf'nitesimal, could really be
> obliterated, the universe, y' know, would cease to exist —
> the cosmic problem would be solved, and the Creator
> would write Q.E.D. across an empty firmament. Our only
> chance of going on with this illusion we call Life, d' ye
> see, lies in the fact that consciousness is like an inf'nite
> decimal point.[21]

Similarly, in *The Bishop Murder Case*, Vance remarks to mathematician Sigurd Arnesson that there is no reality in justice: "Philosophically, of course, there's no such thing as justice. If there really were justice, we'd all be in for a shingling in the cosmic woodshed."[22]

Vance claimed to have a unique psychological method of solving murder mysteries, and it was his success in the Benson case which enabled him to call on Markham's support in later cases. However, he could be insufferable in his affectedness and in his claim to esoteric, recondite learning; the solution of *The Bishop Murder Case* is based on an abstruse literary reference in Ibsen's *The Pretenders*.[23] No wonder Ogden Nash immortalized him in the couplet:

> *Philo Vance*
> *Needs a kick in the pance.*

Possibly that is an appropriate epitaph for Anglophilia that went beyond affection to affectation!

6

Creating an American Tradition

The Hard-boiled Maverick

I

In the name of the real but tainted world in which we live, Raymond Chandler protested against the artificialities of the classical school of detective fiction: "Fiction in any form has always intended to be realistic."[1] Chandler was an unlikely proponent of a style of detective fiction that criticized the predominantly English form.[2] But unlikely or not, his protest in "The Simple Art of Murder" voiced the legitimate objections of a generation of American writers, and his work became the focus for an entirely different style of detective fiction.

> The realist in murder writes of a world in which gangsters can rule nations and almost rule cities, in which hotels and apartment houses and celebrated restaurants are owned by men who made their money out of brothels, in which a screen star can be the finger-man for a mob, and the nice man down the hall is a boss of the numbers racket; a world where a judge with a cellar full of bootleg

liquor can send a man to jail for having a pint in his
pocket, where the mayor of your town may have condoned
murder as an instrument of money-making, where no
man can walk down a dark street in safety because law
and order are things we talk about but refrain from prac-
tising; a world where you may witness a hold-up in broad
daylight and see who did it, but you will fade quickly
back into the crowd rather than tell anyone, because the
hold-up men may have friends with long guns, or the police may not like your testimony, and in any case the shy-
ster for the defense will be allowed to abuse and vilify you
in open court, before a jury of selected morons, without
any but the most perfunctory interference from a political
judge.

It is not a very fragrant world, but it is the world you
live in, and certain writers with tough minds and a cool
spirit of detachment can make very interesting and even
amusing patterns out of it. It is not funny that a man
should be killed, but it is sometimes funny that he
should be killed for so little, and that his death should be
the coin of what we call civilization. All this still is not
quite enough.

In everything that can be called art there is a quality of
redemption. It may be pure tragedy, if it is high tragedy,
and it may be pity and irony, and it may be the raucous
laughter of the strong man. But down these mean streets
a man must go who is not himself mean, who is neither
tarnished nor afraid. The detective in this kind of story
must be such a man. He is the hero, he is everything. He
must be a complete man and a common man and yet an
unusual man. He must be, to use a rather weathered
phrase, a man of honor, by instinct, by inevitability, without thought of it, and certainly without saying it. He
must be the best man in his world and a good enough
man for any world. I do not care much about his private
life; he is neither a eunuch nor a satyr; I think he might
seduce a duchess and I am quite sure he would not spoil
a virgin; if he is a man of honor in one thing, he is that
in all things. He is a relatively poor man, or he would not
be a detective at all. He is a common man or he could not

go among common people. He has a sense of character, or
he would not know his job. He will take no man's money
dishonestly and no man's insolence without a due and
dispassionate revenge. He is a lonely man and his pride is
that you will treat him as a proud man or be very sorry
you ever saw him. He talks as the man of his age talks,
that is, with rude wit, a lively sense of the grotesque, a
disgust for sham, and a contempt for pettiness. The story
is his adventure in search of a hidden truth, and it
would be no adventure if it did not happen to a man fit
for adventure.[3]

This passage is quoted at length because, although
there are probably no better-known words among the
cognoscenti than Chandler's "down these mean streets
a man must go who is not himself mean, who is neither
tarnished nor afraid," they are rarely quoted in context.
However, the context is revealing for both of Chandler's
legitimate claims—his contrast between real life as normal people experience it and the artificial setting of
detection in the classical mode, as well as his call for the
realistic kind of detective-hero to high adventure.

It is ironic that the protest voiced by Chandler and
the *Black Mask* school of detective fiction in the name
of realism did not recognize how totally unrelated such
adventurous escapades were to the humdrum lives of
most of their readers. Drab, even squalid, many lives
are, but adventure and physical heroics of the kind
described in this fiction are totally unrelated to the
experience of most people. Indeed, the charge of being
unrealistic may be returned on the protesters. Sara
Paretsky's tough private eye, V. I. Warshawski, may
have recognized the inconsistency while investigating
the death of Boom Boom, a Chicago hockey star: "I
opted for sherry—Mike Hammer [Mickey Spillane's de-
tective] is the only detective I know who can think and
move while drinking whiskey. Or at least move. Maybe
Mike's secret is he doesn't try to think."[4] That may be a
good reason for arguing that Mickey Spillane had unconsciously separated himself from the tradition that

arose from the Enlightenment and Edgar Allan Poe! But Sara Paretsky could be recognizing that, in striving for realism, writers of the "tough" school of detective fiction sometimes became unrealistic: how can a person think clearly or act decisively under the influence of several belts of neat rye whiskey?

However, this detective writing is important for our purpose. The thrust of this chapter will be to suggest that the American *Black Mask* and hard-boiled school of writing, associated with the names of Chandler himself, Dashiell Hammett, Mickey Spillane, and sundry Macdonalds, represent a resurgence of a tradition that began in *Caleb Williams*, continued in the hero-safecracker, and was ambiguous about society, if not openly critical of it. This is in direct contrast to the British country-house mystery, which maintained the classic tradition that started with Poe, continued with Wilkie Collins and Conan Doyle, and was essentially affirmative about the goals of contemporary society.

II

Here we may be instructed by John Nelson, who, in *Your God Is Alive and Well and Appearing in Popular Culture*, suggested that popular culture is related to the belief system of most Americans in the same way worship services are related to that of church members. He further suggested that "the dominant belief system in American life has found a normative ritual form of expression in 'the Western.' In no other type of mythological drama is this dominant American salvation myth more comprehensively fixed."[5] The typical Western is the story in which a township (representing civilized society) is threatened by some evil but is saved (redeemed) by a single "savior-figure" cowboy who rides into the town and frees it by means of a single violent confrontation with an evil gang of outlaws or other destroyers of civilized life.

Nelson's insights have a particular pertinence because he also recognizes that the tradition of the Western is itself complex and contains a paradoxical emphasis which he calls the "anti-Western"—"a film (or popular-culture unit) that modifies the ritual drama by criticizing the classic form, or that tells the story so as to alter the way we respond."[6] The anti-Western recognizes that the relationship of good and evil is ambiguous, so that the typically black-hatted villain may reveal hidden resources of goodness—or even become the agent of salvation—while the sources of evil are sometimes to be found within the township (i.e., civilization) itself. This is the *Caleb Williams* motif in a more modern form. If the hard-boiled school of American detective fiction may be thought of as an urban variety of the Western cowboy drama, then it is mainly in terms of the anti-Western emphasis that we should consider this school.

The anti-Western element is seen in the relationships between men and women. In the classic Western tradition, the only acceptable relationship between hero and heroine was that of an idealized romantic love, but in the anti-Western, the situation is more complex because it is not always clear who the hero and heroine are supposed to be. Room has to be made for the bighearted prostitute and for the obvious villain who reveals unexpected depths of tenderness as he shows that black hats, like storm clouds, may hide silver linings. This ambiguity is repeated within the urban setting in the tough school of American detective fiction. So sex, as distinct from romantic love, makes obtrusive and fairly regular appearance. The new "realism" provided a foretaste of the post–World War II permissive society, and in that period it enjoyed new popularity. It was also perhaps no accident that both Dashiell Hammett and Raymond Chandler centered the work of their leading fictional detectives in the liberal "film-land" of southern California.

However, we must express strong disagreement with Nelson's own treatment of detective fiction as an exclusive example of American popular culture. In making a semantic distinction between the classical form represented by Conan Doyle, Agatha Christie, and Erle Stanley Gardner and the writing introduced by Raymond Chandler and Dashiell Hammett, he maintains that the former "was more *detecting* fiction than detective fiction."[7] We may readily concede the distinction between these two forms of writing and we may also concede that what we have called the classical form was more concerned with the detecting process than was the other. However, we question whether the later kind of literature has any more right to claim the designation "detective" fiction than the classic literature we have discussed hitherto.

Presumably Nelson's contention is that Hercule Poirot, Perry Mason, et al. are more concerned with the function of detecting than with being, in the twentieth-century sense, live, believable detectives; but it is just as arguable that, however much Sam Spade and Philip Marlowe give us the impression of realism as detectives, they are only minimally concerned with *detecting* as an investigative, rational act. As Chandler himself observed of the detective, "The story is his adventure in search of a hidden truth, and it would be no adventure if it did not happen to a man fit for adventure."[8] One has the impression that writers of the hard-boiled school, although they may be concerned with the ultimate triumph of what they believe to be right over wrong, or justice over injustice, they are not primarily concerned with demonstrating this as the outcome of rationality. Rather their triumph comes as the end result of innately heroic qualities and of the hero's native capacity to overcome all obstacles, physical as well as intellectual; their ultimate rationale is Adventure, with a capital *A*.

III

Reference to some of the fictional detectives of the exponents of the hard-boiled school will illustrate its distinctive emphases.

Sam Spade

Although the beginning of the hard-boiled school
came with the publication of the *Black Mask* crime
magazine in the 1920s, Dashiell Hammett's the *Maltese
Falcon* is generally recognized as the epitome of the
form. It appeared about 1930[9] and was immediately
recognized as a classic, although it has little to do with
classical detection. The story begins when a certain Miss
Wonderly (whose real name is Brigid O'Shaughnessy)
engages Sam Spade and his partner, Miles Archer, to
trace Floyd Thursby, who has eloped with her sister
Corinne Wonderly. Behind the commission is the discovery and possession of the fabulously valuable statuette,
the Maltese Falcon. That original commission leads to the
death of Archer and then to attempts by others such as
the Levantine Joel Cairo and the obese Mr. Casper Gutman to muscle in on Sam Spade's exploits.

If *The Maltese Falcon* illustrates the form of the
new hard-boiled school, Sam Spade is the primary
exemplar of the new kind of detective. He is human and
makes mistakes at almost every level — the antithesis of
the omniscience expected from the great detective. One
of his girlfriends (Effie Perine) remarks, "You worry me.
You always think you know what you're doing, but
you're too slick for your own good, and some day you're
going to find it out."[10] Sam demonstrates a fairly catholic and broad-minded relationship to women. He claims
that he cannot work miracles, but he is able and willing
to take appropriate violent action when necessary.[11] He
is also quite willing to give the impression that he is
working only on his own behalf. When Gutman asks
him whom he represents,

Spade pointed his cigar at his own chest. "There's me,"
he said.
The fat man sank back in his chair and let his body go
flaccid. He blew his breath out in a long contented gust.
"That's wonderful, sir," he purred. "That's wonderful. I do
like a man that tells you right out he's looking out for

himself. Don't we all? I don't trust a man that says he's not. And the man that's telling the truth when he says he's not I distrust most of all, because he's an ass that's going contrary to the laws of nature."[12]

Sam Spade is totally realistic about all the enemies ranged on the other side of his own personal struggle, and there is no false quixotry in his dealings with them; so he declares to Gutman, "Keep that gunsel away from me while you're making up your mind. I'll kill him. I don't like him. He makes me nervous. I'll kill him the first time he gets in my way. I won't give him an even break. I won't give him a chance. I'll kill him."[13] The rational assessment of the relative strengths of his opponents and himself is perhaps the primary function of Sam Spade's reasoning. One curious feature of the story is that whenever Spade engages in the reasoning detection of classic detective fiction, he is always led into personal danger from which he escapes only because of his ability to handle difficulties; he has the ability to brazen out his opponents or to review his assets in such a way that he always negotiates from a position of strength. That is not detection in the classic sense, but as Sam Spade would say, "That's the way it was."[14]

The Continental Op

The same characteristics can be found in Dashiell Hammett's other private eyes. There is Ned Beaumont, the friend and associate of political boss Paul Madvig, who appears in *The Glass Key,* and then there is the character, the Continental Op.[15] Of these two characters, the Continental Op is perhaps the more interesting because he is drawn from Hammett's own experience as a Pinkerton agent. The Continental Op remains a nameless figure who plies his trade as a salaried operative of the Continental Detective Agency. He has never married and is fat and fortyish, but he is the complete professional. He has a carefully trained sense of observation that enables him to assess potential danger at once, and he has the shrewd ability to see the strange or unusual in any given situation.[16] This innate caution, or even skepticism about human nature, gives him an edge when he becomes the target for violence and is able to react appropriately.[17] It is his ability to survive that enables the Continental Op to bring his investigations to successful conclusions, and it is this same ability together with his human capacity for error that make him such a characteristic detective of the hard-boiled school.[18]

Philip Marlowe

Raymond Chandler's Philip Marlowe operates from behind a door labeled "Philip Marlowe . . . Investigations" in an office in Hollywood. Marlowe describes this place of business: "It is a reasonably shabby door at the end of a reasonably shabby corridor in the sort of building that was new about the year the all-tile bathroom became the basis of civilization. The door is locked, but next to it is another door with the same legend which is not locked. Come on in—there's nobody in here but me and a big bluebottle fly."[19] Marlowe could almost be regarded as the epitome of the detective in this school of writing. He has most of the vices of the period: he smokes (both cigarettes and a pipe), he keeps a bottle of Old Forrester whiskey in the file drawer of his desk, and is "neither a eunuch nor a satyr," to use Chandler's own words. Marlowe is also shrewd and—except when confronted with a giant like Moose Molloy, described as "not more than six feet five inches tall and not wider than a beer truck"—Marlowe is well able to take care of any physical demands made on him in the line of duty.[20] Another of Marlowe's qualities is his uncanny insight into the realities of human nature; as he declares to General Sternwood in *The Big Sleep*, "I'm not Sherlock Holmes or Philo Vance. I don't expect to go over ground the police have covered and pick up a broken pen point and build a case from it. If you think there is anybody in the detective business making a living doing that sort of thing, you don't know much about cops."[21] To add to this character sketch, Marlowe describes himself: "I'm thirty-three years old, went to college once and can still speak English if there's any demand for it. There isn't much in my trade. I worked for Mr. Wilde, the District Attorney, as an investigator once. . . . I'm unmarried because I don't like policemen's wives."[22]

On the other hand, he is not noticeably repelled by women, married or not, and when he pays a social call, he is what would have been regarded as "a natty dresser." Marlowe is somewhat cynical and tends to dress this attitude in wise-cracking repartee, but he is also given to saying "Yeah!" which he was told is "common." Despite his college education, he professes ignorance of Proust, but his native intelligence is such that he is sometimes asked for help by the law-enforcement agencies. Above all, he has the uncanny knack for self-preservation, which is also related to a fierce defense of his clients' interests. This private eye knows when to keep his own counsel, especially in his dealings with the police. He has no illusions about death—it is "the big sleep."[23]

Despite his heroic qualities, the Philip Marlowe stories have a decidedly anti-Western stance. Like the chess problem he sets himself, one might say of his profession, "Knights had no meaning in this game. It wasn't a game for knights."[24] In the same way, realism is extended to Chandler's assessment of American society because although it is Captain Gregory of the Missing Persons Bureau who expressed the following critique, there can be no doubt that this view is endorsed by Marlowe and his creator, Raymond Chandler:

> "I'm a copper," he said, "Just a plain ordinary copper. Reasonably honest. As honest as you could expect a man to be in a world where it's out of style. That's mainly why I asked you to come in this morning. I'd like you to believe that. Being a copper I like to see the law win. I'd like

to see the flashy well-dressed mugs like Eddie Mars spoiling their manicures in the rock quarry at Folsom, alongside of the poor little slum-bred hard guys that got knocked over on their first caper and never had a break since. That's what I'd like. You and me both lived too long to think I'm likely to see it happen. Not in this town, not in any town half this size, in any part of this wide, green and beautiful U.S.A. We just don't run our country that way."[25]

Perhaps both the Western and anti-Western, heroic and anti-heroic elements in Philip Marlowe are indicated at the end of *The Big Sleep*. Because he has turned down the offer of $15,000 by Mrs. Vivian Regan (the elder of General Sternwood's two wild daughters) to find her missing husband, she calls him an SOB. To this, Marlowe responds:

Uh-huh, I'm a very smart guy. I haven't a feeling or a scruple in the world. All I have the itch for is money. I am so money greedy that for twenty-five bucks a day and expenses, mostly gasoline and whiskey, I do my thinking myself, what there is of it; I risk my whole future, the hatred of the cops and of Eddie Mars and his pals, I dodge bullets and eat saps, and say thank you very much, if you have any more trouble, I hope you'll think of me, I'll just leave one of my cards in case anything comes up. I do all this for twenty-five bucks a day—and maybe just a little to protect what little pride a broken and sick old man has left in his blood, in the thought that his blood is not poison, and that although his two little girls are a trifle wild, as many nice girls are these days, they are not perverts or killers.[26]

In the attitude of Philip Marlowe to General Sternwood and his two irresponsible daughters, we see his professional stance—he did it for the money, but he was also willing to suffer danger in order to fulfil his professional obligations honorably. We see also the tension between his respect for the status quo (General Sternwood) and his distaste for some of its follies (racketeer Eddie Mars and Sternwood's daughters.)

Travis McGee

The kind of detective who appeared in the writings of Dashiell Hammett and Raymond Chandler was brought up-to-date and set firmly in the "permissive society" for the second half of the twentieth century in John D. MacDonald's Travis McGee, Robert B. Parker's Spenser, and most of the American fictional detectives who have appeared since the fifties.

Travis McGee has all the qualities of the hard-boiled detective that we recognize in Philip Marlowe. He is tall, handsome, shrewd, but above all, a survivor amid all the threats to his life and liberty.

John Wiley Nelson speaks of Travis McGee as "the tarnished knight in modern armor" and points out that the colorful series of stories in which he is the hero are not progressive; his character is as complete in *The Deep Blue Good-by*, the first of the series, which appeared in 1964, as it is in any of the later books. Nelson observes that a consistent system of beliefs operates through all the books, and he then makes the significant comment, "The self-affirmation of the classic Western belief system merges with the self-hatred, guilt, and bitterness of the anti-Western."[27] For a complete analysis of McGee in relationship to our theme, we could hardly do better than refer the reader to Nelson's survey.

McGee is a young Florida beach bum, living on his boat, *The Busted Flush*. He undertakes investigations on the basis of receiving half of any money he recovers for his clients. John D. MacDonald presents a very explicit anti-Western attitude to American society, which is voiced sometimes by McGee and sometimes in the philosophical musings of the elderly economics professor, Meyer. In *The Scarlet Ruse*, Meyer gives a devastating critique of American consumerism:

> You come up against a bleak fact, Travis. There is not

enough material on and in the planet to ever give them what we're used to. The emerging nations are not going to emerge — not into our pattern at least. Not ever . . .

It was okay, Travis, when the world couldn't see us consuming and consuming. Or hear us. Or taste some of our wares. But communication by cinema, satellite, radio, television tape, these have been like a light coming on slowly, being turned up like on a rheostat control in a dark cellar where all of mankind used to live. Now it is blinding bright, cruelly bright. And they can all look over into our corner and see us gorging ourselves and playing with our bright pretty toys. And so they want theirs now. Just like ours, God help them. And what is the only thing we can say? "Sorry. You're a little too late. We used it all up, all except what we need to keep our toys in repair and running and to replace them when they wear out. Sorry, but that's the way it is." What comes after that? Barbarism, an interregnum, a new dark ages, and another start a thousand years from now with a few million people on the planet? Our myth has been that our standard of living would become available to all the peoples of the world. Myths wear thin. We have a visceral appreciation of the truth. That truth, which we don't dare announce to the world, is what gives us the guilt and the shame and the despair. Nobody in the world will ever live as well, materially, as we once did. And now, as our materialism begins to sicken us, it is precisely what the emerging nations want for themselves. And can never have. Brazil *might* manage it. But no one else.[28]

Meyer also blasts the consumerism induced by amoral advertising which causes people to waste money on unneeded items. In an in-depth survey of the economic problems of elderly couples in the Fort Lauderdale area, he has shown that they were "squeezed between the cost of living and their Social Security."[29]

For all his criticism of the American economic system, John D. MacDonald pointed out that McGee was the worst example of improvident citizenry that one could hope to find in a day's march.[30] In this way,

MacDonald was able to deliver his sermon on the evils of capitalism and keep his maverick hero still in business. But the primary reason that made Travis McGee a particular illustration of the hard-boiled school in the latter half of our century is his attitude toward sex. The attitudes of twentieth-century permissive society were normative for McGee in that, within the stories, the sexual relationship itself has a therapeutic—if not redemptive—function, and although McGee's relationship to women appears to be casual, it is dominated by a very clear personal morality. Travis McGee may have fallen in and out of love more or less at will, but he always presented the illusion to his readers that he was essentially a one-woman man. In *The Deep Blue Goodby*, his companion is Lois Atkinson, but she is killed in the end; in *The Quick Red Fox*, it is Dana Holtzer, the efficient secretary of film star Lysa Dean, but she is accidentally hit on the head and that brings her back to her senses; in *Pale Grey for Guilt*, it is Pussy Killian, a gorgeous redhead, who wants to taste McGee's life-style before returning dutifully to her husband, but it is hinted that she will die of a brain tumor. You can't have the best of both worlds, but McGee makes a good stab at it. Thus when he has the opportunity to take to bed Mary Smith, the attractive operator associated with Garry Santo, he relinquishes the opportunity out of his deep respect for his recent loss of Pussy:

> Where is the committee, I thought. They certainly should have made their choice by now. They are going to come aboard and make their speeches, and I'm going to blush and scuff and say, "Shucks, fellas." The National Award for Purity, Character, and incomprehensible Sexual Continence in the face of an Ultimate Temptation. Heavens to Betsy, any American Boy living in the Age of Hefner would plunge at the chance to bounce that little pumpkin because she fitted the ultimate playmate formula, which is maximized pleasure with minimized responsibility. With a nice build, Charlie, with a lot of class, Charlie, you know what I mean. A broad that really goes for it,

and she had a real hang-up on me, Charlie. You never
seen any chick so ready, Charlie buddy, to scramble out
of her classy clothes and hop into the sack. Tell you what
I did, pal, I walked away. How about that?[31]

Here McGee is laughing at himself.

True to all that the public opinion polls have told us
about the twentieth-century attitudes to religion,
McGee places organized religion among those coercive
and repressive aspects of modern society to which he,
the maverick, is opposed; but perhaps true to John D.
MacDonald's earlier Puritan upbringing, McGee seems
to place Jesus among the mavericks. So in explaining
to Sheriff Burgoon why hippies were opposed to the
kind of head-knocking represented by the sheriff and
his faithful deputy, McGee observes:

> "It's a mass movement against head-knocking, Sheriff."
> "What kind of joke is that?"
> "All kinds of head-knocking. Commercial, artistic, and
> religious. They're trying to say people should love people.
> It's never been a very popular product. Get too persistent,
> and they nail you up on the timbers on a hill."
> He stared at me with indignation, "Are *you* one of
> *them*?"[32]

Elsewhere in this story, McGee criticizes commercialized Christmas in America and also the new breed of
manipulators and those who serve them.[33] Outside the
Travis McGee corpus, John D. MacDonald wrote an
expose of commercialized religion in *One More Sunday*.[34]

We see signs of the same attitudes and qualities in
Ross Macdonald's matter-of-fact and somewhat cynical
private eye, Lew Archer, his last name taken from Sam
Spade's ill-fated partner in *The Maltese Falcon*. Discussing his life-style with the wife of a psychiatrist
(whom he subsequently seduces), Lew touches on the
problem of justice which has been so much at the center
of the classical detective story:

"The life is its own reward," I countered. "I like to move into people's lives and then move out again. Living with one set of people in one place used to bore me."

"That isn't your real motivation. I know your type. You have a secret passion for justice. Why don't you admit it?"

"I have a secret passion for mercy," I said, "But justice is what keeps happening to people."[35]

Spenser

In some ways the hard-boiled detective story produced its most acute contemporary example in Robert B. Parker's private eye, Spenser, whose allegiance is to the city of Boston. Spenser illustrates the new mix of the seventies and eighties which makes for a popular story in the American detective genre. He is tough but sensitive, expert in the physical arts but also in cuisine, fond of sex but essentially *decent*, indifferent to or even skeptical about organized religion but deeply involved in religious and moral values. The expletives that are indicated by a simple dash in Hammett and Chandler are now expressed in all their four-letter clarity: the name of Jesus Christ might appear with equal urbanity as an oath or as an authentic commentary on contemporary attitudes.[36] The most significant exchange perhaps is in a discussion between Spenser and his girlfriend, Susan Silverman, on the ethics of killing. This occurs because Spenser has killed two unsavory characters (Doerr and Hogg) and has almost beaten the life out of a third (Lester Floyd).[37] Even more pertinently, Spenser realizes that for many supertoughs like himself and even for superjocks like baseball player Marty Rabb, the older values by which they live are no longer helpful in dealing with the real ambiguities of life. Within modern society, people are searching for a new ethical system that will make sense of their lives and give meaning to their existence. Spenser has said that the only thing that matters is personal honor. The conversation continues:

Susan said, "But aren't you older and wiser than that?"

I shook my head. "Nope. Neither is Rabb. I know what's killing him. It's killing me too. The code didn't work."

"The code," Susan said.

"Yeah, jock ethic, honor, code, whatever. It didn't cover this situation."

"Can't it be adjusted?"

"Then it's not a code anymore. See, being a person is kind of random and arbitrary business. You may have noticed that. And you need to believe in something to keep it from being too random and arbitrary to handle. Some people take religion, or success, or patriotism, or family, but for a lot of guys those things don't work. A guy like me. I don't have religion or family, that sort of thing. So you accept some system of order and you stick to it. For Rabb it's playing ball. You give it all you got and you play hurt and you don't complain and so on and if you're good you win and the better you are the more you win so that the more you win the more you prove you're good. But for Rabb it's also taking care of the wife and kid and the two systems came into conflict. He couldn't be true to both. And now he's compromised and he'll never have the same sense of self he had before."[38]

This was true for the 1970s when the book was written, and today the problem has not disappeared. Robert Parker seems to have a stethoscope on the heart of the great American public that is well on its way to becoming completely secularized, but which is still searching for a contemporary moral system than can effectively take the place of the older religious values on which its culture was based. It is significant that Parker should end *Mortal Stakes* with a serious discussion between Spenser and his girlfriend on such a heavy subject. But there can be no doubt that they are speaking with a very different accent from that of the classic detective story when Susan brings the discussion sharply to a close with the comment, "Enough with the love talk. Off with the clothes."[39]

IV

In our own understanding of detective fiction, we have to cast our net much more widely than Nelson. The American thriller has its own significance just as, I suspect, the British thriller of the same period (such as the work of Edgar Wallace) has, but there is no justification for limiting the term *detective fiction* and excluding everything that does not fit Nelson's definition of that term. Similarly there may well be reasons for regarding the works of this hard-boiled school as distinctively American in their assumptions about life and society, but there is no more reason for regarding them as distinctively *more* American than the works of Erle Stanley Gardner, Ellery Queen, Phoebe Atwood Taylor, and Rex Stout, who were writing at much the same time but who followed a different mode. Perhaps what Nelson observed about Travis McGee is applicable to the greater part of contemporary detective fiction; in it "the self-affirmation of the classic Western belief system merges with the self-hatred, guilt, and bitterness of the anti-Western."[40]

Even the selection of private eyes as the primary kind of detective employed in the hard-boiled school was itself significant. In the very nature of the trade they practiced, professional private detectives were skating on very thin ice as soon as their investigations uncovered a serious crime like murder. They were pledged to protect their clients (who might be the culprits), and yet they were also required to cooperate fully with the police to the point of calling them without delay and handing over all the evidence they had collected. Hence, almost inevitably they were in the ambivalent position of being required both to affirm the lawful authorities of the prevailing society and yet at the same time implying, through their own activities, the inadequacies of those same agencies.

But to understand the real significance of the American thriller, on which John Wiley Nelson concentrated, we need to remember Nicholas Blake's astute observation that detective stories were mostly read by the upper and professional classes and thrillers by those with less money and inferior social status.[41] That is the clue. When *The Maltese Falcon* appeared, America had been disrupted by a series of bank failures and the beginnings of the Great Depression. There were plenty of people who had reason to question the American system, since they had lost their own stake in it, and if they yearned to believe that everything would come right in the end, they were conditioned to think that this was more likely to result from the national qualities of American ingenuity, common sense, and the realistic employment of brute force in key places, than from any faith in the essential rationality of the universe. Indeed the 'God' whom Nelson discovers to be alive and well in American popular culture may be closer to an idol in America's own image than the God of Western Christendom or to the biblical God of America's own Puritan beginnings. Furthermore, Richard Hofstadter has reminded us that there is a persistent strain of anti-intellectualism in American life that is not only skeptical about the solutions offered by pure reason but downright suspicious of those who make a profession out of offering such solutions.[42]

In some ways, the American literature of this period forecast the kind of skepticism about society reflected in Nelson's anti-Western. At first sight, for example, Sam Spade appears to be working simply for money. This is very explicitly stated.[43] On the other hand, money, even the fabulous Maltese falcon itself, would not be adequate reward for the mortal dangers he regularly faces. There is a fuller clue to his motivation in his attempt to explain his position to Brigid O'Shaughnessy:

> You'll never understand me, but I'll try once more and
> then we'll give it up. Listen. When a man's partner is
> killed he is supposed to do something about it. It doesn't
> make any difference what you thought of him. He was
> your partner and you're supposed to do something about

it. Then it happens we were in the detective business.
Well, when one of your organization gets killed it's bad
business to let the killer get away with it. It's bad all
around—bad for that one organization, bad for every detective everywhere. Third, I'm a detective and expecting
me to run criminals down and then let them go free is
like asking a dog to catch a rabbit and let it go. It can be
done, all right, and sometimes it is done, but it's not the
natural thing.[44]

In this chapter, I have argued that the hard-boiled
school belongs to the tradition of the anti-Western, and
that in a detective-fiction form, this goes back to William Godwin's *Caleb Williams*. The hard-boiled school
stands in the American tradition of the Western cowboy, who comes from afar and who rides into town to
find himself elected sheriff and confronted with the
task of trying to reestablish law and order in the face of
a corrupt and ruthless administration.

The form is simplistic and points to a morality that
is essentially individualistic. So much so, in fact, that
when we add to this the often illegal and even immoral
actions of the detective in pursuit of his quarry, we may
be tempted to wonder whether this kind of writing has
anything to do with morality, much less with the spiritual foundations of society that is our main interest.
Critic Frederick Isaac may redress any imbalance at
this point: in "The Changing Face of Evil in the Hard-
Boiled Novel," he argues that the critical work dealing
with this brand of literature has lacked a study of evil as
distinct from crime.[45] Behind this suggestion, one
senses his concern to remind us that ethics should not
be confused with mere legality.

Judged from the point of view of legality, the school
of Chandler and Hammett et al. may fall very short. So
far short, in fact, that those obsessed with a merely
conventional view of morality may be ready to dismiss
Philip Marlowe and Sam Spade as immoral characters.
And this they are not, because although they were on

occasion extremely casual in their treatment of the law, they had a highly developed individual sense of right and wrong. Their activities make the point that law and morality are not always (nor often) synonymous. Isaac argues that there has been clear development in the moral sensitivities of hard-boiled detective fiction. This fiction has evolved from the wholly simplistic and sordid world of crime presented by Micky Spillane; through the more complicated attitudes to society presented by Hammett, Chandler, John D. MacDonald, or Ross Macdonald; to the even more sophisticated and ambiguous understanding of our world and the evil in it in the books of Robert B. Parker. Isaac suggests that Parker understands the simplistic answers which had appeared in earlier detective stories will no longer satisfy the public, and he goes on to say that Parker's own solutions, "while they do not reflect societal norms and are not what we might wish to see, have a consistency and contemporary logic that is missing from almost all other series. The presence of the Code, for all of its situation ethic, is true to our uncertain time."[46]

It might be nice if a simpler ethic that offered alternatives in clear contrasting colors were tenable, but it is not. And since that kind of clear-cut approach to good and evil is no longer possible, "Parker retains the solidity of his own beliefs to oppose the irrationality and insubstantiality of the present reality."[47] I am not too sure what that means, but it does not mean that, because our situation is ambiguous, for Robert Parker ethical considerations cease to exist.

The problem, of course, not only for Parker and his Spenser, but for all the heroes of the "me-against-society-in-the-midst-of-all-this-ambiguity" school of detective activity is that ultimately they have no authority apart from their personal opinion for what is right: the writer is guessing that his individual opinions will be endorsed by the reader. But how are such personal convictions formed or sustained or ultimately justified? In past generations, the Church at least served the useful purpose of providing an objective standard to which all our subjective preferences could be referred, but that does not appear to be possible any longer; and you must pardon me, but your slip is showing!

Part 2

Changing Times

A brave world, Sir, full of religion, knavery and change

—Aphra Behn

7

Change and Decay

I

"Change and decay in all around I see," are words from the well-known hymn "Abide with Me" by Henry Francis Lyte. Erik Routley, who was even more celebrated in the field of church music than as a theological commentator on the detective story, held the opinion that the first three words are the only words which are appropriately set to the music of W. H. Monk's popular tune, "Eventide." And it is those words that provide the theme for this chapter.

We live in a world where older standards of morality are no longer regarded as absolute, and in which standards of ethics and taste appear to be arbitrary or relative. Routley himself spoke quite frankly of the demise of the detective story and thought that its disappearance reflected the anxiety of relatively intelligent people for what was happening in society; the detective story reader "is not a lover of violence but a lover of order."[1] He argued that the period when the detective story held its highest place of influence was a period when the notions of authority and stability in society were beginning to be questioned and to be radically changed. As long as the actual foundations of society did not seem to be attacked, the genre was safe. However, "in the age which succeeded that one, in which it is perfectly clear that very few of the values familiar and precious to people who were born between 1830 and 1930 have the least chance of survival, detective fiction withers. There is now too much anxiety altogether. . . . It is quite likely that the readership of detective stories will be forced further and further towards the fringes of society."[2]

This may be rather too pessimistic, for there are signs that the pendulum is beginning to swing in another direction.[3] We have already seen that even in the heyday of classical detection some prescient minds, like Dorothy L. Sayers, recognized that the literary form of the detective story would not survive without radical change. In some ways the appearance of the American movement that we described in the last chapter suggests that American writers were more aware of the inevitability and dimensions of social change than were those of the Old World, for even in the 1920s in Albert Train's series about the attorney Ephraim Tutt and his junior partner Samuel, American detective stories were not without their critics of society.[4]

However the most devastating forecast of modern Western society and of its changes in relationship to the detective story must have been Ernst Julius Borneman's remarkable essay in detective fantasy, *The Face on the Cutting-Room Floor*.[5] Almost everything about this book is significant in what it forecasts about the course of Western (particularly Anglo-Saxon) societies. Although it was presumably set in Britain, it was also cast within the context of that most twentieth-century of all industries—the film industry. As the dust jacket declares, "The plot is like one of those Chinese boxes, each box as you open it revealing yet another one, and each time with subtle differences of emphasis and new revelations of character. The detective is as deeply involved as is the narrator. When the tale has been told, a commentary follows by an outside observer (Müller)— and he, too, turns out to be deeply involved."

Critics raised fundamental questions about the morality of the story or whether it really was a detective story, but more fundamentally, the story illustrates a sort of nemesis in Western society, raises questions about where ethical values are located and whether anyone could now be charged with guilt or safely acquitted.

The main character in the story is Cameron McCabe, the Anglo-American chief editor of a film company, "thirty-eight years of age, born in the city of Glasgow, grown up in the stone farms of the New Land Beyond the Seas, a worker working on a work that does not help to make the world better, a Christian without belief and without unbelief, neither good nor bad, neither rich nor poor, neither happy nor unhappy, both native and stranger, host and guest."[6] If one wished to interpret the work as an allegory (as Borneman may have intended), this could represent a remarkably accurate description of Western humanity in the mid-twentieth century.

When the major part of the story has been told, a commentary is added by a former German, who possibly represents the polarity in Borneman's own thinking and who is given the significant name Adolf Benito Conrad (Comrade) Müller. The allusion to twentieth-century totalitarianism is clear and through Müller's dialogue with McCabe, the writer is able to introduce his own observations on the effect of world war on the Western nations.[7] Müller also seems to have presented Borneman's remarkably perceptive estimate of Western humanity in his description of McCabe:

> Mr. McCabe was a typical twentieth-century big-city middle-class man, especially post-war [i.e., post–World War I] in his attitude towards that present-day structure of society which he himself helped to build, therefore both creator and creation, unwilling creator and unwitting victim of that social development which began in the eighteenth century, grew up during the nineteenth century, ripened, flowered and showed plainly evident signs of early decay at the beginning of our age and is now fighting a last desperate and losing struggle against odds of its own creation. . . .

I tried to show Mr. McCabe's dependence on the age,
class and environment from which he came: twentieth-
century, middle-class and big-city, a product of the press-
ing need "to earn increasingly more money so as not to
sink into a relative pauperization." This pressure produced a void, which is normally filled—and filled it must
be—with the primitive essentials of human requirements: food and the other sex. Parts of the void are filled
with various kind of dope: with the last fragments of
nineteenth-century religion, with nineteenth- and twentieth-century bogus politics, with pseudo-science, pseudo-art and other substitutional products of modern
civilisation. The result: "a growing disregard for those
human qualities which have not yet become purchasable
and marketable merchandise."[8]

We should look beyond the vaguely left-wing philosophy of history that this passage seems to express, with
its orthodox Marxist belief in the inevitable disappearance of the capitalist system, and we should concentrate on its underlying assumptions about Western
society as it was when the passage was written. So in
Müller's description of McCabe's litany of revelation and
revision, "The old explanations are recanted and new
information is given. This is again recanted in the next
chapter and so it goes on and on: uncertainty and
instability govern. Nothing is firmly fixed, nothing
steadfast, nothing solidly established. Everything is in
the process of change, demolition, destruction, decay:
an exact picture of the man and his age."[9] The identi-
fication between this particular detective story and the
course of Western society was made explicit.[10]

The response of writers to the complexity of the
human dilemma is too universal and too diverse for a
comprehensive analysis, but we may distinguish between two different kinds of evidence about changes in
society. Broadly speaking, the changes that we note in
detective writers during the past few decades seem to
echo the demand that the American "urban cowboys"

voiced for increased realism, but at the outset we have to distinguish between (1) incidental change in social fashions and (2) much more fundamental change in values that suggests the separation of the culture from its religious and ethical roots. These may be interrelated and yet discerned as discrete influences.

By the first I would indicate changes reflected in the literature which may be understood as only the reflection of the society within which the author is writing, although they are the result of more fundamental changes in society's basis for ethical action. So, while the whole climate of sexual permissiveness was certainly due to a change in fashionable attitudes, it also may be the result of something much more basic — of attitudes that assume there are no moral absolutes, for example. In accepting this shift in the mores of society, writers may often be doing no more than jumping on a bandwagon of the prevailing fashions.

On the other hand, the more intrinsic change implies a society that lives under the conviction that there *are* no absolutes, that there is no way of proving ultimate truth, that there are no decisive ways of distinguishing right from wrong. This is obviously much more basic and at root, more theological. Because we shall be looking later at some of the ways in which the changes in society since World War II may be documented, we may simply note at this point how the "permissive society" and other social issues have manifested themselves in detective-story writing during the last few decades.

II

Detective fiction seems no better and no worse than most other forms of modern literature in its treatment of sexual relationships. On the negative side, there are very obvious attempts to engage the prurient interests of prospective readers, but on the more positive side, the treatment of sexual themes recognizes how sex may be a motive for criminal violence, and it also forces the reader to recognize that crime is often squalid and dirty.

One may write much more happily about the recognition of social issues which detective story writers have been quick to pick up once they have become popular. Compare, for example, the treatment of the color question in Rex Stout's *Too Many Cooks* (1938) with its purported sequel *A Right to Die* (1964). Be aware too of the growing consciousness in books after World War II of violence in society, or of the problem of capital punishment. In the 1960s, Britain was arguing the morality of capital punishment, and this ethical debate is reflected in Ngaio Marsh's *Dead Water*, which appeared in 1963. Superintendent Alleyn of Scotland Yard discovered the body of a drowned woman:

> Alleyn had never become completely accustomed to murder. This grotesque shell, seconds before its destruction, had been the proper and appropriate expression of a living woman. Whether here, singly, or multiplied to the monstrous litter of a battlefield, or strewn idiotically about the wake of a nuclear explosion or dangling with a white cap over a cyanosed, tongue-protruding mask—the destruction of one human being by another was the unique offense. It was the final outrage.[11]

Alleyn returns to this theme later to justify his own urge to detection. Discussing the possibility that Miss Cost's death may have been due to an assault by a local half-wit, Alleyn observes that although the latter may have nothing to do with the case, he would have to find out because

> murder . . . is always abominable. It's hideous and outlandish. Even when the impulse is understandable and the motive overpowering, it is still a terrible, unique offense. As the law stands, its method of dealing with homicides is, I think, open to the gravest criticism. But for all that, the destruction of a human being remains what it is: the last outrage.[12]

Alleyn has put himself firmly on the side of the wide-spread movement for the abolition of capital punishment, while justifying the continued necessity for his own detective activity.[13] One doubts whether this kind of speculation would have appeared if the climate of opinion at the time had not raised the considerations in a particularly acute form. In this story, when the criminal knows that he has been discovered, he commits suicide—a useful way of avoiding the awkward moral problem that Alleyn would have faced in view of his expressed views on capital punishment.

The detective literature of the time also reflects increasing concern about (and with) new technology and with the Third World countries (as in Patricia Moyes' the *Black Widower* [1975]). The changes in society and the more fundamental changes in cultural philosophy are also documented in writers from continental Europe and elsewhere. Writers such as Maj Sjöwall and Per Wahlöö (Sweden), Poul Ørum (Denmark), Janwillem van de Wetering (Netherlands) along with English exile Nicholas Freeling—since his stories are set in the Netherlands, Akimitsu Takagi (Japan), Pierre Audemars (France and Switzerland), and Friedrich Dürrenmatt (Switzerland) all illustrate the realism that refused to romanticize detection, sometimes to the point where it leaves the reader with the overall impression of being engaged in a rather thankless irony. Because there is no contrasting ethic, everything is reduced to a colorless grey so that one sometimes wonders why the detective is bothering with such a pointless enterprise. That does not mean that the books are not well written or that the main characters are not believable and even likable human beings.

Martin Beck, the character in the Swedish stories of Sjöwall and Wahlöö, is a most likable person, but in light of his dissatisfaction with his job, his early marital problems, his dyspepsia, and his general dislike of the state of Western society, one wonders why he persists in his job. Something similar might be said of Ørum's Detective-Inspector Jonas Morck of the Copenhagen Flying Squad. The Danish detective enjoys a happier personal life than Beck, but in *Scapegoat*, Morck is plainly disgusted.[14] He is offended by the evidence of police brutality during a protest at the American embassy. Later this disgust is personalized in his revulsion at the bullying methods used by a colleague in securing the arrest of the half-wit, Otto Bahnsen, for the murder of a young girl, and at the psychological bullying used to secure a conviction. One ethical point of the story is that, although Morck did his best to clear Bahnsen of the murder of Kirsten Bunding, he is too late to save the simple-minded boy from the terrible results of his ordeal with the law. More pertinently, Morck himself plays his own part in the charade and therefore must share the blame. If such ethical issues are to be raised in a detective story, then somewhere along the line, there ought to be some explanation of why, at the end of the story, Morck is able to go contentedly to sleep and presumably wake up to continue his job in the morning. It presents an ethos of purposelessness that raises questions for this reader. American police procedurals are no less sordid, probably more brutal, and contain as much personal trauma, and yet they are more optimistic, because one senses that the characters still believe that what they are doing is worthwhile.

In Pierre Audemars' *Slay Me a Sinner*, there is a classic confrontation between the law, represented by a conscientious young officer of the Sûreté, Monsieur Pinaud, and Father Lafarge, the parish priest of Vallorme, who remarks to the officer that they live in two different segments of society which do not meet often enough. This story too is concerned with ethical problems: three times we are assured (by three different people) that the only way to love is to love without reservation. However, the author leaves us in the dilemma of inferring that this justifies one murder and three attempts at murder, because the person who is murdered is utterly evil and the detective is trying to bring somebody to justice for the murder of an evil person.

Father Lafarge is opposed to M. Pinaud's approach to factual truth and asks, "What is this thing you have agreed to call truth? Nothing is immutable—that is the whole secret of life. There are laws and principles—causes and effects—that man has not even started to understand in the brief time he has been on earth. This is surely the greatest truth of all, and one which the wise man should learn to accept."[15] The priest goes on to say, "The law—that is the justice of man. What can the law achieve now? What has it achieved in the past? How can you punish with justice and mercy? Take another life—in revenge—in payment of a debt? What punishment is fitting and suitable for a person who already feels remorse and has asked and prayed for a higher forgiveness?"[16]

Although some modern detective novels have a good deal in them that might be considered amoral, if not downright immoral, the relationship between law and religion persists as a cloudy but pervasive undercurrent, even into the fourth quarter of the twentieth century. And the relationship persists throughout Western society, which is still living on the moral capital bequeathed to it by Christendom.

It persists in the Dutch writer Van de Wetering's story of an extremely "moral" murderer in *Outsider in Amsterdam*.[17] It is reflected in the work of two dogged, run-of-the-mill police officers, Adjutant Grijpstra and his associate Sergeant de Gier. In some ways, this is a police procedural but the main theme concerns the murder of Piet Verboom, the leader of a religious cult and a dealer in drugs, and his curious ex-police Papuan bodyguard, Jan Karel van Meteren. It is also concerned with the ethical distinction between dealing in marijuana and heroin, and with the problem (resolved in a typically un-Western way) of how to deal with a leader who has gone off the rails.

The undercurrent of relationship between law and religion persists, even though it may be represented as old-fashioned. When a streetcar stops in front of the Volkswagen in which de Gier and Grijpstra are trying to make their way through the Amsterdam traffic, the driver, de Gier, utters a mild expletive:

> "Bah," de Gier said, "and bah and bah again."
> He and Grijpstra were in a marked police car, a white VW complete with its blue light, siren, and loudspeaker. They were on normal patrol duty.
> "Three times, bah," Grijpstra said. "Three is a holy figure, the bah of the father, the bah of the . . ."
> "Don't," said de Gier, who was trying to worm his way between a streetcar and a parked tourist- bus.
> Grijpstra laughed.
> "One can't insult the great power above," he said, "He is there and whatever we say fits in with him."
> "Who?" asked de Gier, who had got the car stuck and was waiting for the streetcar to move.
> "God," Grijpstra said.
> "Ah," de Gier said. "I see, you misunderstood me. I don't mind the blasphemous talk. I said 'don't' to the streetcar. It stopped and I wanted it to go on."
> "But you should mind," Grijpstra said. "You are a policeman and a policeman has to do with the law, and the law has to do with religion. Don't you remember that lecture last month?"
> De Gier remembered. A retired state-police general had told them about law and religion. First there was religion, then there was law. Don't misbehave for misbehavior displeases Divinity. It was only much later that the law came down to earth and bold spirits stated that misbehavior displeases humanity.[18]

That is a theological statement—a twentieth-century, secular theology leaning toward humanism, but it is still a theological statement.

However, the residuum of traditional Christianity can have curious manifestations. It is to be seen in the strangely apocalyptic view held by Beuzekom, the drug dealer. In order to discover more about the baffling case, de Gier has allowed himself to become involved in a drinking session with Beuzekom and even hints that he might be ready to work for him. The following exchange takes place:

> "And drugs mean the end of everything," de Gier continued.
> "It was the end of China before the communists solved the problem. Drugs mean dry earth, dust storms, famine, slaves, bandit wars."
> "Yes," Beuzekom said, "that'll be the future."
> "And you want to be part of it?" de Gier asked.
> "Don't be ridiculous," Beuzekom said. "You know what's coming. You can read the statistics, just like I can. We can waste our time being idealists, or refuse to stare facts in the face, but it's coming all the same. It's probably a cosmic apparition, part of the destruction of this planet. But meanwhile we can make a profit out of it and live well, if we live *with* our circumstances, not against them. If you want to fight the general trend I would suggest you buy an antique helmet, find yourself an old horse, and attack the windmills with a lance. There are enough windmills around, you'll be busy for the rest of your life."
> "I saw the dead body of a girl today," de Gier said, "some nineteen or twenty years old perhaps. She had sticks instead of arms and legs and her face was a skull."
> "Heroin?" Beuzekom asked.
> De Gier didn't answer.
> "O.K.," Beuzekom said, "heroin. Heroin is bad for the health. So is quicksilver poisoning. Atom bombs are even worse. And machine guns, tanks, and guided rockets. Very unhealthy. So do you want me to cry? The world is the way it is. And we are on it. We can fly to the moon but we can't stay there."
> "I hope your business is profitable," de Gier said, and closed the door behind him.[19]

There is no doubt where the writer, and presumably his readers, stand. They are all (*we* are all) against heroin dealers. But in the words of Beuzekom, Van de Wetering expresses the apocalyptic despair of many within our own world, and the common rationalization that, if you can't beat the hell-bent rush of this human race, you may as well live it up while you can, and make as much as you can while it is possible.

The roots, even of the despair and frustration underlying modern hedonism, though, are basically theological. At the end of the story, the commisaris (commissioner) and the chief inspector of police are musing upon the curious circumstances that permitted their murderer to slip through their fingers. His escape had been inevitable:

> "Force majeure," the chief inspector said, "you said that just now. Force majeure makes us blameless. We did our best but something happened that we couldn't have foreseen. Caused by a power beyond us. Force majeure means an act of God."
> "Ah yes," the commisaris said, "God."[20]

The book ends there, but we are left wondering about the meaning of the last paragraph. Does it mean that God has taken a hand to save the man who, although technically a murderer, has destroyed a heroin dealer? Or was the author telling us that after all our stories, all our ethical problems, all our despair and cynicism, at the end there is still awaiting us the unprovable fact . . . God?

Perhaps the most perceptive evaluation of modern society to arise out of European existentialism is in the works of the Swiss dramatist and writer, Friedrich Dürrenmatt, who studied theology at the time when the dominant names in European theology were Karl Barth and Dietrich Bonhoeffer. Dürrenmatt is profoundly concerned about the disappearance of ethical values, as a result of the fact that—as he writes in the introduction to the story *Traps* (*Die Panne*)—"Destiny has fled the stage . . . all things have become accidents."[21]

The existentialist stance is clear. Life seems to be governed by sheer accident. "We are no longer threatened by God, by justice, by fate as in the Fifth Symphony, but by an automobile accident, a dam that breaks as a result of faulty construction, the explosion of an atomic plant through the error of some absent-minded laboratory technician, a wrong setting of an incubator."[22] The whole emphasis of Dürrenmatt's introductory chapter is to question whether the writing of real stories that go beyond the subjective experience of the writer in or out of bed is possible any longer, because he recognizes that in order to be accepted as literature, "there is a call for higher values, for moral principles, useful mottoes; something has to be discarded or supported, now Christianity, now popular nihilism."[23]

That is what the public expects. It presupposes conventional theology popularized, and Dürrenmatt indicates that he is not prepared to play games like that. In contrast, he speaks of following our own road through this world of accident, a road bordered by billboards advertising all the irrelevant ways to make our living and spend our money, "but along whose dusty edges we may find a few possible stories, with humanity visible in a commonplace face, with hard luck haphazardly acquiring a universal validity, with justice and the judiciary process displayed, and perhaps even with grace manifesting itself, caught, focused, and reflected in the monocle of a drunken man."[24]

That is where theology enters, whether it is invited or not, because the grace that manifested itself to Alfredo Traps through the monocle of the drunken prosecutor—and what an old-world touch that was; does anyone today look at the world through a monocle?— was also revealed to him as judgment. Traps recognizes himself as guilty, and he not only accepts the sentence on the crimes by which he has boosted his own dubious career, but claims the sentence as his right, and embraces those who have sat in judgment on him. The *implicit* theology in Dürrenmatt's book is in forcing us to recognize, even if it is by some such suprahuman entity as 'Humanity' itself, our search for justice and our need of judgment. As Alfredo Traps recognizes the truth of his own guilt, we read, "Justice—how the word intoxicated him! In his life as a salesman of textiles, he

had envisioned justice only as an abstract pettifoggery;
now it rose like a huge incomprehensible sun over his
limited horizon, an idea only vaguely grasped and for
that reason all the more able to send shudders of awe
through him."[25]

No wonder he protested when his defense attorney
started to make excuses for him and to plead that he
was innocent of the crime with which he was charged.
Traps felt that he was insulted by such excuses. And
that, of course, raises the interesting symbolism of the
defending attorney. He represents the conventional arguments of Western society and its accepted values, and
for Dürrenmatt, he is not an attractive figure. Herr
Zorn, the prosecutor, is slovenly enough, with dueling
scars on his face, a hooked nose, and presenting a lank
and cadaverous mien, but he is merely "an antediluvian
phenomenon," whereas Herr Kummer, the defending
lawyer, is gross and "looked as though he were made of
greasy sausages." In addition he is blowsy, has the
bulbous nose of an alcoholic on which he perches his
golden pince-nez, and we are told that under his sloppy
suit he is still wearing his nightshirt, "probably because he had forgotten to change it."[26] That may represent the writer's view as to where contemporary Western
society rests in its conventional understanding of right
and wrong. Herr Kummer presents the defense of liberal civilization in response to charges against the individual.

Kummer does not pretend that Traps is completely
innocent of sin, because he has already inadvertently
confessed to such peccadilloes as casual adultery, occasional petty swindles, and malicious spitefulness, but
he does have his good points, and "taken all in all, we
cannot detect more than an unethical taint, a slight
spoilage, such as occurs and must occur in so many
average lives." But Traps cannot be charged with Pro-
methean crime, "a culpability that is great and pure
and proud." Kummer maintains that Traps is simply
one of the casualties of society: "He is not a criminal,
but a victim of the age, of our Western civilization,

which, alas, has fallen farther and farther away from faith, from Christianity, from universals, succumbing more and more to the rule of chaos, so that the individual may no longer look up to a guiding star, and in place of order and true morality, disorder and immorality reign, the law of the jungle prevails."[27]

One could hardly have the arguments and the apologia of Western liberal humanism or of modern liberal theology (if they can be distinguished) put any more clearly than that. And what Dürrenmatt seems to be saying is that these conventional excuses must be rejected, so that humanity may now accept the title of "sinner" and so put blame squarely where it belongs — on the individual self.

Something of this, both in its dissatisfaction with the accepted processes of conventional justice and in the profound belief that we ourselves are judge, jury, and executioner when we face evil, also comes through in Dürrenmatt's detective story, *The Judge and His Hangman*, written in the early 1950s.[28] That date is important, because apart from examples of the "tough" school of American urban cowboys, the criticism of conventional justice had little parallel at this time in the Anglo-Saxon world, and those who did the detection in Anglo-Saxon societies would not accept kindly the sophisticated philosophy that motivated Commissioner Barlach of the Berne police.

It all started with what appears to be a straightforward murder mystery in which Barlach tries to discover who shot the brilliant young Lieutenant Schmied, whom he has sent on an undercover operation to investigate the suspicious activities of the international financier and industrialist, Herr Gastmann. There is nothing to suggest any deep philosophy in this: the theme, based on the lifelong rivalry of Barlach (representing good) and Gastmann (representing evil), is one that recalls the confrontation of Holmes and Moriarty.

But other elements are woven into the story. The position taken by conventional society in relationship to the pursuit of real justice is illustrated in the clash between Barlach and Dr. Lutz, his superior at the head of the Berne police, and poignancy is given to the confrontation between Barlach and Gastmann by the fact that the former (in his sixties) knows himself to be dying from an incurable disease and therefore not concerned with advancement. Thus Barlach can react to the situation in a way that not only appears to do justice, but in a way that actually achieves justice. Furthermore, we are not offended when Barlach makes his observations about life and human destiny, because a person in his sixties and soon to die has probably earned that right.

So Barlach illustrates for us the paradox of human life. Sometimes he seems to act in a way that is almost fatalistic,[29] but what appears to be fatalism (his belief in the inevitability of discovering crime within a flawed world and an imperfect humanity) has a more profound basis when we reflect that this holds important convictions about justice itself and the uniqueness of human life. Gastmann also believes in the uniqueness of human life, but it leads him to precisely opposite conclusions.[30] The difference between these two men is the paradox of life, and perhaps the novelist whom Barlach and Tschanz interview gets to the heart of it when he recognizes Gastmann's evil motivations and yet wonders whether "Gastmann has done more good in his life than all three of us taken together as we're sitting here in this garret."[31]

Life is a paradox, but Barlach refuses to be deflected from his discovery of the truth or his pursuit of real justice.[32] Despite Gastmann's nihilism, despite the fact that sometimes there appears to be an inexplicable determinism in human behavior, the earth can be beautiful and being human may still remain an enigma: "What sort of animal is man?"[33] Particularly, we might ask, what sort of animal is it that recognizes beauty in the face of mortality, pursues justice as a desirable end in itself, and which finds life still worth the effort even at the end.[34]

III

There is a further interesting comment in another European detective novel published in the 1970s. In *The Body Vanishes,* Inspector Holz observes to his superior officer Inspector Dulac, at the end of the story, that he finds police work particularly satisfactory because the police have rules and are only required to carry them out: "There's no room for doubts or moral scruples."[35] But we read that Dulac remains silent because he is thinking about one of those who has suffered through the crime which they have been investigating.

That silence reflects the doubts of the second half of this century because the clear-cut objectivity that Holz found so satisfying no longer exists amid the ambiguities of our time. It is possible that the loss of such distinct standards is related to the noticeable disenchantment with the classical form of detective fiction, at least among many writers. It may indeed be a reason for the popularity during the last few decades of writers like John le Carré and of the spy thriller, in which the chase does not have to bother with right and wrong but is concerned only with "them" against "us."

But in order to trace further the movement away from classical detection, we must return to the Anglo-Saxon world where the genre had its genesis. Something of the change of ethos in Britain may be seen in Anthony Gilbert's *Looking Glass Murder.* In the first chapter, the traditional Roman Catholic attitude is indicated in the black funeral draperies and the way in which death is taken so seriously.[36] The decline in the status of religion within British society is noted by Florian, an Italian nobleman, who remarks about the English, "They have abandoned their belief in God, yet think of themselves as gods." Not that the decline in religious influence was limited to the English, for "when he was in Rome Florian didn't even attend Mass,"[37] although he was a Catholic.

Rational skepticism is expressed more pointedly by an English medical man, Dr. Gregg, whose father had been a parson. Gregg lost his faith many years earlier when his father asked him to take something to a parishioner who was dying in hospital. The doctor said,

> She was a nice old girl, and I suppose I wasn't very good at hiding my feelings—I was about sixteen at the time—for suddenly she caught my arm and said, "Don't worry about me. I can stand the pain, because God sends it, and He's my friend." I stood up and told her, "Well you've just procured Him a lifelong enemy; because if he can visit this misery on you, then I'll spend the rest of my days finding ways to thwart Him."[38]

One is reminded of a similar protest by one of P. D. James' characters in *A Taste for Death* where she protests that God can't be less merciful than we are.[39] We will not enter into a theological debate about suffering at this point. We simply note that modern authors recognize that their characters are living in a world where traditional theological assumptions are no longer universally accepted and where the divine is understood more and more in terms of the humane.

The context of Josephine Tey's *A Shilling for Candles* is uncompromisingly English and set in the 1930s, but it reads in a way that makes it curiously appropriate for Anglo-Saxon societies later in the century, when it was reissued.[40] It marks a break from the classical format of detection by featuring an intelligent, matter-of-fact policeman (Detective-Inspector Grant) and a nonconforming teenager (Erica Burgoyne), and it tilts at the spurious values of the mass media.[41] The book also expresses disgust at the sensationalism of twentieth-century culture, dislikes contemporary violence and dictators, and is disgusted by the litter and sprawl of plutocratic suburbia. The writer deplores the continuing influence of privilege and recognizes that we live in an unfair world.[42]

The more fundamental change in ethical attitudes is expressed in Amanda Cross' *Theban Mysteries*, which concerns the traumatic changes that come into an ostensibly conservative girls' school in New York City during the 1960s and 1970s under the headmistress, Miss Tyringham, who is determined to find a happy balance between preservation of the school's older values and a readiness to meet the new world. The detectives in the story are Kate Fansler and her husband, Reed Amhearst of the District Attorney's office. If you can survive the author's obsession with quotations, which seems to force her to drag in nearly every erudite citation she has read since the eighth grade, the book says a great deal about the moral and social revolution in American society of those days. Kate Fansler is a typical New York liberal, with all the attitudes and prejudices of that genus, and is strongly opposed to her brother's old-line conservatism. She supports the radical polarization of the young at the Theban School, favors the rights of minorities, and opposes the Vietnam War; the story involves two boys who are trying to avoid the draft—one by legal means and the other by hiding in the girls' school. By 1971, when the book was published, a fair proportion of the great American public was willing to accept these radical sentiments. From this point of view, perhaps the most significant comment is put into the mouth of one of the teachers at the school, commenting on the sophisticated well-to-do parents of the pupils:

> The most extraordinary change here is never talked about at all. . . . Since your time, or long, long before that, I'm certain this school has always been largely Republican in sentiment; not reactionary, you understand, but sound and vaguely right wing. It astounds me how little support there is for President Nixon, not only among the students but among their parents. And these girls represented some of the most prominent families in the country. Of course, the staff isn't supposed to argue politics with the students, but that's easier said than done, these days. [43]

To this, Kate correctly points out that these girls and their families also represent the "Eastern establishment," which had never been among Richard Nixon's strongest supporters. But however true that may have been politically, liberal changes did come about among intellectuals and not only among members of the Eastern establishment. It was not a change that was typical for the whole of American society, as Nixon's crushing victory over George McGovern in 1972 made clear, but it was true for a significant portion of the hardcover-book-reading public. The values that the author was expressing were addressed to this public. That is not to suggest that Amanda Cross was "insincere" or that the views were not her own, but in 1971 an author could take these stances even in writing a detective story and they would find resonance within a significant majority of readers.

However, it is worthwhile probing behind Amanda Cross' support for causes that had become congenial to her political preferences; there is a theological stance which is much more fundamental. Kate Fansler discusses the situation with the grandfather of one of the students and, in the course of that discussion, she refers to Sophocles' *Antigone*, which the students had been studying: "You think they [the students] are running away from what *you* conceive their destiny to be. But there are no oracles any more to tell us what is fated, or pleasing to the gods. There is no longer a Tiresias. You know, the play Angelica is studying was rewritten in modern times, similar in many ways, but without Tiresias. There is no one today who can tell us the truth."[44] This is the crucial point of divergence between our own age and all previous ages—"there are no oracles any more to tell us what is fated, or pleasing to the gods." A little later in her discussion with the old man, Kate puts the issue even more pertinently: "I believe *Antigone* is a great play. I don't think we agree on what are eternal truths; I'm not sure I believe there are any eternal truths, apart from the facts that a man only learns at a terrible price and there are no easy answers."[45]

The theological message from this story is that there are no absolutes, because no values remain permanent, so even the law tends to become more relative in its operation and pronouncements.[46] But despite the seriousness of her discussion—and its presence in a detective story is at least acceptable enough to her readers for inclusion—Kate Fansler did not recognize how this new fact of our time could undercut the whole enterprise (i.e., the search for reality) in which she was, throughout the story, not only temporarily engaged but existentially *engagée*.

The world reflected by a growing number of writers of the crime novel is no longer sure about right and wrong. In John Buxton Hilton's *Hangman's Tide*, "'It wasn't really dishonest,' Sally said. 'Nothing seems really immoral when you don't think there's a chance of your being found out.'"[47] And yet at the same time, it is no longer a congenial society in which to live. There are a couple of significant comments in Hugh Pentecost's *Death after Breakfast*. Pierre Chambrun, the French manager of a New York City hotel, affirms that it is "not a nice world we live in."[48] After the murder of his girlfriend, Mark Haskell, the public relations officer of the hotel, is questioned by the police. Lieutenant Hardy asks, "Did she have a lawyer. Was she religious? Did she have a priest, a minister, who might know about the family?" "We did not talk about lawyers or God," is Haskell's reply.[49] The exclusion of God from discourse has become increasingly true in the twentieth century, although lawyers may still remain a "hot item" of conversation.

In the late twentieth century, the world is more blatantly violent and cruel. John R. L. Anderson's *Death in the North Sea* shows this. In the book, a bomb has been wired to a corpse, and the body is left in a boat to drift in the direction of an oil rig. The inevitable explosion appears to be directed against capitalism and the North Sea oil project, but it may simply be a way of getting rid of an inconvenient husband. However, the explosion results in the death of two innocent members of the Dutch crew that picks up the corpse from the sea. Surveying the affair afterward, Colonel Peter Blair, who has carried through the detection, discusses it with Sir Edmund Pusey, of the Home Office. Pusey is asked how the culprits must have felt when they found they had killed two innocent people who could not further their plans in the slightest. He responds, "About the killings—I don't know. They were quite unscrupulous, and it seems to be the habit of people who place bombs to accept the deaths of innocent bystanders; it's part of the corrosion or moral values of our times."[50]

Later in the same conversation, Blair blames the drabness and purposelessness of the new town of Seathorpe for breeding frustration in the culprits. He observes, "I think the real trouble was that appalling town, and equally dreadful new university. If you subject human beings to places like those, you get murder," but Pusey will not accept this. He declares:

> No, Peter, there's a far too fashionable view that no individual is ever to blame for anything, that the vilest crimes are all the fault of society, or parents, or someone else, never the fault of the people who commit them. It isn't true. A lot of people live in Seathorpe without becoming murderers, and I dare say a number of them manage to commit adultery quite happily, insofar as adultery can ever be a really happy human state. Most of the undergraduates at new universities get a great deal from them, and even the drop-outs seldom turn to murder. There's a hell of a lot wrong with human society, there always has been. But there's a great deal of sheer human wickedness that's nothing to do with society. These people were very wicked.[51]

One of the most genuinely sinister books that documents the rapid sliding of moral values since World War II is Desmond Cory's *Circe Complex*. It is dismaying, not because it is more gruesome than other stories (although it contains a horrible account of torture), nor because it is too free with sex (although one character blatantly uses sex to get whatever she wants), nor because of its callousness with regard to death (although it is certainly not squeamish). The main reason the book is depressing is that it seems to be built on the cynical remark of Robert Walpole that "every man has his price." Three men who have lived honest lives, Tom Foreman, a jewelry appraiser; Oliver Milton, a consultant psychiatrist (who is also the narrator); and David Bannister (a police sergeant) all sell their honor when tempted by the prospect of acquiring jewels worth £400,000. Also, Ollie, Dave, and "Cat" Devlin (a petty crook) are easily seduced by Valerie Foreman's sexual charms.

But why do people who have lived as respectable citizens succumb? Earlier Ollie had refused to compromise his values by becoming an industrial psychiatrist ("an intellectual prostitute"). After he gives in to Valerie's seduction, she chides him with not being overly principled: "I wouldn't say you were very scrupulous about money in general. Or even about people in general. You're a hard case, I've always thought. Not that I think that's bad. In fact it's a good thing to be . . . in a world like this one."[52]

The assumption is that there is no morality "in a world like this one." The forces of government and of conventional society are therefore hypocritically tuned to keep the status quo "status quoing." After a particularly fatuous case in court in which Ollie had to give expert evidence, he meets Dave Bannister on the steps of the court and over a cup of tea in the local café, Dave remarks that this sort of nonsense sickens him:

"The law is the law," I [Ollie] said.
"The law's a lot of starch-shirted London gobies with plummy accents and fat wallets is what the law is. Sometimes I see what those longhair student revolutionaries are getting at, I really do. It's the system that's all wrong, no doubt about it."

"And a pig is a pig is a pig."
"When he's not a wage-slave of the Fascist reaction-
aries. Well, they could even be right about that."
"Oh, come on," I said.[53]

As Ollie observes to one of his clients, progress is an
outmoded concept, "like British imperialism," and it
seems that with the loss of the old world and its certainties, we are in a world where trust disappears, where
you can trust nobody.[54] Oliver Milton gives expression
to this attitude, musing about the remarkable breakdown that led the honest, respectable Tom Foreman to
go against a whole lifetime of habit and training and
make off with £400,000 worth of jewels and shoot a
policeman in the process:

> All that bull his business associates had put out about
> *not knowing what had got into him* . . . Of course they
> had to say something like that, it's all part of the great
> professional facade and the sticking-together swindle,
> but every damned one of them had known perfectly well,
> "Betraying a trust" is the way they'd have described what
> Tom had done . . . Well, I doubt if there's a psychologist
> alive who could tell you what that word *trust* means. It's a
> non-scientific term. We don't use it. It's something that
> permits you to go to a perfect stranger called a bank
> manager and give him all your money—just like that; or
> to another stranger called a valuation assessor and give
> him all your family jewellery and silver plate; then on the
> mere say-so of another total stranger called a medical
> specialist, you'll allow another, a different stranger to cut
> you wide open and pull your guts out and give you, may-
> be, yet another stranger's kidney to get along with in-
> stead of your own. A sort of mental infirmity, I suppose
> you could call it, which happens to be necessary to the
> running of an organized society and which, therefore,
> through a kind of unspoken conspiracy, psychologists
> have agreed to accept as normal behaviour. It's nothing of
> the kind. It's God you're supposed to trust in. Not in hu-
> man beings.

Why? . . . Because your trust is somebody else's responsibility. And human beings get tired of responsibility, get sick of being trusted. I know how Foreman had felt all right; I knew maybe better than anybody, because in my profession you have to ask for trust. Ah, come on now Mrs. Henderson, tell me all about it. You can trust me. In fact, if you don't I can't help you. Just trust me, trust me, trust me . . .

And why the hell should she? Suppose she does and ends up with her head in a gas oven, as is only too likely. Whose fault is it? Mine? Well, hardly. You can't allow yourself to start thinking *that* way. So it's hers, then. Obviously. That's the only possible answer to the question, unless you're a Laingian or one of those rather outmoded gentry who thinks that *society's* to blame. It isn't really. It's not society that asks to be trusted, it's me.[55]

The passage raises all sorts of interesting questions. Milton's psychology cannot explain or even justify 'trust' and yet the whole of organized, civilized society depends upon it; fundamentally, as even the psychologist admits, trust depends not on the person, but on the concept of something behind the person. Call it God? What happens when that concept no longer has any persuasive power? Then Ollie happens, and Foreman, and Valerie, and Dave Bannister. And we witness the appearance of more Cat Devlins and people far worse than Cat Devlin, since he appears to have a rudimentary idea that there *ought* to be something or someone who could put things right, but Ollie has lost it all. While he and Bannister are interrogating Devlin, the latter is suddenly afraid that he will be sent to Broadmoor (the British prison for the criminally insane). Ollie tells us:

He raised his eyes—for once—towards Bannister's face, almost as if in search of help, or anyway of reassurance. But Bannister's face was the classical policeman's blank. Non-intervention was what he'd promised and that was what I was getting; to all intents and purposes he wasn't there. Not as a person. But he was there all right as a

symbol of established authority, and it's a funny thing
how people like the Cat who've spent the whole of their
waking life kicking against these particular pricks, often
turn towards authority when the chips are really
down . . . maybe as badly shot rabbits very often crawl
towards their hunters.[56]

Devlin's reaction suggests that nobody is totally
devoid of the sense that there *ought* to be order in life,
that there *ought* to be the authority of the one or of those
who can put things right. None of us wants to live in a
universe that makes no sense and where there is never
any hope of justice. The wistfulness of this is present
even in the author, Desmond Cory, himself.[57]

From this survey of writers, all the characteristics
of our society that were forecast by Borneman can be
documented in the way detective fiction developed after
the appearance of *The Face on the Cutting-Room Floor*.
We note society's growing void, and the attempts to fill it
with the primitive requirements of food (note the popularity of cookery books and exotic cuisine) and sex. We
note too the reversion to various kinds of drugs. Even
the last fragments of nineteenth-century religion can
be discerned both within our society and in the continuing popularity of the older, classical writers leading
to what Borneman described as "bogus politics, pseudo-science and pseudo-art," for those human qualities
which have not yet become "purchasable and marketable" are now at risk in the horrendous spread of terrorism and in the crime that stalks our streets.

In most of the chapters that follow, we shall see how
modern writers of detective fiction have tried to adapt
to the changes in society, from those who were content
simply to follow popular fashions, through those who
altered the format, and then to those who grappled with
the fundamental loss of faith within Western culture.

8

The Different Faces of Realism

As we have seen, the movement away from the classical form of the detective story was stimulated by Raymond Chandler's demand for more realism, both in narrating the work of criminal detection and in depicting the detective.[1] But those who followed that path often carried the insight much further; so the sordid began to wallow in squalor and the recognition that most crime is associated with dirt became almost an assumption that all life is sunk in filth: realism gave place to surrealism. There is a very fine line between what may be authentically realistic and what is unacceptable in terms of public taste; but many of the experimenters were unable to discern this distinction, particularly those who were content to follow the fashions.

Followers of Fashion

One of the most striking ways in which society has changed through the last half-century is in its attitude to sex in literature. Robert Barnard's *Death in a Cold Climate* illustrates the change as it affects Ålesund, a city on the coast of Norway.[2] The cynicism and callousness of young people and the casual way in which a girl takes or discards sexual partners are contrasted with the religious attitudes that prevailed only a decade previously. In the novel, Ålesund is compared with the modern city of Trondheim and is described as, "a hard-faced city, which only ten years ago had enjoyed the benefits of near-total prohibition, and whose joyless, life-sapping religion seemed to have moulded not just the faces of the older inhabitants, but the stance, the tone of voice, the choice of clothes and colours as well."[3]

Here one may feel that the references to sexual permissiveness are justified by the society Barnard was describing, but in other books one is less sure; Simon Brett's stories about the middle-aged character actor, Charles Paris, are sometimes obvious examples of a tendency to accept casual immorality and to employ dirty language in the name of realism, but in a way that is not always convincing. Charles Paris, a bibulous, somewhat libidinous middle-aged and not-very-successful actor, is unfaithful to his wife and has a penchant for good-looking young women as well as detection. This latter occasionally becomes little more than "peeping-Tommery."[4] The stories are usually well written, apart from some tendency to use the tenpin method of construction instead of a more carefully worked-out plot (first suspect—no good; second suspect—no good; on to the third suspect—no good; and so on; to the point where the last chapter contains a confession that solves everything). But Brett's tendency to use explicit sex and four-letter words adds little to the story.

In *A Comedian Dies*, Brett gives the impression of working on the same principle for his readers that one of his characters, the old music-hall comedian, Lennie Barber, adopts with regard to his audience at a Sutton nightclub—pour on the dirt and then you can do what you like with them:

> But he was getting through to the audience. . . .
> From being cowed, the audience began to be amused.
> The material remained unattractive, tales of sex and scatology, but it seemed to be what they wanted. Each punch line was greeted with the right shout of shocked laughter.

More and more faces turned to the spotlit figure, sweaty faces with mouths slightly open in anticipation of the next crudity.

And as he won the audience, Lennie Barber began to woo them, to force them to his rhythm rather than bending himself to theirs. He slowed down, stopped pile-driving his jokes, started to use silence and work with his face. Now that he had their attention, he let the audience see his full range of expression. His eyes popped lasciviously in the character of young men, fluttered with false sophistication for tarts, bleared rheumily as impotent dodderers and closed in obscene ecstasy for images of consummation.

But as his spell began to work, he started to dilute his material. Now that the audience was watching him, it no longer needed the hook of dirty words. His jokes became more whimsical, more attractive. Charles [Paris] began to relax. He was in the presence of a master.[5]

This is good writing, and without the use of one obscene word, Brett conveyed all that he wanted to convey. Why then did he give us the objectionable extract from Lennie's act on the previous page? That was unnecessary.

An even more blatant example of using the relaxed standards of the permissive society is to be found in Elizabeth Foote-Smith's *Never Say Die*. The detection is by a private investigator, Will Woodfield, who employs a student assistant, Mercy Newcastle. This young woman wearing tight jeans is able to keep Mr. Woodfield in touch with all the latest youth fads without spoiling his private eye, tough guy image. It is a good ploy, which shows the "straight" Mr. Woodfield (who carries a flaming torch for Miss Newcastle) in the process of being converted by noble-minded youth; he admits that "he was a selfish possessive bastard who was a long way from getting accustomed to the sexual mores of her age group."[6] This may be interpreted as Woodfield wanting to hop into bed with her exclusively, while implying that the more promiscuous approach of "her age group" is sexually more *generous*. Yes, that's the word.

This is a very promising start for a program of literary "with-it-ness," and the program is helped forward by a sprinkling of four-letter words that are unnecessary to the main action, and by reference to other fashionable concepts: psychic experience (the explanation of OOBE—out-of-body experience), fetishism, the revolutionary art of the underprivileged, witchcraft, astrology, women's liberation, homosexuality, lesbianism, natural foods, and reincarnation. The writer is also strongly in favor of rallying to the support of misunderstood young lovers.[7] Some of this, such as the explanation of OOBE, may be germane to the story and some may be justified in terms of its contemporary setting, but most of it is like adding Worcestershire sauce, Tabasco, lemon juice, and vinegar to a Bloody Mary—it is too much.

One can legitimately argue that this *is* the kind of hedonistic, fashion-conscious society in which we live. If a book intends to tell a story set within our present culture, then the writer has every right to describe the culture as it is, and the writer of detection has every right to use the special features of our society in order to bemuse and pull the wool over the eyes of the readers. That is traditionally part of the game. There is no answer to this argument, if that is the game which is being played. But I have a shrewd suspicion that the game has been changed without anyone admitting it. It has been changed from literary detection to the game of "seeing if I can sucker you into buying another book by the same author." It is as if the writer is saying, "Hey you, read me! I know the scene, man! This is where it's at! Let me show you how much I am 'with it,' and titillate your liking for gore, or sex, or the occult while giving you the excuse that you are reading detection!"

There are many more examples of books that rival *Never Say Die* in the use of the prevailing fashions and in its freedom of expression. Leo Rosten's *King Silky* has to have a glossary of Yiddish terms as an appendix; it contains plenty of explicit sex, with hints of all sorts of kinkiness, hard drugs, crooked policemen, and the philosophy that every person has a price. It also contains realism of a more solid order, as in the protest of the southern lawyer Settegard that those accused by the law should not be at risk without the production of proper evidence, and the legitimate claim that some people thereby get away with it "is the price we have to pay for making sure that guilt or innocence are too important to rest on hearsay—or madness."[8]

That is a serious issue, and it reminds us that all examples of realism in contemporary writing are not to be dismissed as merely cynical. The passage underlines the rules of evidence, the importance of human rationality, and our responsibility for making rational decisions about truth or falsehood, innocence or guilt. But this in turn rests on a presumption that we live in a rationally ordered universe. In A. B. Guthrie's *No Second Wind*, one of the police deputies, Jason Beard, objects when a girl criticizes police work as too limited; after all, we all believe in law and order, don't we? Particularly the people who read detective stories. As Jason observes: "People feel a good deal the same way about farmers and ranchers. It's a dumb occupation, not fit for a smart and ambitious man. Those people forget that without agriculture there would be no food on the table. Just as a good police officer has a special concern for society, so does a good farmer have a special concern for the land. We fight weeds, both of us."[9]

At the risk of being accused of special pleading, could not much the same be said about the clergy? There is a story about sowing wheat, some of which was choked out by weeds of one sort or another. At the very lowest level, apart from the claims churches may make for themselves, how much more work would the police officer have if there were no churches or clergy?

Yet, it seems as if it is becoming fashionable simply to sneer at the place religion holds in contemporary society. In Kenneth Giles' *A File on Death*, an exchange takes place during the digging of a grave:

"Was Mr. Lane a Protestant?"

"I 'eard 'im say the whole lot was bloody rot."[10]

This book is a prize example of the cynicism about British society in some modern writers — it tilts at everything, the Church, the public officials, the police, the law, "society"; nothing is sacred, and we are left with the feeling that if the social order is really like this, we would be better without it. It describes the suspicious deaths in Waddington Harbour, home of Sir Hugh Palabras, who is a sort of eighteenth-century lord of the manor with Fascist tendencies, exercising all the medieval *droits du seigneur*.

The dust jacket fulsomely declares, "Kenneth Giles is cherished as one of the keen admirers of the English character who can combine this affection with the ability to combine wayward ways with ingenious, completely fair, amusing murder mysteries." That is not the most sparkling piece of prose, even for a dust jacket, but it suggests that one could expect the eccentrics to be likable. They are not. The detectives, Chief Inspector Harry James and Detective Sergeant Honeybody, are decidedly not heroic characters, having more interest in food and drink than in most other matters. Their superior, Superintendent Hawker, is an obese, ambitious hypochondriac, given to bootlicking his superiors and browbeating his inferiors. The mysterious Mr. Quarles, from MI5, is positively sinister; of Sir Hugh enough has been said. Dr. Tulkingham, the local vicar, is more interested in killing, stuffing, and selling local birds and wildfowl than in his parish duties; Signor Abajo is ninety-three and the last of the *castrati*, with exotic gastronomical tastes; Beedle, his cook, is an African anarchist; General Gould is described as "the most incompetent British General ever"; he is also a sadist and mean with money; Mrs. Peremely-Fox, his daughter, is a sex-starved sadist; while Mill Sloper, the organist of the church and an enthusiastic Girl Guide, is a nasty nosey parker. Nor are the incidental characters much better — Bruggles is the stereotype of a homosexual actor; Bosky Lane, the publican, is not trusted by anyone except Sir Hugh; Dianile Higgins is a crook (although she maintains she is an honest one!); Dirty Douglas is a petty criminal and an informer; Stinting, the maid planted in Sir Hugh's house, is a tough little piece; while Joan Drinkwater, the journalist, is a spy. There is not one likable character in the whole boiling, and instead of being funny, the final effect is depressingly nasty. Perhaps even more fundamentally, it is clear that there is not a pin to choose between the morals and motivation of those who are supposed to be working on the side of law and order and those who are working simply for their own interests. We are left with the impression that it does not matter which way things go, because everyone is out for his or her own ends, and the police are simply engaged in an elaborate cover-up for the British establishment. In the guise of a murder story, and with the implicit plea that it is all very humorous and amusing, we are treated to sexual and scatological allusions that leave us feeling that if British society is really like this, there is little hope for it. It is just plain nasty.

This attitude of cynical disgust about everything that has traditionally been regarded of value in the British way of life, an almost deliberate muddying of accepted values, amorality for the sake of amorality until it becomes decidedly immoral, is seen in the works of Peter Dickinson. And sometimes Colin Watson, for all his genuinely humorous gift, comes close to it.[11]

Robert Barnard illustrates the decline of respect for religion when he spoofs theological and ecclesiastical fashions in Blood Brotherhood. In this novel, he brings a group of ecclesiastical stereotypes together, in an Anglican monastery in the north of England, to discuss the fashionable subject, "the social work of the Church in the modern world."[12] The group is led by a suave, theologically radical bishop (the Bishop of Peckham), who is given to witty comments. Group members include a far-left-wing vicar (Stewart Phipps), a vicar hung up on youth culture (Philip Lambton), an American interdenominational minister whose major interest is finance, an uncivilized African bishop who is very willing to cash in on the Western nations' interest in the Third World (the Bishop of Mitabezi), and two women Lutheran ministers from Norway—one young and good-looking (Bente Frøstad) and the other a dried-up prig with a viciously charitable smile (Randi Paulsen). Add to these a mysteriously impressive head of the order, Father Anselm, and a bigoted nincompoop in Chief Inspector Plunkett, and it is clear that Barnard has dreamed up a suitable context in which to deliver "the many unorthodox things" one of his reviewers says he has on his mind.

At first it is all lighthearted jest, and Barnard is able to poke fun legitimately at the religious stereotypes that have inflicted themselves upon the churches during the past two or three decades. But the fanatics are all a bit too much (Plunkett and Paulsen), the African primitivism is a bit too gruesome, and the radical liberalism is a bit too gelatinous. Finally, the "solution," which virtually condones covert homosexuality in the monastery and which discovers the culprit to be one of the least attractive of Barnard's caricatures, is more than a bit too much. The air of cynicism about all religion not only breathes through but seems to be the main thrust of what Barnard is trying to say. It is illustrated by Inspector Croft's reaction when he receives the report from America on Simeon P. Fleishman (surely it is no accident that he bears the name of an American brand of margarine?), "Oh, God, thought Croft, another committed Christian."[13]

This irreverent method of poking fun at society through detective fiction perhaps reaches its *reductio ad absurdum* in America in some of the works of Donald E. Westlake.[14] The principal quality of the grand larceny that he artfully introduces is its frank escapism and the "detection" becomes an overly flaunted skill and craft, like the artist's portrayal of voluptuous and bouncing wenches in a mural by Rubens, or an exuberant carving of a cornucopia by Grinling Gibbons. However, there are signs that the writers themselves at times are tempted to cry *Enough* or even *Too Much!*[15]

However, we cannot disparage all those who openly follow the new fashions of sexual permissiveness. They cannot be entirely discounted when they use their method to support a serious plea for social change. Some of the characters in Lionel Black's *Ransom for a Nude* think nothing of hopping in and out of bed with a variety of partners, but there is a strong motif running through the book concerning the remorse of a World War II ex-bomber pilot for the bombings in which he took part and his newly acquired social conscience to help the underprivileged. Sir David Bullen dies at the end of the story apparently in an act of atonement for his wartime career and with the assurance that "in the end, everything is fitting, all is well."[16] Before his death, he describes his trust fund and the stolen Velasquez painting which was to have been "given to the Sawdon Trust. Which means it really belongs to all the homeless families we can cram into our hostels this year, next year, and ever after—until England becomes a country where every man can expect a roof for his wife and children. That's why I hope whoever took the painting will give it back."[17]

Sir David's statement is a change of fashion that offers an altogether more optimistic impression of British society, and it may represent one reason why even trend seekers cannot be entirely discounted. There is evidence that some writers may be wearying of the unnecessary bad language and gratuitous sex that has been imposed on the genre. There is a passage in Lucille Kallen's *Introducing C. B. Greenfield* in which a black architect (Gordon Oliver) and his wife Shirley are discussing a play they have seen recently at the Lincoln Center:

> "I think he [the playwright] was just using the kind of language and imagery those kind of people would normally use," Shirley said.

"He used that language and that imagery," Gordon replied, "because they are normal to *him*. He's a lazy think-
er, he has a poverty-stricken imagination, and he
substitutes shock and titillation for literacy and inven-
tion."

"You're a prude, Oliver, that's your trouble." Shirley bit
hugely into a buttered bagel.

"It's a matter of aesthetics," Greenfield observed. "Gordon isn't prudish, merely chaste."[18]

Just Doing a Job

One of the most important aspects of the movement
toward realism in detective fiction is that of humaniz-
ing the detective. Writers were no longer tempted to
make their detective heroes infallible and omniscient.
Obviously the detectives would become more human as
the writers concentrated more on the routine of police
work or on the equally mundane work of a private eye in
a detective agency. As Dora, the wife of Ruth Rendell's
Detective Chief Inspector Wexford, reminds him, "You're
not God."[19]

For the rest, the procedural as a form of detective
fiction—whether a police procedural or a P.I. procedural—is simply a slice of life, not apple pie or fruit cake
but, if American, Chicago-style pizza, sometimes topped
with jalapeño peppers and a dash of strychnine. The
formula tends to be the same whether the city is Los
Angeles (Elizabeth Linington and her several alter
egos, Dell Shannon, Lesley Egan, etc.) or London (John
Creasey and his), whether the original language is a
regional brand of English (June Thomson and Ruth
Rendell), Dutch (Janwillem van de Wetering), Swedish
(Maj Sjöwall and Per Wahlöö) or that of Ed McBain's
eighty-seventh precinct in an imaginary American city.
Nor need the procedural be limited to the urban environment, although undoubtedly crime stories of this
nature are usually set in the "urban jungle." Some
British writers have adapted the police procedural to
the local constabularies—Catherine Aird's Inspector C.

D. Sloan and Peter Alding's Inspector Robert Fusil show that detection as followed by the British county police forces is not very different from that followed by the metropolitan forces described by John Creasey or the American writers. All procedurals are concerned to show us that, like ordinary life, the work of the professional detective is never romantic, rarely undertaken without pressure and often sordid. Some writers preserve the illusion that the successful solutions are mainly due to the intelligence or intuitive processes of their leading character (e.g., Alding's Fusil), but in the true procedural the reader is constantly reminded that most crimes are solved by dull routine, by tips received from informers, and occasionally by the culprit's stupidity or the detective's lucky break.

John Creasey's books show the interrelationship of police work; it is not the kind of detection where the detective can concentrate on one case, and (in his writings as J. J. Marric) he shows us that Commander Gideon's function as a senior officer of Scotland Yard is to take an overall view and to see where patterns emerge within the sequence of cases, and this is the way real detection operates. It depends less on clues from the scene of the crime than upon clues from the whole of society. The Gideon stories are less the account of single crimes than the weaving together of many separate strands, but the reader is finally left wondering whether this is any more fundamentally realistic than the classic stories of detective fiction, because the question remains whether the montage of criminal activity in real life provides such neat patterns as that which provides the solutions in most procedurals.

Ed McBain's *Hail, Hail, the Gang's All Here!* is the story of twenty-four hours in the activity of the detective squad in the eighty-seventh precinct, faced with every kind of problem from tracing a missing child to dealing with a phony suicide or arresting two trigger-happy robbers who have already shot a policeman.[20] Some of the problems are solved immediately when the culprits confess, but others take the whole twenty-four hours before they are solved. But solved they are, and the fact that all the investigations are brought to a successful conclusion is still the most unrealistic element in the procedural. What they manage to hide in the stale cigarette smoke and the dregs of cold coffee is that most crimes are never satisfactorily resolved; but perhaps that is understandable, since, to admit that, would be to assassinate the goose that lays the golden eggs.

However, the rest claims to be life as it is lived, and we are forced to recognize the squalid, real world, as in the following description with which the writer introduces the night shift:

> The morning hours of the night come imperceptibly here.
> It is a minute before midnight on the peeling face of the hanging wall clock, and then it is midnight, and then the minute hand moves visibly and with a lurch into the new day. The morning hours have begun, but scarcely anyone has noticed. The stale coffee in soggy cardboard containers tastes the same as it did thirty seconds ago, the spastic rhythm of the clacking typewriters continues unabated, a drunk across the room shouts that the world is full of brutality, and cigarette smoke drifts up toward the face of the clock, where, unnoticed and unmourned, the old day has already been dead for two minutes. The telephone rings.[21]

Beautiful. This is obviously a story that is down-to-earth (asphalt), bedrock (concrete) realism in which we can expect the writer to lift the stones of the city and show us what is crawling underneath, because this is where real crime flourishes; these are the people who deal with it day and night, and this is the way they go to work.

That kind of realism is to be found in the private eye procedural, illustrated in *File #1: The Mayfield Case* by Joe Gores.[22] It is an account of the first case investigated by Larry Ballard, a new member of Daniel Kearney Associates, a firm that specializes in recovering cars on which borrowers have defaulted. It is a sordid business, and as Dan Kearney shows Larry, nothing matters except the recovery of the automobile for their clients. The nature of this kind of detection may be summed up in this comment at the end of the story: "Dan Kearney nodded to himself. A girl had died; a man had had his first bitter taste of reality. And in the process D.K.A. bought themselves an investigator. Maybe, with a few more rough edges knocked off, a damned good investigator."[23] As you read the story with its matter-of-fact description of the offices of D.K.A. in the basement of a building that was once a bawdy house, you learn that when Larry has gained some experience, he will be expected to handle seventy-five cases at a time without losing track of any of them. This, together with the daily, never-ending task of filling in reports, the cynicism and lies of his colleagues as they make their pitch to get information, is what detection means: a firm such as D.K.A. really does operate on the basic principle that *nothing* matters, apart from getting the job done. That is the way it is.

Moreover, it should be clear from the foregoing that there is another important difference between the procedural and every other kind of detective fiction. Not only are the detectives ordinary professionals, operating in a mundane and ordinary environment, but these professionals, whether they belong to regular police forces, or to a firm of investigators, do not have the luxury of being able to concentrate on one particular case in isolation. They are at the mercy of whatever demands are made on their time and whatever cases appear. For the police, detection takes place under constant pressure—pressure from politicians looking for a quick solution that will win them votes at the next election; pressure from the media looking for material to fill another editorial or a 6:00 p.m. newscast, while hoping to keep enough interest alive to carry their audience over to the following day; pressure from the public that is more than willing to be titillated, even as it demands to be given a greater sense of security; but over and above all, the pressure that comes from the unscheduled, random, and often crazy way in which things happen and events pile up. That is an insistent theme in all procedurals: the multitude and the variety of the claims made upon the detective's attention and time. As Lesley Egan expressed it, through one of her police officers, Sergeant Clock, "He wished real life would behave more like the paperback mysteries, where cops were let alone to solve one crime before they got handed another."[24]

The dominant theme of procedurals is to emphasize the human characteristics of the detective, the humdrum and routine nature of detective work. Detectives are doing a job—a necessary job for the sake of society. As one writer has put it, "The basic characteristics of any good investigator are a plodding nature and infinite patience."[25] Beyond this we cannot do better than refer the reader to Raymond Chandler's description of police work in the words of Captain Gregory to Philip Marlowe in *The Big Sleep.*[26]

Realism and Religion

The foregoing represents a movement away from the story in which the primary accent is on solving a single puzzle to one which provides a realistic if frenetic view of the police or detective agency at work. Both are based on the popular ethics of their time, but the procedural relies on the fact that society needs some of its citizens to be set aside to maintain law and order. The genre is low-keyed and veers away from profound philosophical reflections.

Religiously, the detectives of the procedurals seem to reflect faith and skepticism in about the same proportion as their contemporaries at large. So Dell Shannon insists that her detective hero, Lieutenant Luis Mendoza has no religion, while Ruth Rendell's East Anglian detective, Chief Inspector Wexford, rather regretfully notes that his quotation from the Authorized (King James) Version of the Scriptures is completely unrecognized by representatives of the modern generation.[27]

One of the most striking examples of modern agnosticism in a crime novel is to be found in William McIlvanney's *Papers of Tony Veitch*.[28] The story is concerned with sinister and sordid crime in Glasgow, and yet it probably contains as much serious theological reflection as many books conceived in theological faculties. It is well written, ineffably (is this *le mot juste?*) full of four-letter words exploding in functional sex or casual blasphemy, and admits no squeamishness when describing either the horrors of gangland warfare in the gray city of Glasgow or the dirty little sins that hide under the sheets of a bedroom and the cassocks of a confessional. And yet, despite all the sordidness of the life it describes, it is full of theology.

The reason for that is its chief character, Chief Inspector Jack Laidlaw of the Glasgow police, and his determination to catch criminals: somehow or other this brash and often bloody-minded police officer—the examplar of arrogant opinions with a failing marriage and skeptical attitudes to religion—has to come to terms with the apparent meaninglessness of life, his own drive to reach the truth, and his disgust with those who gratuitously hurt others. Laidlaw's life and activity as a detective pose the basic question—what point is there in ethics, or in distinguishing between good and evil, if this existence is all there is? Behind his search to find an answer to the enigma of Tony Veitch is his own desperate search to find an answer to that personal question.

In his skepticism about traditional answers, and in his desperation to find real answers, Jack Laidlaw shows himself as typical of the British mood in the second half of the twentieth century. Although he rejects the idealism of the young Tony Veitch that makes him seek absolute certainty, Laidlaw is in the same kind of hunt, despite the fact that he settles for the doubts imposed by his uncompromising realism.[29] He has been through the "wherefore-are-we-put-upon-this-earth phase" of adoles-

cence and questioned "the meaning of life," but all that
has brought him to is "a rueful smile."[30]

McIlvanney rightly gauges the modern tendency to
reject traditional answers. He is no more enamored of
Scotland's residual Calvinism (or the anomalies caused
by the Scottish Sabbath) than the young Tony Veitch.
He speaks of "an eroding certainty about what God's
like," and when one character describes a small boy's
horror at the ghastliness of the crucifixion, McIlvanney
groups this observation with other reminiscences as
part of a "home-made wreath of already withering flowers."[31] Laidlaw speaks of the impossibility of 'God'—"if
there's a God"—preconceiving the world. And one has a
feeling he is obsessed with the theological problem,
because while throwing a chair at Mickey, the man with
the knife, its lucky trajectory "was almost enough to
make him believe in God"; but not quite—because
reflection on the injustice of life, at Tony Veitch's funeral, made him feel that if, as the minister declaimed,
God had taken that young man to his bosom, then it
was "some bosom, an embrace like kissing a shark."[32]

Realistically the answer is not to be sought in any
kind of idealism, religious or political; through Laidlaw,
McIlvanney rejects all kinds of orthodoxy, religious or
Marxist, and McIlvanney maintains a state of insistent
social outrage against the welfare state's myth of having eliminated poverty.[33] The characters who reflect at
all maintain hatred of the discriminations imposed by
distinctions of wealth and poverty. But that social
disparity had an ethical question at its heart—the
distinction between real compassion and real rectitude. McIlvanney is clearly critical of Britain's social
establishment.[34]

Why do ethics matter? *Truth* matters: "the only
healthy climate is the truth."[35] *People* matter—even
the most worthless-looking life matters, even Eck Ad-
amson's. No death is irrelevant.[36] Either everyone matters or no one. Laidlaw "could recall giving up any belief
in an overall meaning to living because any such meaning would have to be indivisible, unequivocally total,

giving significance impartially to every drifting feather, every piece of paper blowing along a street."[37]

But perhaps that issue cannot be resolved, because "Eck was like one of those pieces of paper," and try as he might, Laidlaw cannot get rid of the conviction that Eck matters, and the only nobility possessed by humans is to "defy the meaningless of our lives by mutual concern."[38] His theology is essentially humanistic, because it is centered in human caring. "The more people who cared, the closer you came to some kind of humanist salvation. There was no other he could believe in."[39] Laidlaw's problem with his own skepticism is that he cares for people, and he knows there are others who care—the people whom he calls "decency's martyrs," who "were the best of us because they gave of their good, quite naturally, in actions. They weren't dedicated to God or high political principles or some idea but to an unforced daily generosity of giving, a making more bearable for others and themselves. And they were legion."[40] His humanism shows its theological face in a remark he makes to Jan, the young woman who makes up to him what he misses in a bad marriage, "You know what I believe? There's no centre as such. The sum of the edges is the centre. You have to keep walking the edges."[41]

Some contemporary theology may be making a similar statement. In the words of the Harvard theologian Harvey Cox, "whereas theology was once manufactured at the center for distribution in the provinces, the direction of the flow is now being reversed. *It is the periphery which is now impacting the center.*"[42] Is that to be dismissed simply as the accidental use of the same metaphor? There *is* a valid critique of the conventional standards that comes from the edges of our society, but as Jack Laidlaw recognizes, and to some extent even exemplifies, there is something more than that. What about all that inexplicable goodness, that crucial decency that one discovers on the edges and which so obviously ought to belong in the center? How is it to be explained. Jack Laidlaw may have been right—we cannot explain it satisfactorily and we may no longer explain it in traditional terms but it is there, and it demands explanation just as much as does the dirt, the cruelty, and the squalor.

The trouble with realism is that its interpretation depends so completely on our own social perspective. As the nineteenth-century novelist Ouida is reputed to have observed: "Realism! The dome of St. Peter's is as real as the gasometer of East London, the passion flower is as real as the potato. I do not object to realism in fiction; what I object to is the limitation of realism in fiction to what is commonplace, tedious, and bald."[43]

There is nothing more real to us than human existence and our own conscious rationality inevitably points to the cosmic question mark behind existence. Because of its subject matter, detective fiction cannot help raising that issue, and although it may be anticipating our final chapter, it is worth noting that there are strong exponents among the modern writers who have tried to face the issue at a more profound level than that which is purely skeptical or flippant. Just as the first words of Henry Francis Lyte's hymn "Abide with Me" point to the rest of the verse in which they appear, so the "change and decay" in society illustrated in recent detective fiction point to the ethical imperatives in detection, and they in turn point to something else. As Arthur Upfield expressed it, through his Australian aboriginal detective, Napoleon Bonaparte:

> It doesn't matter two hoots whether the form of the evil is murder or an unjustly harsh act. Evil is always countered by God, or Good, or Providence, or whatever name you might choose to give it. You and I know, as well as other sensible and experienced men, that Evil never blesses, and the evildoer never prospers. I recognized that eternal law years ago . . . which is why I am an investigator of crime and not a supermaster of crime.[44]

9

Realism Turns
to Religion

As he crossed the bridge and looked away down the lake toward Lausanne, Henry knew that his life could never be quite the same again. Old, unquestioned values had been turned upside down. The black-and-white view of morality which he had accepted as his middle-class heritage had gone forever. He forced his mind to consider the facts, clearly and brutally, so that they might have their full, salutary impact.

—Patricia Moyes, *Death on the Agenda*

Not all the attempts to reflect the new ethos of realism in detective fiction can be dismissed as simply following the fashions: the permissive society is a fact that cannot be ignored, but there is a discernible mood in modern writing that makes it different both from the classic detective fiction of earlier times and from the patterns discussed in the previous chapter. We would call it "chastened conservatism" or "chastened realism": some writers, while accepting the ethical and religious skepticism of recent decades, indicate that they are not altogether happy with the trend and would welcome a return to clearer ethical norms. This is indicated either in terms of nostalgia or by calling for a new basis on which ethics can be established and rooted in civilized society.

The Consciously Religious Perspective

This may explain the appearance of detective stories written from a consciously religious perspective such as the work of the Jewish writer, Harry Kemelman, and the Protestant, Charles Merrill Smith, but some of the most striking examples have been written from a Roman Catholic position; Jane Dentinger's Jocelyn O'Roarke describes herself as "mentally flagellating herself as only an ex-Catholic can," and her friend, Lieutenant Phillip Gerrard, remarks to her that "for a self-professed agnostic, your Catholic guilt reflex is still pretty sharp."[1] That is true not only in regard to feelings of guilt but also in her respect for the old-fashioned institution of marriage, and perhaps even more significantly, her philosophical belief—shared by Gerrard—in an essentially rational universe.[2]

A similar conservative stance may be seen in the struggles of Ralph McInerny's Father Dowling, Leonard Holton's Father Joseph Bredder, O.S.M., and William X. Kienzle's Father Koesler to relate themselves to the world since Vatican II.[3] This viewpoint is also expressed in the struggle of Lawrence Sanders' earthy ex-chief of detectives, Edward X. Delaney, to operate with integrity in the changing conditions of the New York City streets that he has loved and served:

> It was the freedom, Delaney said somberly to Monica [his wife]. It was partly the drugs, he agreed, but mostly it was the freedom. Complete, without any restraint. There were no rules, no laws, no prohibitions. Moral anarchy. The kid was really surprised, Delaney said [of a young culprit], when he finally realized he was going to be punished for what he had done. He couldn't understand it. It didn't seem to him all that big a deal.
>
> The Chief told Monica that it frequently happened that way with people who couldn't handle freedom. They didn't know self-discipline. They acted on whim, impulse. They couldn't sacrifice the pleasure of today for the satisfaction of tomorrow.[4]

His first wife Barbara, who had died, thought he had become a cop because "he saw beauty in order, and wanted to maintain order in the world."[5] This is confirmed a little later when we read, "In fact he found a curious satisfaction in this task of 'putting things in order.' That's what a cop's job was all about, wasn't it? To restore and maintain order in a disordered world. Not only in society, but in the individual as well. Even in the cop himself."[6]

For Delaney, beauty is to be revealed only in truth. He realizes this when he reflects on the quality that makes certain paintings so attractive to him. Technique is not enough. "To be truly satisfying, the painting had to move him, to cause a flopover inside him when he looked upon life revealed. A painting did not have to be beautiful; it had to be true. Then it was beautiful."[7]

Obviously Delaney still accepts the older ethics. We read that his sympathy disturbs him because a cop is not paid to be compassionate:

> A cop had to see things in black and white. *Had* to. Explanations and justification were the work of doctors, psychiatrists, sociologists, judges, and juries. They were paid to see the shades of grey, to understand and dole out truth.
>
> But a cop had to go by Yes or No. Because . . . well, because there had to be a rock standard, an iron law. A cop went by that and couldn't allow himself to murmur comfort, pat shoulders, and shake tears from his eyes. This was important, because all those other people—the ruth-givers—they modified the standard, smoothed the rock, melted the law. But if there was no standard at all, if cops surrendered their task, there would be nothing but modifying, smoothing, melting. All sweet reasonableness. Then society would dissolve into a kind of warm mush: no rock, no iron, and who could live in a world like that? Anarchy. Jungle.[8]

When Detective Sergeant Boone expresses doubts

about the way in which the investigation is going, Delaney has no doubts because "our cause is just."[9]

Father Joseph Bredder is explicit in his support of traditional values. During a discussion with a fellow priest about the modern movement away from spiritual concepts, we read,

> "Why do they [scientists] shy away from the word 'spiritual'?" he [Bredder] asked.
> "Bigotry, my dear fellow," replied Father Armstrong cheerfully. "Pure bigotry parading as learning . . . as it always does. We have entered the spiritual Dark Ages. Or perhaps we never really got out of them. Six hundred years ago people used to recite little rhymes to ward off the Devil, and now they recite little equations, and with the same objective. What is called Science had replaced God and the Devil, and men's souls are reckoned as nonexistent because they cannot be found with photoelectrical equipment."[10]

So later, in a conversation with his friend, Lieutenant Minardi of the L.A.P.D., Bredder declares, "Reality demands eternity. Without eternity there is no significance to anything," and Minardi responds,

> "Well, the significance of a crime is that a law has been broken and it is the job of the police to discover who broke the law and punish him to discourage others."
> "The significance of a crime is that a law of God, exemplified in the formation of society, has been broken and the crime remains until the offender repents," said Father Bredder. "The state will pass away. God will not."[11]

These are all Roman Catholic sentiments grounded in traditional theology.

The questioning of the sixties and seventies in Britain is illustrated in the writing of James Fraser. It belongs to the permissive society, but the change of style is profound. Ingeborg Cattell, a young woman with whom Detective Inspector Bill Aveyard gets involved, confesses, "I'm just not certain about the marriage thing. I don't go for drugs, protest marches, the Civil Liberties bit, but a lot of things are changing. You'd be surprised, even in these dull backwaters, how much we keep in touch with what's going on. It seems to me two of our institutions need redefining. One's the Church, and the other's marriage."[12] The point is reinforced by the appearance of an unattractive clergyman, but we see both the recognition of a new kind of society and a demand for the revision of—but not the total rejection of—older institutions. In the same story, Detective Sergeant Bruton is forced to reflect on the depths to which human nature can sink:

> Thinking men refuse to accept the depth to which the human ethos can sink. "How can they do that?" they ask, but it's a futile question. Bruton knew, and Aveyard eventually would come to know, for it was the nature of their job, that the human mind has been created with an infinite capacity for good and evil, in equal amounts, and though the good men do is often transcendental, the evil can wallow hog-like in inconceivable mire.[13]

The loosening hold of religion may in part account for the rapid rise of the spy story as a separate genre, for in the story of espionage, we do not need to make any attempt to follow absolutes of 'truth' or 'justice', because the distinction between right and wrong may be very simply resolved in terms of "them" and "us."[14]

Although Peter Dickinson's story of a tiny "Livonian" government-in-exile in London may not be dismissed simply as a spy story, it accepts many of the values and reflects the more blasé attitudes that are common to that genre. Because there seems to be so little purpose in life, the young prostitute, Procne Newbury, is far from shocked at the murder of her mother, and observes:

> "He [the murderer] did her a good turn, I been thinking. I mean, where she is now, if she knows it'll be a big

thrill, won't it, being a murder victim; even up there there's not a lot of them can say that. And if she don't know, it's no skin off *her* nose, is it? She'd had a smashing life, her way. I mean there wasn't much to it, but she made it smashing, didn't she?"

"Yes. I suppose that's what matters." [says Lydia.]

"Course it is."[15]

That expresses a common mood: if there is anything beyond this life, fine; but if not, there's not much you can do about it, and it is "no skin off *your* nose," so "live it up!"

Lydia (Lady Timms) is the owner of the decaying boardinghouse where the Livonians have their headquarters, and she discusses the political issues between free societies and communism with Mr. Diarghi, of the Russian embassy.[16] But at the end of the story she expresses the political disillusionment of many of her contemporaries as she muses that

all governments, to her, were abominable, but not equally so. She didn't care whether there was any logic in her instinct to support the tiny and defunct government upstairs against the vast and far-reaching neo-Stalinist engine in the Kremlin. She simply knew that their smallness made them incapable of more than little lies and minor mischiefs, whereas in Russia there were probably ten thousand Aakus and a million Mrs. Newburys. . . . Her dealings with Superintendent Austen confirmed her belief that the government of Britain was only marginally better than that of Russia, because an historical accident had left the individual citizen with a little more power against it; but the police state was there, waiting to be released into domination, like a djinn in a bottle.[17]

On the other hand, the continuation of traditional values may be seen in the ongoing popularity of older writers such as Edmund Crispin (Bruce Montgomery) with his stories of Gervase Fen.[18] Crispin is profoundly influenced by the Christian history of England and the morality associated with it. As far as we know religion never obtrudes in the exuberant career of Gervase Fen, but he always treats it with respect, if not affection. On one occasion, in dealing compassionately with the sorrow of a young girl who has learned of the suicide of her friend, he comes close to an expression of Christian doctrine that would have done credit to Father Brown. Fen brushes aside rather brusquely her hope that the death of her friend was not suicide. "Then seeing that the headlong gallop towards a nerve-storm was for the time being arrested, he added more gently: 'It's distressing and horrible, I know, but there's nothing you or any of us can do about it.' And half to himself he murmured: 'We owe God a death.'"[19]

Undoubtedly, the traditional position taken by Gervase Fen represents the basic position of his creator, but it is a position with which his readership had some sympathy. Although a freer attitude towards moral and ethical questions rapidly developed after World War II, it did not suddenly win the support of the whole population, for there were still many whose preferences and even prejudices were still largely influenced by the standards of the past. Fen's personal conduct was wholly traditional; we read that "he is—unlike so many other detectives of current fiction. . . . entirely faithful in his marriage," and although Dolly, his wife, disappears from the later books, "a divorce seems in highest degree improbable."[20]

Fen also represents the older values in his detective motivation. In *The Case of the Gilded Fly*, the first of the Crispin stories about Fen, which appeared in 1944, we hear of Fen's reaction to the death of an innocent bystander that had been an act of brutal murder:

That wanton, useless act roused in Fen something which was neither heroism, nor sentimentality, not righteous indignation, nor even instinctive revulsion; and having stated the negative side, it is difficult to put into words, what, actually, it was, since it is not a common emotion in mankind, and since it lies at the basis of Fen's personality. I suppose that as near as anything would be to say that it was a kind of passionless sense of justice and of proportion, a deeply rooted objection to waste.[21]

The austere ethical residue of older attitudes and of the societies supported by them may not be as pronounced as in Crispin but it is still discernible in many British writers of the last half of this century such as Michael Innes (J. I. M. Stewart), Catherine Aird, Elizabeth Lemarchand, John R. L. Anderson, Ruth Rendell and others, but a few examples will suffice. W. J. Burley's Detective Chief Superintendent Wycliffe, on a Sunday morning, feels dissatisfied with his life and his job and points out to his wife that police officers, like other people, "want to do their Sunday thing: gardening, fishing, sleeping, taking the kids and dogs for walks, even going to church."[22] Going to church may now be the last of the options, but at least it is still a possibility. Elizabeth Lemarchand's Detective Chief Superintendent Pollard reflects on the change that has taken place in the English village and observes, "It's unfortunate that both old Bellamy and the former vicar are dead. There's nobody with recognised status and long inside knowledge of the community that one can talk to about people's reliability and moral calibre."[23] Michael Innes' Sir John Appleby still holds an old-fashioned attitude to truth and evidence. In conversation with a shady art dealer, Egon Raphaello, he says,

"My technique is quite simple. It consists in persuading people that it's to their advantage to tell the truth. The graver the crime, the more obvious surely, that is. I don't suppose people often get convicted of murders they didn't commit as a consequence of being insufficiently candid about precious little enterprises of their own, but it can land them in a very awkward situation."[24]

In contrast with American society, in which the secular orthodoxy makes it distasteful, if not dangerous, to recognize any official place for the Church in society, English society has been built on the recognition that the Church has an indispensable place and is at its center. In Lemarchand's *Nothing to Do with the Case*, the role of the Church is implicit: "The ground sloped up gently to the church, and she stood for a few moments looking at the tower. It was sturdy rather than lofty, and had an air of watching protectively over the village."[25]

"What Is Truth?" Pilate's Question Reconsidered

However, we have the impression that few writers in the second half of the twentieth century could afford to ignore that there have been radical changes from the traditional view of society.

One of the first changes was the appearance of a different kind of detective. When a writer or his or her readers have difficulty in believing in God, or in any eternal and immutable principles of justice and truth, there is little need for these qualities to be personified in an omniscient detective or promoted in the doctrine of the character's infallibility. Truth today is a much more tentative matter than our immediate forefathers believed, and when we have ceased to "walk humbly with" our God, it often seems easier to love mercy than to do justice (Cf. Mic. 6.8).

Typical of the change of fashion in detectives is Richard Lockridge's Jewish detective, Lieutenant "Nate" Shapiro of Homicide South in New York City. In contrast to the sublime omniscience of Hercule Poirot and Nero Wolfe, and even to the omnicompetence of Peter Wimsey and Perry Mason, Lockridge's sad-faced hero makes a decisive break with the Sherlock Holmes tradition of the great detective: for Shapiro *nothing* is elementary. Captain William Weigand, his immediate superior officer, insists on sending him into cases for which Shapiro protests that he has absolutely no aptitude or competence, such as the world of avant-garde art (*Murder for Art's Sake*, 1967), fundamentalist evangelism (*Preach No More*, 1971), or that of literary best-sellers

(*Write Murder Down*, 1972). Shapiro's typical reaction as he surveys the scene of the crime is to declare that he is completely out of his depth, and when he ultimately solves a mystery that has baffled everyone else, he is likely to say that he has only reached the truth by accident and that any number of people could have solved the problem more quickly than he had.

The Appearance of Violence and Terror

A further characteristic of our age is the appearance of terrorism and violence. This is not so much the terror caused by Mickey Spillane and other representatives of gore and violence who try to establish their own ideas of reality by means of brute force, but rather the violence of those hostage takers and others who seriously represent terror and cruelty as part of modern life.

A most striking example is David L. Lindsey's *Heat from Another Sun*, which indicates the traumatic effect of the Vietnam experience on the American public.[26] It is not a book for the squeamish, but it is a book in which the writer uses four-letter words, scatological references, and violence in such a way that they are necessary to the action and to the development of his characters.

At several levels, it is concerned with the twentieth-century obsession with violence in its most obscene forms. This appears in the frightening obsession of the financier Roeg at the heart of the story. But it is also present in a more sophisticated way as the hero, Detective Stuart Haydon, wrestles with his own past and with the circumstances involved in his job as a homicide detective. It raises some acute theological questions for our society, but they are handled at a far different level from the simplistic treatment of earlier writings. Lieutenant Robert Dystal, who may be regarded as typical of twentieth-century American society, is described as not given to much soul-searching:

Questions of ethics and morality, problems of theodicy that teetered on the sharp edges of philosophical deliberations and could not be resolved by the useful exercise of good common sense, were of no value to him. He quietly believed that the consideration of such questions was nothing more than pretentious posturing, of no use to himself and with no practical application to the living of life. The truth, Haydon thought, would be as uncomfortable for Dystal as it was for him, though certainly for different reasons.[27]

What sets Lindsey's work apart from most of the other realistic writing of our period is that he is consciously a writer with religious faith, plumbing the depths of the potential for evil in ordinary people and "trying to set the reader's mind on fire with the obscenity of violence."[28] Yet the story ends, "Haydon inhaled deeply of the night air, which carried the sounds and smells of a world both ancient and newborn, a world no better and no worse than the best and worst of men could make it."[29] It leaves the reader with a memory of creation that contains the hope of re-creation.

It is ironic that the American trend to toughness and violence should have appeared originally as a protest against British writers of the genteel, country-house, cerebral type of murder mystery, since recently, some of the toughest and most violent examples of realism in detection have come from the pens of British writers: the stories of Peter Alding's detective from the north of England, Inspector Fusil; William McIlvanney's Jack Laidlaw; and the horse-racing milieu of Dick Francis or the writings of Desmond Cory. However, for all the recourse to violence and the frank secularity, this style of writing can come close to religious feeling and theological expression. Detective Inspector Fusil, regarded by many of his contemporaries and neighbors as "a reet bastard," is obviously moved when he visits a cheap boardinghouse that caters to some of life's derelicts: "How many of the blasted lives had once appeared so promising? Was fate the villain, or each man his own? He hated criminals with the sharpness of someone who believed in the Old Testament's unforgiving definitions of good and evil, but for wrecked lives like these, he had a deep compassion in which good and evil could often not be separated."[30] This is reminiscent of Desmond Cory's *Circe Complex*, and the same tone is found in Cory's *Bit of a Shunt up the River*, which is worth a more extended comment.[31]

It is the story of an English loser—a racing driver divorced from his wife, who has given up racing to become an unsuccessful proprietor of a garage in Brighton. Tracy—he is known by his surname as his Christian names are Cuthbert Delamere—recognizes himself as a failure. He never quite made it to the top in racing, is unsuccessful in marriage and business, and never has any luck with women. Also, he is completely happy only when he is working with machinery.

A mysterious Mr. Green hires him to deliver a Lamborghini as a birthday present to his daughter, Bernadette, and Tracy is to take her to Wales where she will discuss divorce with her husband, Tommy Pope. In the course of this excursion, Tracy becomes involved in a murder and with its perpetrator, "Bony" Wright, a convicted murderer who has escaped from prison with the full intention of adding a few more corpses to his tally. Tracy is responsible for frustrating Bony's plans against Tommy and is instrumental in bringing the convict to his death. The poignancy comes from the curious empathy that Tracy and Bony share from their love of cars and racing. The story, with its language that would have been frowned upon in the Sunday School I knew as a lad, and the sexual angle of the trip with Bernadette, has all the makings of a hard, fast-moving, realistic yarn that is thoroughly modern and secular. The basic attitude toward life in these hedonistic times is suggested by Tracy as he thinks covetously about Ferraris, Corniches, Maseratis, and other exotic automobiles that were his stock-in-trade. "Nice cars, really. If you were lucky, you could get one for a birthday present. Just as if you were unlucky, you could get some part of a racing car all mixed up with your brains. You had to believe in luck. What else was there? Money."[32]

But at a deeper level, Tracy has to face the contemporary uncertainty about ethics. Can we still accept the easy distinctions that we have been in the habit of making between the respectable (good) and the disreputable (bad)? Is cruelty to be found only in people like Bony Wright? As Tracy is held at knife-point by Bony, he is forced to listen to a strong denunciation of the sadism that sometimes animates members of the judicial bench.[33]

At a deeper level still, the empathy that Tracy has with Bony leads him to new insights about his own personal destiny and identity. At the end of the action, there is a shoot-out in which Tracy is wounded and Bony is killed, but we are left questioning whether Bony deliberately allows himself to be shot so that Tracy could escape. Then while Tracy is lying in bed, in the curious state between consciousness and dreaming, he imagines that Bony has come to tell him that in death you have all the possibilities that were denied you in life. "I mean, I'm infinite. Everybody's infinite. They just don't realize it."[34] That is a new thought for Tracy who is only too conscious of his own finitude and failure in this life:

> A million Tracys, all too tired to. . . . No, that wasn't
> right. All the others had to be asleep already, because
> Bony hadn't talked to any of the others. Or had he. . . ?
> Sleep itself is a turning, anyway. Like death. You'd have
> of course an infinite number of deaths, and presumably
> only one of them was perfect—the one that rounded off
> the perfect life. . . . Had anyone ever *lived* that perfect life
> before dying that perfect death? There was supposed to
> be an answer to that one, wasn't there? That, when you
> thought about it, was the whole point about him. But
> then he was God. That had to be different.[35]

Well, there it is, and we are obviously close to a religious statement. Perhaps we are too close to religion for the average reader, because the end of the story surfaces in our normal greedy world, with Tracy taking the offer of "five hundred jimmy o'goblins" (pounds sterling) for keeping his mouth shut. He then disappears from the story as he began, "this wifeless, friendless, impecunious, none-too-bright Tracy," but with the curious hope that "what *hadn't* been just possibly had been, too."[36]

Unrepentant Conservatives in a Religionless Society

But where shall we place the work of Emma Lathen, the corporate nom de plume of the American team, Mary Jane Latsis, the economist, and Martha Henissart, the lawyer?

It is clearly in a class of its own.

The two began writing in 1960 and therefore the books, whether written under the name of Emma Lathen or of R. B. Dominic, belong unquestionably to the post–World War II era, a fact that is reemphasized in the comprehensive review of contemporary social and political issues that appears in the stories. But in relation to style and even to content, they belong to the classical period. It has been recorded that Lord C. P. Snow, in a review of one of the Emma Lathen books, observed: "She is probably the best living writer of American detective stories. . . . The detail . . . is investigated with the enthusiasm of Balzac. . . . She is very witty, in a wry and downbeat manner. The whole of her writing is in fact exactly what in our vanity we like to think of as proprietorially English."[37]

In an informative interview which the two writers granted to John C. Carr, they pointed out that they were prepared for their career in writing by their own early immersion in Victorian novels, "everything from Jane Austen through Sherlock Holmes."[38] They claimed that this influenced their writing in several ways, from the structure of their syntax to their ability to populate the world they described with believable characters.

Emma Lathen, according to Carr, "has preserved the benign and therefore highly entertaining aspects of the tradition: technical knowledge; unity of character and action and time, if not always of place; and the avoidance of the quotidian banalities of life, and of graphic descriptions of sex and violence."[39] In these ways Emma Lathen's works are unrepentantly conservative and at times, she seems to have had Dorothy Sayers consciously in mind—if not as a pattern to be copied, then certainly as a standard to be maintained or possibly surpassed.[40]

On the other hand, the books are uncompromisingly contemporary. They invariably employ contemporary institutions as their subject matter: the Emma Lathen books are set in the context of banking and the high finance of Wall Street, while the R. B. Dominic stories center in the politics of Washington, D.C. The writings of Emma Lathen, featuring John Putnam Thatcher, senior vice president of the Sloan Guaranty Trust, provide a running commentary on the social and political issues that have involved the American public since the 1960s.

A Place for Murder (1963) explores issues that were alive at that time in tax writeoffs among the very wealthy with their Connecticut "farms"; Accounting for Murder (1964) is about finagling in high financial circles in the matter of army contracts, but by 1967, when Murder Against the Grain appeared, we are in the midst of the United States–Russia wheat deal. Death Shall Overcome (1966) revolves around the relationship of big business to the ethnic issue and the Civil Rights movement. A Stitch in Time (1968) involves shady medicine and Murder to Go (1969), the questionable possibilities in large-scale, mass-produced food franchises. When in Greece (1969) reflects the political troubles in that country, and The Longer the Thread (1971) wrestles with the problem of American political and industrial interests in Puerto Rico. Pick Up Sticks (1970) revolves around land sales promotions in New England, and Ashes to Ashes (1970), the post–Vatican II problems in the Roman Catholic Church. By 1973, in Murder Without Icing, we are in the bright world of sports (ice-hockey) franchises. In *Sweet and Low* (1974), we are introduced to the chocolate industry and to cocoa futures in view of unstable conditions in Africa, and in *Double, Double, Oil and Trouble* (1979), to the involvement of Texan oil companies in British offshore North Sea oil exploration. *Going for Gold* (1981) features a financial swindle during the winter Olympics, and *Something in the Air* (1988) is involved with expansion and takeover bids in commuter airlines.

Lathen's stories are set firmly within the context of contemporary American society and the issues in which it is involved—"money is the name of the game." It is in the urbane pursuit of *cui bono* that John Putnam Thatcher owes his success as an amateur detective. This is the basic realism that excludes all secondary motives:

> Wall Street transcends the short, narrow thoroughfare in the Borough of Manhattan. Wall Street is a creed, linking true believers on the Rue de la Bourse and the Paseo de la Castellana. Every noncollective onion sold in Moscow proves that the Real Presence can materialize anywhere.
>
> John Putnam Thatcher of the Sloan Guaranty Trust knew this very well. Unlike many people, he also knew that the best place to exploit his knowledge was on Wall Street proper, the Borough of Manhattan, the City of New York.[41]

But this theme occurs time and time again. We read that

> as senior vice-president of the third largest bank in the world, Thatcher had file cabinets bulging with evidence of an incontrovertible truth. Initialing contracts, programming computers, and underwriting pilot programs are occasionally arduous, often inconvenient, and always insufficient to extirpate the Old Ned lurking below.
>
> In fact, Thatcher had long since decided that Wall Street saw more of the real man than most other locales. With all deference to Sigmund Freud and the animal ap-

petites, Wall Street—and the world it serves—proves that
sex is not the only outlet for deep-rooted, life-shaping
forces. There are also buying and selling.[42]

This acceptance of the money motive at the center
of modern society is the unchangeable article of faith
that enables John Putnam Thatcher to cut through all
the obfuscations of racial prejudice, ill-placed patriotism, or sexual infatuation to get to the central problem
in every story. And yet one has the feeling that all the
time he regards himself somewhat ironically, or even
with slight distaste; but the reality of life in our society
forces him to accept the primacy of the cash motive
although that does not mean that he necessarily ap-
proves. He may believe that capitalism provides the
best possible form of economics, but even though his
loyalty to the Sloan is devoted, it is not uncritical.
Rather like the deep but passionless commitment that
many Britons have to the monarchy—while not uncritical of certain features—it would be difficult to imagine
a livable world where it did not exist.

This underlines the most important reason for considering the works of Emma Lathen here: their complete absence of conventional religion as stimulating
any kind of personal commitment; or rather, the tacit
admission that Western society has made a religion of
its secularity—it has become openly idolatrous. The
Church is considered as an institution, particularly in
Ashes to Ashes, which involves John Putnam Thatcher
and the Sloan in the social turmoil that afflicted the
Roman Catholic Church after Vatican II. In the novel,
neither Thatcher nor any of his colleagues makes any
remark that indicates any religious commitment or any
reflection that can be interpreted as theological. However, in introducing the birth control question that
erupted in *Ashes to Ashes*, Emma Lathen includes the
following reflection:

Man proposes, God disposes.
For many centuries it was widely accepted that the

course of human events was shaped by this division of labor. Then one of the bolder spirits of the Middle Ages put faith to the test. Does man propose? Hundreds of succeeding years were spent debating the proposition.

Then, probably because Charles Darwin and Sigmund Freud between them made man uninteresting, attention was returned to the second member of the partnership. How can God dispose, somebody wondered in print, when God is dead? The subsequent outpouring of intellectual thought strained library facilities throughout the world.[43]

That is outrageously Chestertonian and simplistic. One might reflect upon some of the bolder spirits of the Middle Ages like Mirandola, who saucily hinted that humankind might be able to do some of the disposing; and if Charles Darwin and Sigmund Freud made humanity uninteresting, they did at any rate strip away some of the false mystery with which human nature had been surrounded.

However, Emma Lathen went on to describe something of the new humanism that was disrupting the equanimity of the Church and society in the comment, "Between man, whatever he is, and God, if He exists, there had erupted a new and frightening entity—the crowd. Flensburg, New York, was about to bear witness to the consequences of this interposition."[44] That suggests the characteristically agnostic attitude of people in the second half of the twentieth century. We live in an increasingly secular society.

If detective fiction during the earlier classical period drew its readers mainly from supporters of the bourgeois values in Middle America and from those in Europe who were nostalgic for the certainties of the past, and if the procedurals and more flamboyant writings drew support from the campuses and from those who felt alienated from Western society, perhaps Emma Lathen/R. B. Dominic derive support from those who live in a society that they recognize as blatantly secular, whatever the conventional beliefs of some of their contemporaries. This writing represents the realistic world of finance and high-pressure politics for an upwardly mobile society and for those who have to make their way in it and have to give some obeisance to its gods.

Chastened Conservatives in a Religionless Society: Between Unbelief and Faith

With the books of Dick Francis, the Welsh ex-professional jockey, we are back closer to the writings of authors like Desmond Cory and to the recasting of the crime novel during the second half of this century in Britain. For despite the fact that Dick Francis claims affiliation, at least on a formal, conventional basis, with the established Church of England, his world is thoroughly secular and his stories often contain elements of violence that are not for those with weak stomachs.[45] John C. Carr, in the introduction to his interview with Francis, observed that "some of the pain the heroes must have inflicted on them is just a little too much. Past the gag limit at times."[46] On the other hand, it has been pointed out that pain (and the recognition that it exists and has to be faced by practically everyone) has a significant part to play in Francis' writing. By using characters who have been hurt, sometimes physically, but more often emotionally, Francis enables his characters to develop, and this gives his stories added depth.

At first sight, Francis appears to operate within a somewhat limited circle of experience, since his plots are all set within the restricted area of horse racing (usually British). There is a recognizable "Francis formula" in which a narrator (first-person hero), who has been hurt in some way in the past, triumphs over those who are determined to make money out of the "sport of kings" and who are totally unscrupulous about crushing any who get in their way. This normal pattern means that the stories fall into the indeterminate area between detection and thriller, because the antagonists are known early in the story, and the quest remaining is how the hero will discover their plans and win against all the odds that seem to be stacked against him. As

John C. Carr recognized, this is very English and is an adult version of the kind of encouraging schoolboy literature that used to grace the pages of the *Boys' Own Paper*.[47]

But it is adult in the sense that the suffering of Francis' characters is a necessary part of their development into maturity. Francis endows his characters with a richness of interest that goes beyond conventional requirements. As Michael Stanton pointed out:

> Emotionally starved or physically damaged (or both) as his protagonists are, it is not too much to say that Francis's fiction is about learning to love. One function of the plot or action is to teach people (often but not always the hero) to be fully human. Exciting as the action is, its end is not itself—its end is to show characters how to open their closed hearts.[48]

This is a perceptive comment because, although Francis' characters often engage in actions that earlier cultures would have regarded as immoral, the reason for such action arises directly out of the situation that is being portrayed and the insight that concerns Francis—tracing love in human relationships—carries us close to the humanism noted in other modern writers. In *The Craft of Crime*, John Carr also wrote, "Francis's realism about violence can be refreshing. His kicked around heroes take the whole novel to recover from a good beating and that certainly adds, rather than detracts, if we are to have sympathy for them—and Francis's heroes uniquely command our sympathy."[49]

Basically, the insight that "it is not too much to say that Francis's fiction is about learning to love" and "to teach people . . . to be fully human" means that the writer is reaffirming the fundamental and potential goodness of the human spirit and its need for love in relationship to others. In *Bonecrack* (1971), we see the fundamental need for human love reflected in father-and-son relationships—first between the protagonist Neil Griffon and his own father and then in the unhealthy relationship between Enso Rivera and his son Alessandro.

A further trait of the books is our innate need for justice, and not simply for legality. As Stanton observed, "The struggle is not simply between legal and illegal; it is between right and wrong, or good and evil. A moral polarity exists in Francis's novels—a polarity which is not exactly simple but is usually very clear."[50] Dick Francis' stories illustrate the basic need not simply for the justice of the courts, but for a justice that will be open and appropriate. Some of his heroes could have echoed the sentiments of W. S. Gilbert's *Mikado:*

> *My object all sublime*
> *I shall achieve in time—*
> *To let the punishment fit the crime—*
> *The punishment fit the crime.*

Although it should be added that the retribution meted out by Francis' heroes goes considerably beyond causing the guilty party to become a source of "innocent merriment." So Steven Scott plots his counterattack on the "bad guys":

> "Gee, dammit," said Allie, finally and explosively, "I just don't see why that guy should be allowed to rob you and make people despise you and get away with it."
> "Give me time," I said mildly, "and he won't."
> "Time?"
> "For thinking," I explained. "If a frontal assault would land me straight into a lawsuit for slander, which it would, I'll have to come up with a sneaky scheme which will creep up on him from the rear."[51]

And *Nerve* ends in a classic tale of revenge. In this case, Rob Finn takes his revenge against the embittered journalist who has brought about the end of his career and that of several other jockeys.[52]

Dick Francis points us back to an understanding of society that is basically ethical and maybe even theological. If "learning to live fully means learning to love" then we are close to the anthropological center that is to be found in a great deal of modern theology.[53] For the rest, Michael Stanton's comment sums it up, when he suggests that the satisfaction from reading Francis' novels "really comes not through their adherence to a formula but through their adherence to a set of values: the price of learning to need, the value of being vulnerable, the inestimable worth of human love."[54]

Cri de Coeur

In their attempt to place literary detection fully within the setting of a "post-Christian" society, some writers probe even more deeply. They recognize the confused mixture of faith and agnosticism characteristic of our time, and they seem to reveal in their dealing with social and ethical matters an odd mixture of nostalgia and wistful longing—Sehnsucht—that may lie beneath so much of the professed realism and the open hedonism of the modern mood. Of no writer is this more true than of P. D. James (Phyllis Dorothy James White), an English writer of whom it has been said that she is "one of the few authors who deserves a permanent place on the bookshelves of all those who treasure literary craftsmanship."[55]

The relationship between theology and the society she describes in her stories is illustrated in one of her earlier books, *An Unsuitable Job for a Woman*. This novel has a British setting, and in common with the feminist interests of the seventies, the detection is by Ms. Cordelia Gray, who after the suicide of her partner (formerly of the C.I.D.), suddenly finds herself the proprietor of Pryde's Detective Agency but possessing very little else. Cordelia's education illustrates the religious/social mix of British society. Her education was catholic if not eclectic, for although she was the daughter of a peripatetic Socialist lecturer with professed atheist leanings, she was raised in at least one foster home run by a woman who was a strong Protestant Nonconformist. She had been educated almost by accident, however, in a Roman Catholic convent school. In a later book, Cordelia says that she was never converted to Catholicism, but she had liked the convent because "I suppose it was the first time I felt secure. Life wasn't messy any more."[56] She explains her own personality as "the result of having an atheist father, a convent education, and a nonconformist conscience."[57] This shows how the different religious influences in English history affect society and leave Britain with a social conscience, a background of morality, and also a nostalgic feeling towards the ancient faith.

But there is also the skepticism of the modern age. This is particularly illustrated in Cordelia's thoughts when she suddenly finds the body of her former partner, Bernard Pryde; she reflects that since Bernard was dead he could not know anything:

> Her second fostermother, Mrs. Wilkes, would have said
> that Bernie did know, that there was a moment of inde-
> scribable glory, shining towers, limitless singing, skies of
> triumph. Poor Mrs. Wilkes! Widowed, her only son dead
> in the war, her small house perpetually noisy with foster
> children who were her livelihood, she had needed her
> dreams. She had lived her life by comfortable maxims
> stored like nuggets of coal against the winter. Cordelia
> thought of her now for the first time in years and heard
> again the tired, determinedly cheerful voice "If the Lord
> doesn't call on his way out, He'll call on his way back."
> Well, going or coming, He hadn't called on Bernie.[58]

Oh? How do you know that, Cordelia? The writer has already lined up Cordelia—albeit regretfully—on the side of contemporary agnosticism. After these doubting reflections, however, we read that "she said a brief convent-taught prayer to the God she wasn't sure existed for the soul which Bernie had never believed he possessed and waited quietly for the police."[59] But perhaps like most reluctant unbelievers in the Western world and certainly a large part of the British public,

Cordelia has doubts even about her doubts; she wonders about the propriety of her willingness to take the oath in court. "There were moments, usually on a sunny Easter morning, when she wished that she could with sincerity call herself a Christian; but for the rest of the year she knew herself to be what she was—incurably agnostic but prone to unpredictable relapses into faith."[60]

These reflections underline themes that permeate almost all of P. D. James' stories—we live in a time when religious faith is difficult and agnosticism must be acknowledged; we have no answer for the evil and suffering that exist in the world. On the other hand, because of these doubts, we have little comfort in the face of death; and ethically we can only do the best we can. But there seems to run through the whole of the corporate consciousness a feeling of nostalgia, a wistfulness for a time when the laws that govern our life were accepted as absolute.

There is an incident in *Death of an Expert Witness* where Commander Dalgliesh of Scotland Yard finds it necessary to interview the teenage daughter of a suspect and they find themselves discussing what happens to people convicted of murder. That in turn leads to a discussion of crime and punishment and Eleanor Kerrison, the girl, says she thinks it is wrong of the state to punish a person for many years when his or her victim might have lived only a week. She goes on to say, "I suppose it was different when people believed in God. Then the murdered person might have died in mortal sin and gone to hell. The seven days could have made a difference then. He might have repented and had time for absolution." To this Dalgliesh replies, "All these problems are easier for people who believe in God. Those of us who don't or can't have to do the best we can. That's what the law is, the best we can do. Human justice is imperfect, but it's the only justice we have."[61]

Here is the uncertainty of the modern mood and the relativity of the world view that is common throughout Western civilization; there are no longer any absolutes, and where there is no belief in God, there can be no reason for absolutes. One may compare this with the certainties of the past, as Dalgliesh reflects on them in the work of a parish priest in *The Black Tower*, "Of the more corrosive, petty, mean-minded delinquencies in all their sad but limited variety, he, like any other parish priest, would have had his fill. He had his answer ready, compassionate but inexorable, offered . . . with all the gentle arrogance of absolute certainty."[62]

The agnosticism also comes through in Cordelia's dealings with Clarissa Lisle, the central figure in *The Skull Beneath the Skin*. Clarissa frankly admits that she cannot believe in God, and perhaps it is not surprising that she has handed on her unbelief to her adopted son, Simon, who "found himself praying, petitioning the God in whom he no longer believed, with all the desperate urgency, all the artless importunity, of a child."[63]

Similarly, in *The Black Tower*, we see that it is possible for unbelief to be passed from one partner to another in marriage. The invalid Ursula Hollis, shunted by her husband into Wilfred Anstey's communal settlement where she is unable to interfere in his interests and preoccupations in London, reflects on her Catholic training:

He [her husband] had forgotten that he had taught her to do without God. Her religion had been one of those possessions that, casually, neither understanding them nor valuing them, he had taken from her. They hadn't really been important to her, those consoling substitutes for sex, for love. She couldn't pretend that she had relinquished them with much of a struggle, those comforting illusions taught in St. Matthew's Primary School, assimilated behind the draped terylene curtains of her aunt's front sitting-room in Alma Terrace, Middlesborough, with its holy pictures, its photographs of Pope John, its framed papal blessing of her aunt and uncle's wedding. All were part of that orphaned, uneventful, not unhappy childhood which was as remote now as a distant, once-

visited alien shore. She couldn't return because she no
longer knew the way.[64]

The unbelief is here, but clearly also, the nostalgia.
This skepticism is also the attitude of one of the
victims in *Innocent Blood*:

> Mavis had lost her God. Like all other believers she had
> made Him in her own image, a Methodist God, benign,
> suburban in his tastes, appreciative of cheerful singing
> and mildly academic sermons, not demanding more than
> she could give. The Sunday morning chapel had been
> more a comfortable routine than an imperative to wor-
> ship. Mavis had been brought up a Methodist, and she
> was not a woman to reject early orthodoxies. But she had
> never forgiven God for letting Julie die.[65]

Wilfred Anstey, in *The Black Tower*, seems to per-
sonalize the problems of the Church. He has established his philanthropic work by deluding himself that
he received a miracle at Lourdes, although he never
really suffered from disseminated sclerosis, but only
from a form of hysterical paralysis. However, he saw
himself as a kind of medieval abbot dispensing good
works and hospitality in an atmosphere of asceticism
and spiritual discipline while making sure that his own
cell had every little comfort. When Dalgliesh met Wilfred, Dalgliesh's first thought

> was that he looked like a bit-player acting with practised
> conviction the part of an ascetic bishop. The brown
> monk's habit suited him so well that it was impossible to
> imagine him in any other garb. . . . The gentle question-
> ing eyes with their suggestion of other people's suffering
> meekly borne were young eyes, the blue irises very clear,
> the whites opaque as milk. He smiled, a singularly sweet
> lopsided smile spoilt by the display of uneven and dis-
> coloured teeth. Dalgliesh wondered why it was that phi-
> lanthropists so often had a reluctance to visit their
> dentist.[66]

Even more devastating in its implied criticism is Dorothy Moxon's disenchantment with Wilfred Anstey. When she remonstrates with him for handing over his work to another authority, without regard to those who had supported him in the venture, he says:

> "Dot dear, you and I have to accept that we cannot always choose the way in which we are called to serve."
>
> She wondered how she had never noticed it before, that irritating note of unctuous reproof in his voice. She turned abruptly away. The hand, thus rejected, slipped heavily from her shoulders. She remembered suddenly what he reminded her of: the sugar Father Christmas on her first Christmas tree, so desirable, so passionately desired. And you bit into nothingness; a trace of sweetness on the tongue and then an empty cavity grained with white sand.[67]

P. D. James probably had no conscious intention of making that a commentary on twentieth-century religion, but the figure of Wilfred Anstey is appropriate for the religion of our time, particularly a liberal, unrooted Protestantism intent on good works and determined to carry them through in a way that best meets its own need for spiritual satisfaction—often hanging on to the trappings of the ancient faith but without any real commitment to its discipline.

The problem of evil remains the unanswerable theological enigma. It is put forcibly by the embittered former science teacher, Victor Holroyd, in an exchange with one of the crippled patients in Wilfred Anstey's community of medical misfits. He dismisses "dull, repressed, religious" Grace Willison's habitual good humour as simply a condition of her disease.[68] Grace, very much hurt, declares that she does not claim her happiness as a virtue but says that even if it were only a symptom, she could still give thanks for it. Victor retorts acidly:

> As long as you don't expect the rest of us to join in, give thanks by all means. Thank God for the privilege of being

no bloody use to yourself or anyone else. And while you're about it, thank Him for some of the other blessings of His creation; the millions toiling to get a living out of barren soil swept by flood, burnt by drought; for pot-bellied children; for tortured prisoners; for the whole doomed, bloody, pointless mess.[69]

Skepticism raises the basic problem of how we are to view our own death. Cordelia Gray, in *The Skull Beneath the Skin*, thinks it is interesting

the way in which death had replaced sex as the great unmentionable, to be denied in prospect, endured in decent privacy, preferably behind the drawn curtains of a hospital bed, and followed by discreet, embarrassed, uncomforted mourning. There was this to be said about the Convent of the Holy Child: the views of the sisters on death had been explicit, firmly held, and not altogether reassuring; but at least they hadn't regarded it as in poor taste.[70]

Clarissa Lisle is almost unhinged by fear of her own death, and she makes an interesting comment that probably indicates lack of faith even among professedly religious people:

I've noticed that about the God people. They're just as frightened as the rest of us. They cling on just as long. They're supposed to have a heaven waiting but they're in no hurry to get there. Perhaps it's worse for them: judgments and hell and damnation. At least I'm only afraid of death. Isn't everyone? Aren't you?[71]

Of course, in a murder mystery, the participants are bound to be brought face to face with the reality of death, so after the death of Father Michael Baddeley, the sybaritic Julius Court, the epitome of cynical unbelief, observes:

We were alike in one thing. Neither of us feared death. I

didn't know where Baddeley thought he was going as he
just had time to make that last archaic sign of his allegiance [he had put on his stole], but wherever it was he apparently saw nothing to fear. Neither do I. I know just as
certainly as he did what will follow my death. Annihila-
tion. It would be unreasonable to fear that.[72]

As Dalgliesh tells Eleanor Kerrison, in a world where
there are no longer any absolutes, we can only do the
best we can and human justice, although it is imperfect, is the only justice we have. The theme is repeated
in a different set of circumstances in the same story on
the question of the ambiguity of evidence. A group of
the staff at Hoggatt's Forensic Science Laboratory has
been discussing evidence given in court by expert witnesses, but the conclusion is drawn that, despite all the
susceptibilities of jurors, it is the best we can do. As one
of the characters remarks, "It's the same as democracy.
A fallible system but the best we've got."[73]

But the most striking characteristic of P. D. James'
books is her recognition that with loss of religious
faith, society itself has lost something vital at its heart.
There is a sense in which Ursula Hollis' experience of
"lost-ness" cited above might be taken as a parable for
the whole of society. A passage in *Innocent Blood* puts
this into an illustrative figure when Philippa contemplates the east window of a church:

She had bought a cheese and tomato roll for her lunch,
and found herself suddenly hungry, but was reluctant to
offend the susceptibilities of other visitors by eating
it there. Instead she fixed her gaze where God the Father
sat in majesty among His creation, glorified in the splen-
dour of medieval stained glass. Before him was an open
book. *Ego sum alpha et omega.* How simple life must
be for those who could both lose and find identity in
that magnificent assurance. But for herself that way was
closed. Hers was a bleaker and more presumptuous
creed; but it was not without its comfort, and she had no
other.[74]

There is something of regretful nostalgia in the attitude of Dalgliesh as he contemplates the basic decent honesty of Grace Willison: "Ruefully, he recognized in Miss Willison the type of unusually honest witness whom he had always found difficult. Paradoxically, this old-fashioned rectitude, this sensitivity of conscience, were more difficult to cope with than the prevarications, evasions or flamboyant lying which were part of a normal interrogation."[75]

The foregoing suggests that P. D. James' detective stories, at a deeper level, may represent the search of our hell-bent twentieth-century society for solid ethical grounds on which to reestablish itself. This is brought together in a remarkable way in *A Taste for Death*.

If we grant the possibility of this extended parable form, it is significant that the story begins and ends in the vestry of a shabby London church, which in its Anglo-Catholic orientation suggests the Western Catholic roots from which our culture has sprung. The story itself seems to pose the unspoken question of whether, in order to survive, that is where we should return.

The theme is repeated at several levels. The story begins with Commander Dalgliesh's disillusionment with police work and his disgust with the horror of death, but at least it ends with the solution of the death of Sir Paul Berowne.[76] It also starts with the discouragement of the parish priest, Father Barnes, and the declining authority of the Church of England in the inner city; but at length, Father Barnes experiences a new sense of purpose and has reason for encouragement.[77] But the paradox can point in the opposite direction, because at the beginning there is the devotion of Miss Emily Wharton to the parish of St. Matthew's, Paddington, and her love for the waif, Darren Wilkes, but the story ends with her disillusionment.

There is also the intriguing puzzle of Paul Berowne's religious experience which had begun in the conventional Anglicanism of his social class but which had brought him close to the beatific vision. His mother, Lady Ursula, regards his search to find meaning for

existence as a fruitless quest.[78] Throughout the story
there is an undercurrent of agnosticism represented in
the conventional attitudes of Lady Ursula, the open
medical skepticism of Stephen Lampart, the virtually
total alienation of Lady Barbara Berowne from her husband and such casual references to the modern mood as
the reflection that the use of the word *God* as an answer
will always put a stopper to rational conversation.[79]

This change with regard to religion is strength-
ened and maintained in incidental references: in the
recognition that divorce is no longer any final obstacle
to the ambitions of a modern politician; in Mrs. Minns'
recognition that she does not expect to see Sir Paul
Berowne in any future world; in Inspector Kate Mis-
kin's frank admission that she does not understand
religious experience and finds no need for it.[80] There is
also the expressed unwillingness of the twentieth-century person to accept some of the horrors of earlier
orthodoxy—hell and damnation—because, as Teresa's
mother says: "God can't be less merciful than I am. I
can't believe that."[81]

When all this is added together, it presents a fairly
comprehensive picture of religion in decline and docu-
mentation of the claim that "the world is full of people
who have lost faith." But the context in which that
statement is made shows that the malaise is much
wider than simply a concern with religion and the
articles of Christian orthodoxy. As Lady Ursula observes:

> The world is full of people who have lost faith; politicians
> who have lost faith in politics, social workers who have
> lost faith in social work, schoolteachers who have lost
> faith in teaching and, for all I know, policemen who have
> lost faith in policing and poets who have lost faith in po-
> etry. It's a condition of faith that it gets lost from time to
> time, or at least mislaid.[82]

That which is at stake in the loss of religious faith
affects the whole of society so that Dalgliesh is able to

liken the Church to the preparation of evidence for a criminal case. Of the case in hand, he says, "You could say it's like the church, an ingenious edifice erected on an unproved supposition, logical within its terms, but only valid if one can accept the basic premise, the existence of God."[83]

This suggests that, for P. D. James, the issue is not an unrelieved indictment of religious faith; it is much more complex because, although we may be skeptical about religious experience and its hope for a world beyond this life, we cannot altogether discount the testimony of those who have experienced faith.[84] And perhaps the only sensible advice the writer would give to modern society is the advice given in a sermon recalled by Emily Wharton: "If you find that you no longer believe, act as if you still do. If you feel that you can't pray, go on saying the words."[85]

P. D. James' parable of Western civilization may be indicated when the culprit uncharacteristically spares the life of the boy, Darren, and he "sprang to his feet then almost ran to the tunnel end suddenly desperate to gain that half-moon of light before the darkness closed in on him for ever."[86]

What a pity he did not reach that light.

10

Illustration of the Theme

The Agatha Christie Pilgrimage

It may appear curiously fortuitous to have begun this chapter when Agatha Christie's play *The Mousetrap*, after 14,149 performances, had commenced its thirty-fifth consecutive year in the London theater.[1] It is appropriate because, just as the play presents a continuous piece of social history, the detective stories of Agatha Christie are an illustration of the developments in detective fiction and its relationship to society since the time of Conan Doyle.

Agatha Christie was born in 1891, when the fictional Sherlock Holmes was still living in Baker Street, and she died in 1976, long after World War II had exerted its decisive influence on the form and content of the genre. Her first detective story—the first Hercule Poirot story—was published in 1920, and from 1924, she wrote at least one book a year. She did not dispose of her two major creations—Hercule Poirot and Jane Marple—until around the time of her own demise, since the final chapters in the lives of each were made public just before her death: *Curtain*, the denouement of Poirot in 1975, and *Sleeping Murder*, the final Miss Marple story

in 1976. Any writer spanning that length of time in the
present century was bound to reflect the changing
patterns of the craft, but Agatha Christie was a writer of
singular power and inventiveness and therefore becomes a striking illustration of the social significance
of detective fiction which we have been tracing. As H. R.
F. Keating has said, "She served her public," and this
made her uncommonly sensitive to the changes in the
society in which she lived and to the fashions of taste
exhibited in her reading public. She was sensitive to
her readers, but she did not feel that she always had to
submit to their tastes. Fortunately, her public was large
enough and faithful enough that she did not need to
have her characters adopt a life-style that she would not
personally approve or encourage. Hercule Poirot and
Jane Marple grow older, wiser, more socially conscious,
and perhaps less stereotypes of themselves with the
years—despite his arthritis Poirot mellows like a fine
claret, and Miss Marple sparkles like a dry Chablis. But
Agatha Christie does not try to change their characters.

I

Agatha Christie was a profoundly religious woman,
but one of her biographers observed that only those who
read the romantic novels written under the pseudonym
Mary Westmacott "are aware of what a strongly religious
person Mrs. Christie was. Prayer was a way of her life
and the presence of God an integral part of living."[2]
However, she never tried to preach in her detective
fiction and if her fundamental convictions came through,
her concern reveals itself essentially as a search for the
spiritual foundations of Western society—a search for
that ethical groundwork that makes justice possible,
makes the concept of law viable, and underlies the
social yearning for order. As Poirot remarks, "I have a
bourgeois attitude to murder. I disapprove of it."[3]
Agatha Christie affirmed society as she found it.

Keating likens her to a clown at a circus, who
knows precisely the right time to produce the silk hand-

kerchief, so we are forced—despite ourselves—to clap. But I suggest she served her public in a more profound way—by revealing some of our deepest hopes, fears, and anxieties about society and by serving the issues to us in the palatable form of a detective story. The important service she unconsciously rendered was not so much the production of the unexpected handkerchief, but demonstration that the successful outcome is obtained by obedience to the same rules that we expect and cherish in life. As one of her characters, Ariadne Oliver, declares to another, Mr. Parker Pyne, "The public is conservative, Mr. Pyne; it likes the old well-worn gadgets."[4] If Poirot and Jane Marple offer the mystifying spectacle of order out of injustice and chaos, the results they achieve are *not* simply the exercise of magic. Her work endorses Ian Rodger's perceptive comment in the *Guardian*, mentioned earlier, that "novelists are unpaid sociologists who make up for their lack of statistical evidence with inspired guesses," and how inspired Agatha Christie's guesses sometimes were!

All that we have said about the assumptions of the nineteenth- and early twentieth-century detective story, the social and ethical presuppositions of the golden age and the gilded cage, are clearly illustrated in Agatha Christie's early works. These works are ethically simplistic; they reflect the prejudices of their society and their time. The great detective hero/heroine emphasizes the superior quality of ratiocination; assumes the good, solid middle-class values and virtues; and supposes both that truth can be discovered if all the facts are known and that justice will be done. The moral fabric of society depended on that.

In 1953 a journalist, Joyce Egginton, conducted an illuminating interview with Agatha Christie for the London daily paper, the *News Chronicle*. She wrote, "Her approach to Whodunits is intensely moral—crime is committed, villain discovered, right triumphs in the last chapter. Their appeal, she believes, is that of the old morality play, Hercule Poirot being the spiritual descendant of Good Deeds. Only nowadays Everyman pays his share of the royalties."[5] Joyce Egginton's comment about the morality play is extremely perceptive, although the reference to Good Deeds in *Everyman* is nonsense, since that is the one character in the play who is entirely passive. Poirot's function is much more like that of the Voice of God which sets the whole play in motion, forces the culprit to face the issue of death and to render his account. But if Agatha Christie recognized that her writing at the time served much the same moral function as the medieval morality play, then she had an insight into the social implications of her art which was as acute as it is unusual in writers of the genre. Those who support the status quo in any society—in this case the reading public—want to be assured that justice exists, that it is inexorable, that therefore God is in his heaven and that all is right with the world.

At the same time Agatha Christie was so predictable in reflecting the social prejudices of her time that it is embarrassing to read some of her stories from the twenties and thirties. In the collection of short stories *The Regatta Mystery*, she reflected the snob values of Britain in the early 1930s—butlers who know their job *never* knock on doors, and music-hall comedians could *never* be "gentlemen."[6] There is a strong residual prejudice from World War I against foreigners, particularly against Germans.[7] However, Agatha Christie certainly would not have recognized any conscious prejudice when she entitled one of her stories, in 1939, *Ten Little Niggers*, or when it appeared for the American market, *Ten Little Indians*; its current title is *And Then There Were None*.

At the same time, Poirot does not remain completely unchanged by the society in which he is placed, particularly in terms of the changing technology, for in one of the stories we read, "He walked up the steps to the front door and pressed the bell, glancing as he did so at the neat wrist watch which had at last replaced an earlier favourite—a large turnip-faced watch of earlier days."[8] The values which Poirot and Miss Marple exemplify are those of the settled British society of the times in which they are placed, so Poirot's overwhelming motive is the desire to reach the truth. When one of the characters in *Three Act Tragedy* of 1935 questions Poirot about his motivation for detection and suggests that it might be the excitement of the hunt, we read:

> Poirot shook his head.
> "No—no—it is not that. Like the *chien de chasse*, I follow the scent, and I get excited, and once on the scent I cannot be called off it. All that is true. But there is more. . . . It is—how shall I put it?—a passion for getting at the *truth*. In all the world there is nothing so curious and so interesting and so beautiful as truth."[9]

Jane Marple has very similar motivations, for at the successful conclusion of one of her cases, after pity has displaced anger, we read, "There came a surge of triumph—the triumph some specialist might feel who has successfully reconstructed an extinct animal from a fragment of jawbone and a couple of teeth."[10] The parallel between detection and the scientist's search for truth is not accidental. Sherlock Holmes had used the same argument and a similar illustration, and the advances of science through the search for empirical truth had been one of the most important legacies of the Enlightenment cultures which had seen the birth of detective fiction.[11]

Agatha Christie's books all emphasize the detective story's growing recognition that human nature is complex and is primary evidence in the solution of any crime puzzle. All her stories contain the possibility that anyone, however respectable, could become the culprit.[12]

Jane Marple endorses the same concern for truth and justice that we find in Poirot and by using her extensive memory of petty sinners in the village of St. Mary Mead, she has no difficulty in representing herself as a kind of nemesis for evildoers.[13] Therefore she is not at all squeamish on the subject of capital punishment. In a story that appeared in 1932, she states emphatically her satisfaction that a culprit had been executed for his crimes: "'Sanders was hanged,' said Miss Marple crisply. 'And a good job too. I have never regretted my part in bringing that man to justice. I've no patience with modern humanitarian scruples about capital punishment.'"[14]

This ruthlessness was typical of the mind-set of that time, and it was a particular characteristic of the 1930s when the British public was facing the possibility of the devastating war which was beginning to appear inevitable. There is a strange conversation in which Agatha Christie was involved with several of her husband's friends and helpers while on one of his archaeological digs in the North African desert. The discussion had been concerned with the issues of life and death and how desert peoples accepted death so much more casually than more sophisticated societies. The issue centered in the Good Samaritan story and revolved around helping one's neighbor in a life-threatening situation. Sir Max Mallowan (Christie's husband) asked, "How many of us would really succour another human being in conditions where there were no witnesses, no force of public opinion, no knowledge or censure of a failure to extend aid?" After some initial shock, most members of the party thought they would stop what they were doing to help another person in need. But one young man declared that he would not interrupt his journey but would press on regardless. However, when Agatha Christie asked what he would do if the victim were not another human being but a horse, we read: "'Oh, a horse,' says Mac, becoming quite human and alive, and not remote at all. 'That would be quite different, of course. I'd do everything I possibly could for a horse.'"[15]

Of course one could draw all sorts of dubious conclusions from this incident. One could infer, for example, that the British prefer horses to people, but there are two particular aspects that make it interesting. First, the discussion took place in the 1930s when the British public was having to rethink many of its accepted assumptions about life, in view of the threat from totalitarian philosophies in Europe. These philosophies had appeared like meteors in the political sky and the Western democracies felt themselves poised between two forms of efficient ruthlessness—fascism and communism. Many were beginning to question the assumptions of liberal, humanitarian Western culture. That does not mean that they became Fascists or Communists, but it does mean that the spirit which produced the October Revolution, *Mein Kampf,* and Guernica was in the air and causing some heart-searching. Secondly, civilization does make a difference and does condition the way in which we think of life and death.

But these reflections could be carried further. Where did the idea of a civilization that is not only just but even compassionate originate? Who first told the story of the Good Samaritan? And why is it that, within Western society, many or even most people would feel qualms about leaving another human being to die? Why, indeed, do we feel that to help the afflicted, heal the sick, provide for the needy, and educate the ignorant are necessary features of civilized societies? A very different set of standards controls societies that have arisen in geographical areas where such humane feelings are not valued. These were basic questions that were being raised, and during the last decades of the twentieth century, with the advent of international terrorism, those questions may have a new pertinence for us. When the humanitarian concern and feelings of compassion begin to erode, what has happened to the society involved?

II

The Moving Finger (1943) is one of the Miss Marple stories. It concerns a poison-pen outbreak in the sleepy country town of Lymstock, which leads to murder. The novel provides an interesting mixture because it reflects something of the changing theological presuppositions during World War II.

Several of the characters represent the standards of the prewar society, particularly Emily Barton. In a conversation with Jerry Burton, an airman recovering from an accident, Miss Barton suggests that the recent troubles in Lymstock "have been permitted—by Providence! To awaken us to a sense of our shortcomings." Jerry mildly suggests that Providence might have chosen a less unsavory method, to which Miss Barton counters that "God moves in a mysterious way." That causes Jerry to expostulate, "No. . . . There's too much tendency to attribute to God the evils that man does of his own free will. I might concede you the Devil. God doesn't really need to punish us, Miss Barton. We're so very busy punishing ourselves."[16]

There are delightful touches of humor in the book, such as the description given by one of the villagers, of the anonymous letters: "Wicked letters—indecent, too, using such words and all. Worse than I've ever seen in the Bible, even."[17] There is no doubt that the Anglican parish church was still very much at the center of village life, and one of Agatha Christie's most attractive characters is Mrs. Dane Calthrop, wife of the vicar, the Reverend Caleb Dane Calthrop. She is described as a person who "never poked her nose in anywhere, yet she had an uncanny power of knowing things and I soon discovered that almost everyone in the village was slightly afraid of her. She gave no advice and never interfered, yet she represented, to an uneasy conscience, the Deity personified."[18] Agatha Christie's humor is also seen in the description of the anonymous letters Mrs. Dane Calthrop receives with regard to her husband's relationship to the local schoolmistress:

> "I forget exactly what they said. Something very silly about Caleb and the schoolmistress, I think. Quite absurd, because Caleb has absolutely no taste for fornication. He never has had. So lucky, being a clergyman."
> "Quite," I said, "Oh quite."
> "Caleb would have been a saint," said Mrs. Dane Calthrop, "if he hadn't been just a little too intellectual."[19]

This book appeared in 1943, in the middle of World War II, but it still reflected a relatively stable society of settled values, albeit with some hints of future change in attitudes. Agatha Christie understood that and catered for it. A stable society was the basic assumption of her earlier writing, but World War II would disrupt that comfortable setting and the accepted ethical values would change perhaps even more radically. Because, as Erik Routley has pointed out, Agatha Christie was extremely sensitive to the changes of her time and place, we would expect to see these changes reflected in her later writings.[20]

III

Some recent critics think that Agatha Christie's best works were the earlier stories and that after World War II, her detective fiction suffered a rapid decline. Robin W. Winks, for example, declares that "from *Passenger to Frankfort* onward it was apparent that Agatha Christie had (as surely so long a productive career entitled her to do) lost her touch, and the mantle was ready to be passed on."[21] And Colin Watson describes what he calls "the Christie, or Mayhem Parva, school" of writing as essentially escapist: "There would exist for these people none of the sordid and intractable problems of the real world, such as growing old or losing faith or being abandoned or going mad. Even that favourite plot device, the incurable disease, would be introduced smoothly and painlessly."[22]

One may concede that there is probably an element of escapism in reading any detective novel, but that cannot wholly explain the immense popularity of Christie's style and format over so many years. These and similar views are far too disparaging. Had she indeed lost her touch, or was she not rather trying to gain touch with a new and frightening world, in which she sensed the need for a totally new format for her art? The old one no longer provided her with the framework that enabled her to say what needed to be said. So while readily agreeing with

Julian Symons that the level of Agatha Christie's work varied greatly, I radically dissent from the statement that "most of her finest performances belong to the 1920s and 1930s. The following decade more or less maintained this high level, but after that the decline was steady and near the end it was steep."[23]

On the contrary, if Agatha Christie produced some of her best efforts during the 1920s and 1930s, the same period also produced some of her most dated work and perhaps we should evaluate her writings, not so much in terms of improvement or decline, but in terms of sensitivity to a changing world. Early in the 1960s, Poirot offered a fascinating brief review of the detective story in *The Clocks* (1963), in which he surveyed the earlier works of Anna Katharine Green (*The Leavenworth Case*), the writings of LeBlanc and Leroux, and then went on to consider the work of Agatha Christie herself and of some of her contemporaries, under pseudonyms.[24] This passage suggests that at the time, Agatha Christie was consciously reconsidering the earlier classics.

As early as 1933 she had written "The Fourth Man" (republished in 1948), a story which one of Christie's editors has observed was "definitely much more of a story of the supernatural than of mystery."[25] Although it should be noted that in it, she raised the basic theological problems of our mortality, of human destiny, of the ultimate purpose of life, and of our responsibility for the good and evil of life. The problems of human goodness and wickedness obviously fascinated her, and in her chosen genre she had found an almost perfect medium in which to explore these issues fictionally.

During the years that followed World War II, particularly during the 1950s and 1960s, few writers of her reputation and output experimented more boldly than Agatha Christie, as she searched for the new format in which the detective mystery could be cast. Christie may have conducted this experiment consciously. In the announcement of *So Many Steps to Death* (or *Destina-*

tion Unknown, as it was titled in England), which appeared in 1954, the publisher claimed that the creator of Hercule Poirot had "departed from the canons of classical detection." Indeed she had, for Christie played on the fears engendered in the West during the period of the cold war by the defection of several important scientists to Russia. However, the underlying motif of the book is that the political and ideological polarity into which the world had fallen was of less significance to human destiny than the dangers humanity faced through its own mushrooming science and technology. Ultimately ethical questions were posed by the exercise of *power*, and financial and scientific power were just as dangerous as political power. Christie did not stay with this style or theme, however, and that itself is significant, because it suggests that the issues with which she was attempting to deal were those of a period of social uncertainty and instability rather than those of a civilization conscious of its roots and established in its values.

Throughout her experimentation, Agatha Christie seems to have known she was engaged on an essentially theological and ethical task—she was engaged in nothing less than trying to illustrate the ethical and spiritual basis of a civilization that had come into existence almost overnight. Sometimes this led her to a kind of despair as she was forced to allow for the possibility that Western civilization and the traditional values were breaking up in the grip of new and uncontrollable cosmic forces. Sometimes it was politics that represented the devil incarnate, as in *Passenger to Frankfurt* (1970), or political intrigue, in the revival of the Tommy and Tuppence Beresford series (*Postern of Fate*, 1973); and sometimes the theme was epitomized in spiritual forces closer to the occult.[26] But during this period, Agatha Christie was simply reflecting the anxieties that many people sensed, along with the growing feeling that society was wrestling "not against flesh and blood, but against principalities, against powers, against the rulers of the darkness of this world, against spiritual wickedness in high places."[27] But if a note of apocalyptic entered into her writing, many of her readers had experienced it, and one of her biographers has observed that her books "of the 1960s and the early 1970s reflect the mores of those years," and that she "writes of a London that is worlds away from . . . the years right after World War I."[28]

As Christie searched for a new basis for social ethics and a new literary format in which to illustrate it, she did not simply capitulate to prevailing standards. Moreover, she never ceased to remind us, without self-consciousness, of all that was good and decent and invaluable within the older society that was passing away. Without conscious preaching, her books were still able to warn her readers against those who were prepared to tear up their birthright with their birth certificates.

IV

In her later years, Agatha Christie's personal pilgrimage seems to have caused her to explore the problem of evil in even more varied forms. One can hear her speaking in the words of Colonel Pikeaway to Tommy Beresford when he persuaded the latter to reengage in the service of his government in *Postern of Fate:*

> You know what the world's like—well, the same thing always. Violence, swindles, materialism, rebellion by the young, love of violence and a good deal of sadism, almost as bad as the days of the Hitler Youth. All those things. Well, when you want to find out what's wrong not only with this country but world trouble as well, it's not easy. It's a good thing, the Common Market. It's what we always needed, always wanted. But it's got to be a real Common Market. That's got to be understood very clearly. It's got to be a united Europe. There's got to be a union of civilized countries with civilized ideas and principles.[29]

The person speaking here is a character in a detective

story, but it is not stretching the evidence too far to think that it is also Agatha Christie herself, and beyond the writer, it is the long-suffering public, whose views she was expressing and whose mood and fundamental beliefs she had so accurately gauged.

But evil can take many forms, and Agatha Christie became fascinated by its complexity—with evil as a sin *against* love and evil as a sin *of* love. It was possible for Elvira Blake to be a "child of Lucifer," a beautiful but loveless sinner with a heart of stone, about whom at the end Jane Marple can only say, "May God have mercy on her soul."[30] But love too can become a perversion of itself, and this Christie examined in *Nemesis* (1971) and the following year in *Elephants Can Remember*. The world was no longer simple, and even violent crime could no longer be resolved by simple clear-cut answers; and Christie recognized that. She occasionally returned to something like the old format with Poirot, Ariadne Oliver, or Jane Marple.[31] But more and more, the stories began to express the complexity as well as the reality of evil.

V

In two of her most insightful later books, Christie broke entirely from her traditional format, and no books show her theological sensitivity to more advantage or give us a clearer picture of the problem of evil with which she was concerned.

1. *Ordeal by Innocence* first appeared in 1958.[32] It is a story that illustrates the ambiguity of all human actions and relationships. Dr. Arthur Calgary has been the unwitting witness to a murder, but before he realizes the significance of his testimony, he enlists on an Antarctic expedition. Some years later he returns to find that, because of his own sin of omission, an innocent man was condemned for the murder and then died in prison. At that point, Dr. Calgary sets out to clear the memory of this man who was unjustly sentenced.

That is where trouble starts in earnest, because the

family that had accepted the earlier conviction is now plunged into the throes of a new terror as the members realize they are all again under suspicion from others and among themselves. Calgary is then forced to continue his search (even when he would have foreclosed on it to avoid causing further trouble) in order to clear those who are truly innocent. In this situation, we face the ambivalence of a "good" action that can have evil results, against all the canons of the earlier Poirot series. To search for and discover the truth is *not* necessarily the final happiness nor does it necessarily achieve real justice. The ambiguity of human relationships is shown at a different level in the same story, when it explores the theme of misguided love and the evil that can be caused by "goodness." *Ordeal by Innocence* originates in the generosity of Mrs. Argyle and in her family of underprivileged refugees. However, this generosity, instead of producing a reciprocal love and gratitude, actually engenders hatred. In dealing with resentment caused by a gratitude demanded of people who cannot return it, Agatha Christie was dealing with one of the deepest theological issues in the Christian understanding of sin—the need for forgiveness and the doctrine of Atonement. This novel gives a profound commentary on the human condition in the light of God's grace.

2. In 1967 Agatha Christie published another novel that was unlike anything she had written previously. In *Endless Night*,[33] she went even further afield than in *Ordeal by Innocence*. Not only is there no Poirot, no chasing of clues, no vindication of justice, but there is in the normal sense of the term, no detection at all.

Endless Night is reminiscent of an earlier work by Anthony Berkeley (writing as Francis Iles), *Malice Aforethought* (1931): as the reader picks up the clues throughout the story, it becomes clear that a murder is being planned. But *Endless Night* is more than that, because it is the story of how Ellie's love for Mike and also his perhaps unconscious love for her are ultimately defeated by the evil in his own character. It is the story of how his selfishness, his driving ambition, his faithlessness cause him to grab everything he wants and how—because of a passing infatuation with Greta—this greed will eventually cause him to kill the one he loves. Mike himself is the narrator and at the end, he declares:

> Was it me Ellie was afraid of? I think it must have been, though she didn't know it herself. She knew there was something threatening her, she knew there was danger. Santonix knew the evil in me, too, just like my mother. Perhaps all three of them knew. Ellie knew but she didn't mind. She never minded. It's odd, very odd. I know now. We were very happy together. Yes, very happy. I wish I'd known then that we were happy . . . I had my chance. Perhaps everyone has a chance. I—turned my back on it.
>
> It seems odd, doesn't it, that Greta doesn't matter at all?
>
> And even my beautiful house doesn't matter.
>
> Only Ellie . . . And Ellie can never find me again—Endless Night . . . That's the end of my story.[34]

In one sense we seem to be back to the temper and mood of the morality play, but oh, with what a difference! Perhaps it would be closer to Agatha Christie's intention if we were to think of this story as a twentieth-century *Faust*. But if Western society is the leading character, it is a *Faust* in which the leading part is also played by Everyman.

11

Verdict and Sentence

Sherlock Redivivus?

Umberto Eco, whose *Name of the Rose* is one of the greatest events in the detective fiction of the 1980s, once observed, "It is possible to study even spaghetti from a very serious point of view."[1] We would make a similar claim for detective fiction, since a study of it during the last century and a half of its existence makes us recognize the integral relationship between religion (ideology) and society. Therefore C. H. B. Kitchin was probably correct when he declared, "A historian of the future will probably turn, not to blue books or statistics, but to detective stories if he wishes to study the manners of our age. Middle-class manners perhaps. But I am old-fashioned enough to enjoy the individualism of the middle class."[2]

I

If this were a classic detective puzzler, we would now have reached the stage for our denouement, a final chapter when the great detective brings together all the suspects, and after reviewing the case against each, reveals the culprit in the last few paragraphs. Obviously that would claim more for the present work than would be warranted—although the previous chapters appear to substantiate, as other writers have suggested, that the history of detective fiction itself provides an exercise in detection in which Western society is both the victim and the culprit, and in which "John Q. Public" is cast as both jury and judge.[3]

This survey also provides clues about what happened to the great detective and the classic puzzler. First, we have seen that detective fiction itself bears unwitting testimony to Arnold Toynbee's insight regarding the essential part played by religious or quasi-religious ideologies in the rise and fall of civilizations: a testimony to the integral relationship between the ethics that sustain a civilization and the ideological justification for the ethical system.[4] Secondly, we have substantiated the contention that detective fiction manifests itself in two basic forms. There is the classic ratiocinative puzzler, generated by Edgar Allan Poe, which was popularized supremely in Conan Doyle's Sherlock Holmes. And then there is a hard-boiled, nonconformist school of writing that was prefigured in William Godwin's *Caleb Williams*, but which, with few exceptions, was not seriously—and then not consciously—developed until the American *Black Mask* writers of the twentieth century and those who followed Dashiell Hammett and Raymond Chandler. The significance of this bifurcation is that, whereas those who followed the "classical" pattern were essentially supportive of the status quo, the other school was just as essentially critical of it.

Especially since World War II, the distinctions between these two forms of the genre have become markedly less pronounced. Stories that begin from the basic premises of the classic form have found it less and less possible to ignore elements that would normally belong to the tough, hard-sell type of mystery, and particularly those aspects of plot and character that are critical of the status quo. Whereas before World War II, classic detection habitually affirmed the reality of justice, now we are not so sure, and even Michael Innes' Sir John

Appleby declares, "Justice . . . No I don't believe in that at all . . . I believe in injustice. That we are constantly in danger of committing it. And not merely in courts of law."[5] But equally, stories that appear to be centered in the other camp have also found that they cannot totally ignore classical values, particularly the rational methods and positive social affirmations that we recognize as belonging more properly to the classic form. So Dashiell Hammett's character, the Continental Op, argues for a rational explanation for the troubles of Gabrielle Leggett, the central figure in *The Dain Curse*, but this lengthy novel is really the account of his search for rational explanations for events that were often inexplicable, sometimes appeared supernatural, and were always bizarre.[6]

II

There are three fundamental reasons for this unconscious confluence of interest.

1. The proliferation of violence throughout the Western world has brought danger and horror close to people who expect society normally to insulate them from personal threat. We all now live in societies in which we recognize that although we may admire sweet reasonableness, we may at any time find ourselves in situations where only much more active and physical qualities are likely to be effective.

We can no longer produce neat, self-contained plots that maintain a fixed distinction between a modern, classic puzzler and *Black Mask* motifs. Nor can we draw sharp distinctions between British and American societies as in the past, because although handguns are still not generally available in Britain, they are not unknown, and the works of Dick Francis, Desmond Cory, and others indicate how violence infects the most stable societies. But perhaps the most hopeful feature of detective fiction today is to be seen in those writers whom we have recognized as chastened conservatives and whose mood we would describe as chastened realism.

2. Indeed, far from the assumptions of the Victorian and Edwardian epochs, there is a growing consciousness that life is not wholly rational. Movements such as the theater of the absurd, the Dustbin Theater, and recent trends in art and music have revealed a breakdown of recognized norms for evaluating worth and beauty; rational answers are no longer regarded as necessarily true answers, even less as good answers.[7] With sports and entertainment stars earning more money than the teachers who educate our children or the lawmakers who govern our destiny, a decided element of irrationality is to be found at the center of Western societies.[8] Relativity, which arose first from Einsteinian mathematics and astrophysics, now pervades the whole of life, including ethics.

Yet the human condition at the end of the twentieth century presents us with a paradox which almost reaches the dimensions of a contradiction: on the one hand, we recognize the apparent irrationality (absurdity) of society, but despite that, we cannot question the value of the rational processes themselves without questioning all reality. They provide the only way we have of reaching for truth. But if life is not always meaningless, where are the values that give it meaning? Where are the entities worthy of our respect, let alone our worship?

3. These questions underscore a feature of Western society that lies at the root of the development of detective fiction. We have become more openly secular because religion has less hold on us than formerly. Julian Symons once remarked that "the psychological reason for the weakening of the detective story in recent years is a weakening in the sense of sin."[9] Whether or not there has been a weakening in detective fiction will depend largely on a personal interpretation of society. There can be little doubt of the decline in the consciousness of sin, however, at least in its traditional forms. Life is, even for many church people, more frankly secular, and recently, secularity has been a quality claimed for religion. Indeed, there *is* a proper quality of secularity in the Judeo-Christian tradition arising

from the concept of humanity and from insistence that true religion must be world-affirming rather than world-denying. Rabbi Small, in Harry Kemelman's *Monday the Rabbi Took Off,* claims that the whole thrust of orthodox Judaism

> is toward a practical ethics rather than an absolute idealism. That's how Judaism differs from Christianity, as a matter of fact. We don't ask of our people that they be superhuman, only human. As Hillel said, "If I am not for myself, who will be for me?" Traditionally, we have always felt that *parnossah,* the making of a living, was necessary for a good life. We have no tradition of an idealistic asceticism, or superhuman dedication as in monasticism or self-imposed poverty.[10]

Doubtless later writers, using the genre for religious apologia, would make similar claims about religion in relationship to poverty in the liberation theologies of the 1980s. But the emphasis upon secularity was no less pronounced in an avant-garde Protestant writer like Friedrich Dürrenmatt or in the reflections of a contemporary Roman Catholic writer like William X. Kienzle on the impact of Vatican II.

The secularity is more openly acknowledged in writers who have no religious axe to grind, and in the majority of writers, it represents open recognition that the presuppositions of our culture are now nonreligious, if not frankly agnostic. So Elizabeth Linington's West Coast detective, Maddox, mused that although as a child he had not minded Sunday School, "there was something inexpressibly awful about church itself."[11] The religious implications for society in the secularity of popular detective fiction stand clear, because agnosticism in matters of belief cannot avoid support for relativistic ethics.

In *The Franchise Affair* (1948), Josephine Tey, an obvious exponent of the classic detection mode, forecasts the new postwar society in Britain.[12] She is particularly apt—even prophetic—in her description of how religious leaders tend to follow popular fashions.[13] Yet in a short dialogue between Marion Sharpe and her solicitor, Robert Blair, Tey expresses the questioning of some writers about the implications of skepticism for society:

"You believe in the ultimate triumph of Good."
"Yes."
"Why?"
"I don't know. I suppose because the other thing is unthinkable."[14]

Atheism *is* for many unthinkable because it undercuts the basis for rationality and reduces all ethics to nonsense: the ultimate stupidity.

We face an impasse, an insoluble problem for our logic. The religious glue that held earlier cultures together no longer holds. The basic affirmation of religion cannot be proved, as a problem in mathematics may be proved, despite the sanguine hopes of H. F. Wood's Inspector Byde, and the rational processes demonstrated by Sherlock Holmes.[15] Reason does not bring us ultimately face to face with absolute reality, but leaves us with a cosmic question mark. There is no way in which the processes of classical detective fiction can be entirely reconciled with the truths of revelation that evoke a response of faith.

The ethical problem remains. How are we to distinguish between good and evil, which experience convinces us are antipathetical realities that exist very much as matter and antimatter exist for nuclear physicists? Is our existential ethical situation simply reduced—as the world of international politics and of spy thrillers affirms—to "them" against "us," or to one political ideology against another? What is the ultimate ground of goodness, the denial of which determines evil? Or is everything now so relative that the distinction between these values is totally irrelevant?

We might be tempted to agree that these values are irrelevant, judging from the trends in our society, but something within the human situation persuades us otherwise and causes most people to draw back from recognizing relativity as the only absolute. We reach a point close to that of the chastened realism in chapter 9: on the one hand, we acknowledge a vigorous skepticism with regard to simple faith affirmations, but on the other hand, we see a growing recognition that without faith commitment to something (Someone?) beyond human capacity, beyond human rationality, and perhaps beyond human knowledge, humanity itself is left wallowing in a sea of uncertainty and ethical irrelevance.

Alan Hunter's compassionate detective, Chief Inspector Gently, expresses this chastened realism. He reminds us that even contemporary detectives have to recognize moral purpose in the universe in order to pursue their work, when he introduces the artist Reymerston to the metaphysics of scientific philosopher Edwin Keynes. There is a curious little episode when Reymerston, in reaction to the circumstances in which he and his loved ones find themselves, expostulates, "What a bloody mess . . . I'll tell you the last belief of a noble mind. It is that somewhere there's a moral purpose." That leads Gently to mention the metaphysics of Keynes and to point out that the movement from hatred to love, which could be equated with the dispersal of energy in nature, may suggest a cosmic purpose essentially moral.[16]

It is unnecessary and inappropriate to discuss the rights and wrongs of such a concept, but its significance here is that it should be introduced into a *detective* story. It is almost irrelevant to the plot and to the detection, but it underlines our insistence that it is virtually impossible to justify the subject matter of detective fiction unless there is moral purpose, not only behind detection as such, but sustaining the human context in which it takes place.

III

It is time to return to Sherlock Holmes.

There are indications for thinking that a large part

of the reading public, on both sides of the Atlantic, welcomes a return to the detective fiction set in earlier times. Peter Lovesey thought that "the fascination of a mystery set in the remote past is easily explained: it provides an escape from modern life. But we are not at the mercy of a science-fiction writer's fantasizing. The world we enter is real and under control."[17] Catherine Aird, through one of her characters, pointed out that murder was a very primitive crime and a crime essentially against society; moreover, that the appetite of the criminal grew so that later deaths were perpetrated increasingly casually, but she added, "By then the murderer was outside the tribe and beyond salvation too."[18] I suggest that the new popularity of earlier periods of history as settings for detection represents nostalgia for times when the issues were clear-cut, when evil received its due deserts, and when it seemed patently obvious that justice would be done by the law and its officers.

We have already noted the contemporary popularity of historical settings for detection.[19] They range from Van Gulik's fictional reconstruction of seventh-century Imperial China, through various incursions into the medieval world, the revival of Dr. Samuel Johnson as a detective in his time, the era of the Bow Street Runners, into the classical period of the 1930s and 1940s and to the British Raj in India.[20]

For many of these historical periods, our earlier criticism still stands: fictional detection could not develop properly until the Renaissance/Enlightenment had cleared people's minds of superstition, destroyed the "ordeal" method of determining guilt and innocence, and produced a legal system that accepted reason as absolute in the treatment of empirical data.

But the most popular period, which has received a great deal of attention from recent writers, was the period when the scientific method was beginning to demonstrate results, when detective fiction reached new heights of popularity, and when Sherlock Holmes first made his London appearance; that is, when all seemed to be set within the best of all possible worlds. The interest in this era has been particularly marked in some contemporary women writers and in the creation of nineteenth-century female detectives to challenge the primacy of the misogynous sleuth of Baker Street.[21] However, no writer has re-created the spirit and values of Victorian England more accurately and in a more satisfying way than Peter Lovesey in his Sergeant Cribb series.[22] Sergeant Cribb is *not* Sherlock Holmes, he is *not* an amateur superman, and he is *not* omniscient or omnicompetent. Cribb is not even a nineteenth-century edition of the debunking policeman we encounter in the later character of Sergeant Beef.[23] He is an average, working policeman who does his job simply, efficiently, and without unnecessary bravado. He supports the Victorian status quo in its responsibility for law and order, but like Inspector Pitt, the husband of Charlotte Ellison in Anne Perry's novels, the problems engendered by his social origins are a standing criticism of that society. He therefore brings together, within the unlikely setting of nineteenth-century Victorian London, both the classic tradition of detective fiction and the nonconforming reaction that would later be taken up in America.

But when all is said, the character of Sherlock Holmes so dominates detective fiction at the end of the nineteenth century that there have even been attempts to revive him.[24] There has also been an attempt to transfer part of his career to the United States.[25]

Possibly on the basis of Umberto Eco's thoughts on spaghetti, there has also been a serious endeavor to examine the character of Sherlock Holmes psychoanalytically and to explain his detective work in terms of Conan Doyle's sexual repressions. The perpetrator of this idea, Samuel Rosenberg, suggests that, as Holmes represents Doyle's superego, so the Moriarty-Moran element represents all those personal drives that were repressed within the restrictions of Victorian respectability.[26]

More significant for us is Robert Lee Hall's remarkable attempt to revive Sherlock Holmes and to analyze his work and popularity in *Exit Sherlock Holmes: The Great Detective's Final Days*.[27] This book is quite different from the other attempts to re-create Sherlock Holmes' mysteries, not least because the American writer has a remarkable ability to evoke the atmosphere of early Edwardian London, but also because the real detection is conducted by Dr. Watson. This is necessary because, fourteen years after the "death" of Professor James Moriarty at the Reichenbach Falls (and eleven years after Holmes' own reappearance), Moriarty himself reappears and Holmes is forced to go into a false retirement to prepare for the final confrontation with his enemy. Watson, however, is lured into action by Moriarty and during his attempt to find out where Holmes is hiding discovers that during the earlier years, Holmes was extremely secretive about his past, and that many things Watson believes about his friend are untrue. Why is there a mystery about Holmes' early life? Did he once attend Cambridge University? Is Holmes even English? Why has the old actor, Alfred Fish, been pressed into service to act the part of a nonexistent Mycroft Holmes simply to deceive Watson? Why did Holmes keep his secret laboratory in the basement of Mrs. Hudson's house?

The story begins as a typical Sherlock Holmes mystery, with rain, fog, and an indefinable threat to the security of England, but it ends in pure science fiction. Its special interest from our point of view is that not only does it become an epitome of the changes that have taken place in detective fiction since the time of Conan Doyle's best sellers, but it also reflects, in fictional form, the equally great changes that have taken place in the theological and philosophical assumptions of the general public. It is the progress (or if that is too positive a word, change) caused by Dr. Watson's disillusionment from a simplistic acceptance of an epic distinction between good (Holmes) and evil (Moriarty) to the point where he does not know what he believes about either. This is represented in a dream in which Watson sees the figures of Holmes and Moriarty changing into each other as they seem eventually to merge into a single ambiguous personality "who caused the great wheel to move."[28] Could that also be a theological reflection?

All possible permutations of the facts are tried by Watson and his helper, the young actor Wiggins, a former Baker Street Irregular. So at first, Watson suspects that Holmes and Moriarty are brothers, then he wonders if they could be the same person, and Wiggins even suggests that Moriarty might have been simply another figment of Holmes' fertile imagination.[29] Wiggins declares that, despite all the appearances of deception on the part of Holmes, "I believe Sherlock Holmes is a good man," and Watson, in his narrative, adds the wistful comment, "I fervently wanted to believe this and confessed as much." There the response of faith and involuntary twentieth-century agnosticism stand side by side: one can almost feel the wistful longing of a person who has been losing faith but who desperately wants to believe; it is a parable of faith in the twentieth century.

Let us look at the stages of this saga a little more closely.

1. The story begins in the nineteenth century when everyone accepts the principle that absolute good and absolute evil exist and that they are locked in an eternal struggle. The disciple of goodness (Watson) stoutly maintains that the champion of good (Holmes) will finally triumph. After all, that is what faith and discipleship are all about. So we read,

> I remained ignorant of everything except that the most dangerous criminal and the foremost champion of law of their generation stalked one another. I could not help reflecting how alike they were in every way—two single-minded geniuses, with but one difference to distinguish them forever: one was dedicated to the destruction of all that was good, the other to preserving and protecting it.[30]

But despite his unwavering faith and loyalty through

many years of close friendship, Watson's doubts eventually cause him to speculate: "I began at last to wonder if somewhere, unknown to me or the world, Holmes and Moriarty had already met, fought, and Holmes had met his match. At that thought a sense of sorrow, rage, and frustration overwhelmed me."[31] Doubts in the omnipotence and omniscience of his champion already exist for Watson. But note the cosmic terms in which the confrontation is cast in his mind. It is almost as if he is projecting the scene preceding the grim opening of Milton's *Paradise Lost,* but with an opposite result— Satan's victory and the total defeat of the Angels of Light: a precosmic "Fall" of goodness in defeat.

2. Then follow the revelations, not only of the uncanny identity of Holmes and Moriarty, but also of Holmes' unknown past and of his deliberate deception of Watson who was thus forced to question the integrity of Holmes himself.[32]

There is the nightmare in which the personalities that Watson has hitherto accepted as perfect antitheses of good and evil become confused and merge into a single ambiguous figure—an apt expression of the cosmic doubts of our century, caused by the explosion of scientific knowledge. If the traditional simplistic categories are dead, can good, evil, God, and the Devil any longer be distinguished?

3. That leads to the stage where Watson and Wiggins speculate on all possible explanations for the composite mystery of Holmes and Moriarty. For a theological comparison, reflect on the succession of theological speculations experienced in recent decades—death of God theology, secular theology, urban theology, theology of hope, process theology, and the various forms of liberation theology. The average person is apt to wonder where it will end.

4. On the other hand, there is Wiggins' simple affirmation that Sherlock Holmes is a good man and Watson's heartfelt admission that he wants to believe that. There is the affirmation that Holmes (as the champion of goodness and justice) has come into the world to

accomplish a specific task on which the fate of humanity depends.[33] To read significance into this could be seen as a reflection of the average person's faith that there *is* a distinction between good and evil and that there is a decent purpose behind life's charade, which must end in the triumph of good.

5. Finally, there is a resolution of all the doubts, and an explanation of the questions, not by a return to the former simplistic beliefs about Holmes and Moriarty, but in a plausible science fiction answer. This is in tune with the twentieth-century desire to provide rational explanations for things that are otherwise inexplicable, even for the distinction between good and evil. There are many people today who would not confess any belief in God, but who are perfectly ready to entertain the possibility of intervention into our history by beings from some other galaxy.[34]

It would be entirely wrong to suggest that Robert Lee Hall consciously set out to trace the history of twentieth-century belief and doubt; his book would be much less significant from our point of view, if he had. But because in the earliest confrontation with Moriarty, Sherlock Holmes *was* cast in the nineteenth-century absolute terms of good confronting evil, the book has unconsciously reflected the course of speculations about this theme during our century; and it ends on the significant note—Holmes has gone forever, and from now on, the world's struggle with evil will have to be faced and resolved by people like us and Dr. Watson.

IV

One of Margery Allingham's characters, Jimmy Sutane, a dancer, describes his own responsibilities to the public as "a dizzy cathedral balancing on a joke."[35] But if the evidence is added together it is not an inapt description of Western society—we seem to be poised between the aspiration of a society of unimaginable beauty and justice and the possibility of falling into the ultimate absurdity of self-destruction.

Enlightenment rationalism seems to have brought us full circle: on the one hand, we are forced to recognize its limitations and the consequent absurdity of modern life, while on the other hand, to deny the truths reached by reason would send us reeling into an absurdity even worse. How do we recognize the proper authority of human reason without making it absolute?

In the 1960s, the detective stories of J. B. Priestley, the English Socialist writer, were also expressing concern about the course of British society.[36] Fifteen years after the end of World War II, he published a survey of modern literature, entitled *Literature and Western Man*, in which he put the issue very bluntly. At the end of that book, he confessed his own agnosticism, shared, he claimed, by the majority of his literary friends, and he maintained that contemporary society "is not merely irreligious but powerfully anti-religious. . . . So we have no religion and, inside or outside literature, man feels homeless, helpless and in despair."[37] However, the book includes a passage that is as fine a piece of religious apologetic from a professed agnostic as has appeared in this century:

> Religion alone can carry the load, defend us against the de-humanising collectives, restore true personality. And it is doubtful if our society can last much longer without religion, for either it will destroy itself by some final idiot war or, at peace but hurrying in the wrong direction, it will soon largely cease to be composed of persons.[38]

That is the cultural dilemma to which our own survey of detective fiction seems to point. So Agatha Christie's Mike goes out into the hell of the eternal darkness he has made for himself because he cannot accept the simplicity and purity of Ellie's love. Or we may cite Charles Dickens' equally damned Jonas in *Martin Chuzzlewit*, who when he eventually faces his own reality, sees that, as "thatched roofs of poor men's homes were in the distance," so too "an old grey spire, surmounted by a Cross, rose up between him and the coming night."[39]

As Dorothy L. Sayers described it in *The Nine Tailors*, as P. D. James hinted in *A Taste for Death*, as our own return to Sherlock Holmes suggests, and as many other writers in the detective fiction genre have vaguely made us aware, that alternative—revived faith or cultural darkness—may be facing Western civilization. We can only end at the same point as that reached by J. B. Priestley:

> We must wait. Even if we believe that the time of our civilisation is running out fast, like sugar spilled from a torn bag, we must wait. But while we are waiting we can try to feel and think and behave, to some extent, *as if* our society were already beginning to be contained by religion, as if we were certain that Man cannot even remain Man unless he looks beyond himself, as if we were finding our way home again in the universe.[40]

Notes

Index

Notes

Introduction: The "Wrights" and "Wrongs" of Detective Fiction

1. Margery Allingham, "Party of One," *Holiday Magazine* 34 (September 1963): 11–15.

2. Howard Haycraft, ed., *The Art of the Mystery Story* (1946; reprint, New York: Carroll & Graf, 1983), 18.

3. Willard Huntington Wright, from his introduction to *The Great Detective Stories*, ed. Willard Huntington Wright (New York: Scribner's, 1927), which introduction can also be found in Haycraft, ed., *Art of the Mystery Story*, 33–70.

4. Serious criticism of the detective story did not begin until the end of the 1920s, when E. M. Wrong wrote his introduction to *Crime and Detection*, (New York: Oxford Univ. Press, 1926), which introduction can also be found in Haycraft, ed., *Art of the Mystery Story*, 18–32, and Willard Huntington Wright published his introduction to *The Great Detective Stories*. They were followed by others—Dorothy L. Sayers' superb introduction to *Great Short Stories of Detection, Mystery and Horror*, 2 vols. (London: Gollancz, 1928), 1:9–47; Marjorie Nicolson's "Professor and the Detective," which first appeared in *Atlantic Monthly* in April 1929 and can also be found in Haycraft, ed., *Art of the Mystery Story*, 110–27. Early in the following decade the first full-length study of the genre, H. Douglas Thomson's *Masters of Mystery* (London: Collins, 1931), appeared. One should add to this the work of Howard Haycraft, *Murder for Pleasure: The Life and Times of the Detective Story* (New York; D. Appleton-Century Co., 1941), and the volume he edited, *Art of the Mystery Story*.

5. "Who cares?" was precisely the reaction of Edmund Wilson in his article "Who Cares Who Killed Roger Ackroyd?" which first appeared in the *New Yorker* (20 January 1945) and

can also be found in Haycraft, ed., *Art of the Mystery Story*, 390–97.

6.   Harrison R. Steeves, "A Sober Word on the Detective Story," in *Art of the Mystery Story*, ed. Haycraft, 513–26.

7.   Ibid., 515.

8.   Ibid., 520.

9.   Ibid., 514.

10.   Cf. Marjorie Nicolson, "The Professor and the Detective," and Howard Haycraft, "The Passing of the Detective in Literature," in *Art of the Mystery Story*, ed. Haycraft, 110–27 and 511–12.

11.   Lawrence Sanders, *The Tenth Commandment* (New York: G. P. Putnam, 1980), epigraph page.

12.   R. Austin Freeman, "The Art of the Detective Story," and Willard Huntington Wright, "The Great Detective Stories," in *Art of the Mystery Story*, ed. Haycraft, 13–14 and 35.

13.   Haycraft, ed., *Art of the Mystery Story*, 7.

14.   William S. Maltby, *The Black Legend in England* (Durham, N.C.: Duke Univ. Press, 1971), 10.

15.   Robin W. Winks, ed., *Detective Fiction: A Collection of Critical Essays* (Englewood Cliffs, N.J.: Prentice-Hall, 1980), 7.

16.   Edmund Crispin, ed., *Best Detective Stories* (London: Faber & Faber, 1964), 10.

17.   Anthony Boucher is the pseudonym of William Anthony Parker White. Boucher's words are quoted by Allen Hubin in *Boucher's Choicest: A Collection of Anthony Boucher's Favorites*, ed. Jeanne F. Bernkopf (New York: E. P. Dutton & Co., 1969), 10.

18.   Erik Routley, *The Puritan Pleasures of the Detective Story* (London: Gollancz, 1972). Rodger's quotation is from the *Guardian*, 20 December 1967.

19.   Martin Cruz Smith, *Gorky Park* (New York: Random House, 1981).

20.   William L. De Andrea reviewing Stuart Kaminsky's *Death of a Dissident*, "Paper Crimes," *The Armchair Detective (TAD)* 15 (1982): 50.

21.   Routley, *Puritan Pleasures*, 203. Much the same was said in 1931 by H. Douglas Thomson in his pioneering book, *Masters of Mystery*, cited previously. He wrote: "I doubt wheth-

er morality has ever had her case more loyally or more consistently upheld than in this Tweedledum and Tweedledee combat of anarchy and order over her sleeping body," 22–23.

22. Allingham, "Party of One." Dorothy L. Sayers made the same point when she observed that "of all forms of modern fiction, the detective story alone makes virtue *ex hypothesi* more interesting than vice, the detective more beloved than the criminal" ("Aristotle on Detective Fiction," *Detective Fiction,* ed., Winks, 26–27).

23. Alexander Pope, *Essay on Man,* epistle 4, line 49.

24. Elliot L. Gilbert, *The World of Mystery Fiction: A Guide* (San Diego: Univ. of California in association with Del Mar Publishers, 1978), 32.

25. Ellis Peters is the pseudonym of the novelist Edith Pargeter. Examples of Brother Cadfael's detective work are to be found in *One Corpse Too Many* (New York: Morrow, 1979) and other titles under the Ellis Peters pseudonym. The same argument is true for the detection in Umberto Eco's *Name of the Rose* (New York: Harcourt Brace Jovanovich, 1983) and for the stories about Judge Dee, Robert Van Gulik's Chinese detective-magistrate of the Tang dynasty.

26. Wrong's introduction to *Crime and Detection,* in *Art of the Mystery Story,* ed. Haycraft, 18.

27. Cf. Wrong's introduction to *Crime and Detection.* But the point is made more comprehensively in A. E. Murch, *The Development of the Detective Novel* (New York: Philosophical Library, 1958) and Julian Symons, *Mortal Consequences: A History from the Detective Story to the Crime Novel* (1972; reprint, New York: Schocken Books, 1973).

28. Routley, *Puritan Pleasures,* 22.

29. John Wiley Nelson, *Your God Is Alive and Well and Appearing in Popular Culture* (Philadelphia: Westminster Press, 1976), 163.

30. Jacques Barzun, "Detection and the Literary Art" (1961), in *Detective Fiction,* ed. Winks, 145.

31. *Masters of Mystery,* 57.

32. See Sayers' introduction to *Great Short Stories of Detection,* especially 1:10, 15, and 44.

33. Cf. William Bradley, "The Ethics of James Bond," *Hartford Quarterly* 7 (Spring 1967): 33–46.

34. The question to Laplace about where he found room for God in his view of the universe is reputed to have drawn the skeptical reply, "Sire, we have no need for that hypothesis."

35. Some of the ideas in this section repeat and modify material that appeared in my article, "Theology of Detective Fiction" for *Hartford Quarterly* 6 (Spring 1966): 21–28.

36. Rex Stout, "Murder Is No Joke," in *The Delights of Detection*, ed. Jacques Barzun (New York: Criterion Books, 1961), 326–27.

37. Cyril Hare, *When the Wind Blows* (1949; reprint, New York: Perennial Library, 1978), 243–44.

38. Dorothy L. Sayers, *Busman's Honeymoon* (London: Gollancz, 1937), 387–98.

39. Agatha Christie, *Murder with Mirrors* (London: Collins, 1952). (American title: *They Do It with Mirrors*.)

40. Jacques Barzun, "Detection and the Literary Art," 145, 150.

41. Ngaio Marsh, *Death at the Bar* (1940; reprint, Harmondsworth, Eng.: Penguin, 1949), 194–95.

42. Dorothy L. Sayers, *The Nine Tailors* (London: Gollancz, 1934), 81–82.

43. Nicholas Blake is the pseudonym of poet Cecil Day Lewis. Blake's character, Strangeways, is quoted in *End of Chapter* (1957; reprint, New York: Perennial Library, 1977), 28–29.

44. Arthur Upfield, *Death of a Swagman* (1945; reprint, New York: Scribner's, 1982), 131.

45. Patricia Wentworth, *The Silent Pool* (1954; reprint, New York: Pyramid, 1965), 191.

46. I am inclined to think that this adherence to eternal absolutes came through philosophical idealism, from the fact that the accepted background for theology in England was more likely to be "Greats" than any other course of study. This is the program of study in *Litterae humaniores* at Oxford, based on the classical Latin and Greek authors and languages, and heavily weighted in the ancient philosophers.

47. Patricia Wentworth, *She Came Back* (1945; reprint, New York: Bantam, 1981), 86.

48. Michael Gilbert, *Blood and Judgment* (1958; reprint, New York: Perennial Library, 1978), 90.

49.   Joseph Wood Krutch, "Only a Detective Story," in *Detective Fiction*, ed. Winks, 45, or in *Art of the Mystery Story*, ed. Haycraft, 184.

50.   Sayers, introduction to *Great Short Stories of Detection*, 1:38.

51.   Erle Stanley Gardner, *The Case of the Drowning Duck* (London: Cassels, 1942), 43. See also Ngaio Marsh and Henry Jellett, *The Nursing Home Murder* (1935; reprint, Harmondsworth, Eng.: Penguin, 1945), 193–94. A useful theological point of reference might be Emil Brunner, *Justice and the Social Order* (London: Lutterworth Press, 1945), 16–17.

52.   Lesley Egan [Dell Shannon], *Look Back on Death* (London: Gollancz, 1979), 167. (Dell Shannon also writes under the pseudonyms Elizabeth Linington and Egan O'Neill.) Ruth Rendell, *Some Lie and Some Die* (Garden City, N.Y.: Doubleday, 1973), 100. The same point is made by Michael Innes in reference to the historian Plucknose in *The Weight of the Evidence* (London: Gollancz, 1943), 58.

53.   Robin W. Winks, ed., *The Historian as Detective: Essays on Evidence* (New York: Harper & Row, 1968). See also *Detective Fiction*, which he edited, and his *Modus Operandi: An Excursion into Detective Fiction* (Boston: David R. Godine, 1982).

54.   The tramp as victim: Dorothy L. Sayers, *Whose Body?* (London: Gollancz, 1923); the convict as victim: Sir Arthur Conan Doyle, *The Hound of the Baskervilles* (London: Newnes, 1902); the cabinet minister as victim: Ngaio Marsh and Henry Jellett, *The Nursing Home Murder:* the noble peer as victim: Agatha Christie, *Lord Edgware Dies* (London: Collins, 1933), (American title: Thirteen at Dinner); the nonentities as victims: Agatha Christie, *One, Two, Buckle My Shoe* (London: Collins, 1940), (American title: *The Patriotic Murders*).

55.   Agatha Christie, *Appointment with Death* (1938; reprint, Harmondsworth, Eng.: Penguin, 1949), 101.

56.   Christie, *One, Two, Buckle My Shoe*, 249.

57.   Delano Ames, *She Shall Have Murder* (1949; reprint, New York: Perennial Library, 1983), 117.

58.   G. D. H. and M. Cole, *Scandal at School* (London: Collins, 1935), 199. (American title: *The Sleeping Death*.)

59. Michael Gilbert, *Close Quarters* (London: Hodder & Stoughton, 1951), 53–54.
60. *One, Two, Buckle My Shoe*, 251.
61. The story of Saul and the Amalekites appears in 1 Sam. 15, and the quotation appears twice, in 1 Sam. 15.23 and 26.
62. Marjorie Nicolson, "The Professor and the Detective," 125, 127.

1. Those Eminent Victorians

1. G. K. Chesterton, "A Defence of Detective Stories" in *Art of the Mystery Story*, ed. Haycraft, 3–6.
2. There are accounts of the history of detective fiction in several of the works previously cited: the writings of E. M. Wrong, Robin W. Winks, H. Douglas Thomson, Elliot L. Gilbert, Dorothy L. Sayers, A. E. Murch, and Julian Symons. Of the older works, the most complete are H. Douglas Thomson, *Masters of Mystery;* Howard Haycraft, *Murder for Pleasure;* A. E. Murch, *Development of the Detective Novel;* Julian Symons, *Mortal Consequences* (New York: Harper, 1972), (English title: *Bloody Murder,* rev. ed. [Harmondsworth, Eng.: Penguin, 1984]) and Dilys Winn, *Murder Ink* (New York: Workman, 1977; and rev. ed. 1984).
3. *Mortal Consequences*, 23.
4. Wrong, introduction to *Crime and Detection,* in *Art of the Mystery Story,* ed. Haycraft, 18; cf. Haycraft, *Murder for Pleasure,* 1-4; H. Douglas Thomson, *Masters of Mystery,* 60; John Ball, "Murder At Large" in *The Mystery Story,* ed. John Ball (1976; reprint, Harmondsworth, Eng.: Penguin, 1978), 1–3; Julian Symons, *Mortal Consequences,* 27–35; A. E. Murch, *Development of the Detective Novel,* 67–68.
5. Conan Doyle is quoted in Murch, *Development of the Detective Novel,* 83.
6. The case of Mary Cecilia Rogers in New York in 1841. In reality this was an unsolved murder case; Mary Rogers may have been murdered or she may have died accidentally following an abortion.
7. *Masters of Mystery,* 85, 86.
8. Poe's "Murders in the Rue Morgue," as in *The World of Mystery Fiction,* ed. Elliot L. Gilbert (San Diego: Univ. of California, 1978), 47.

9. Gilbert, *World of Mystery Fiction: A Guide*, 29.

10. Gilbert, ed., *World of Mystery Fiction*, 63. This volume also includes "The Purloined Letter" and "The Tell-Tale Heart."

11. "The Mystery of Marie Roget," in Sayers' *Great Short Stories of Detection*, 1:161.

12. H. Sheldon Smith, Robert T. Handy, and Lefferts A. Loetscher, *American Christianity*, 2 vols. (New York: Scribner's, 1960–63), 1:495. Cf. also Octavius Brooks Frothingham, *Transcendentalism in New England* (New York: G. P. Putnam, 1876) for an account of the pervasive spirit of transcendentalism in Germany, France, England, and New England at that time.

13. Smith, Handy, and Loetscher, *American Christianity*, 2:136–40.

14. Ibid., 2:140–47.

15. The poet was William Ellery Channing (1818–1901), who was named after his more distinguished uncle. Cf. Perry Miller, ed., *The American Transcendentalists, Their Prose and Poetry* (Garden City, N.Y.: Doubleday, 1958), 1.

16. Francis M. Nevins, Jr., *The Mystery Writer's Art* (Bowling Green, Ky.: University Popular Press, 1970), 1.

17. The fullest account of rationalism in detective fiction is in A. E. Murch, *Development of the Detective Novel*, 36–62, but there are useful contributions in the works of Haycraft, Ball, Thomson, and Gilbert.

18. Emile Gaboriau, *Le Crime d'Orcival*, 9th ed. (Paris, 1873), 130; our translation.

19. Murch, *Development of the Detective Novel*, 11.

20. Emile Gaboriau, *L'Affaire Lerouge*, 13th ed. (Paris, 1873), 50; our translation.

21. Routley, *Puritan Pleasures*, 55.

22. Ibid., 55–56.

23. H. F. Wood, *The Passenger from Scotland Yard* (1888; reprint, New York: Dover, 1977), 117.

24. Wilkie Collins, *The Moonstone* (1868; reprint, New York: Bantam, 1982).

25. Ibid., 388.

26. Ibid., 9.

27. T. S. Eliot is quoted from the cover of Collins' book (Bantam edition). Dorothy Sayers is quoted from her introduction to *Great Short Stories of Detection*, 1:25.

28.   The three stories are "The Loss of the Diamond, 1848";
"The Discovery of the Truth, 1848–49"; and "Epilogue, The
Finding of the Diamond, 1849."

29.   Collins, *Moonstone*, 63.

30.   E.g., Murthwaite recognizes at once the importance of the
diamond being placed in a bank vault, *Moonstone*, 266–68.

31.   Ibid., 265–74.

32.   Ibid., 269.

33.   E. F. Bleiler said this in his introduction to the Dover
edition of *Passenger from Scotland Yard*, v–vii.

34.   *The Big Bow Mystery* has appeared in anthologies, e.g.
in Hans S. Santesson, ed., *8 Keys to Murder* (New York: Dell,
1970) and in *The Locked Room Reader* (New York: Random
House, 1968). It has also appeared with an introduction by E.
F. Bleiler in *Three Victorian Detective Novels* (New York: Dover
Publications, 1978).

35.   *Passenger from Scotland Yard*, 270.

36.   Ibid., 293–94.

37.   Ibid., 182.

38.   Ibid., 183.

39.   Ibid., 211.

40.   Arthur Conan Doyle, "The Resident Patient," in *The
Complete Sherlock Holmes*, 2 vols. (Garden City, N.Y.: Doubleday, 1930), 1:423. Hereafter cited as *CSH*.

41.   Routley, *Puritan Pleasures*, 57.

42.   Cf. Wayne Wall, "The Theology of Sherlock Holmes,"
Baker Street Journal 29 (September 1979): 134–46, hereafter
cited as *BSJ*.

43.   E.g., in J. R. R. Tolkien's trilogy, *The Lord of the Rings*
(London: Allen & Unwin, 1966) or in C. S. Lewis' seven-volume
series, *The Chronicles of Narnia* (1950; reissued, New York:
Macmillan, 1970.)

44.   Cf. Wayne Wall, "Was Holmes Converted to Religion?"
BSJ 23 (December 1973); 237–45.

45.   Charles Bradlaugh (1834–91) was an extremely popular speaker in the atheist cause during the second half of the
nineteenth century in Britain. George Jacob Holyoake (1817–
1906) was an agnostic who launched *The Reasoner*, a weekly
secular newspaper in 1845. Cf. Warren Sylvester Smith, *The
London Heretics, 1870–1914* (New York: Dodd, Mead & Co.,

1968), 27–83. Holmes terms the idea of a universe produced by chance "unthinkable" in "The Adventure of the Cardboard Box," *CSH* 2:901.

46.   Conan Doyle, *A Study in Scarlet, CSH* 1:81–83.

47.   Conan Doyle, "The Boscombe Valley Mystery," *CSH* 1:217. As William S. Baring-Gould has pointed out, these words were wrongly attributed to the Puritan divine Richard Baxter. They were uttered instead by John Bradford (1510–55) when he caught sight of a criminal on the way to the gallows, and perhaps the words are all the more poignant because Bradford was a Protestant martyr in Mary I's reign. Cf. William S. Baring-Gould, ed., *The Annotated Sherlock Holmes*, 2 vols. (New York: Clarkson N. Potter, 1967), 2:152 and note 28, hereafter cited as *ASH*.

48.   Conan Doyle, "The Adventure of the Veiled Lodger," *CSH* 2:1101.

49.   Wall, "Theology of Sherlock Holmes," 137–38.

50.   Conan Doyle, "The Adventure of the Illustrious Client," *CSH* 2:989.

51.   Ibid., 2:998.

52.   Conan Doyle, "The Adventure of the Retired Colourman," *CSH* 2:1113.

53.   Conan Doyle, "Adventure of the Cardboard Box," *CSH* 2:901.

54.   Conan Doyle, "The Naval Treaty," *CSH* 1:455–56.

55.   Dale is quoted by George Jackson in *The Preacher and the Modern Mind* (London: Charles H. Kelly, 1912), 3–4.

56.   Cf. Geoffrey Wainwright, ed., *Keeping the Faith* (Philadelphia: Fortress Press, 1969), xix.

57.   *Encyclopaedia Britannica*, 1965 ed., s.v. "Darwin, Charles."

58.   Conan Doyle, *A Study in Scarlet, CSH* 1:20–22.

59.   Cf. Conan Doyle, "The Adventure of the Creeping Man," *CSH* 2:1082–83.

60.   Prologue to Tennyson's "In Memoriam," which was written in 1849. My italics.

61.   Isaac Asimov, *More Tales of the Black Widowers* (Garden City, N.Y.: Doubleday, 1976), 169.

62.   Conan Doyle, "The Adventure of the Copper Beeches," *CSH* 1:317.

63. Conan Doyle, "The Five Orange Pips," *CSH* 1:224–25. Cf. also what Holmes said could be deduced from a single drop of water in *A Study in Scarlet, CSH* 1:23.

64. Conan Doyle, "Adventure of the Cardboard Box," 2:889. The Boer War (1899–1902) had invoked a tremendous outflow of British patriotism, and there would be even more when World War I broke out in 1914.

65. Conan Doyle, *The Hound of the Baskervilles, CSH* 2:681.

66. Wall, "Theology of Sherlock Holmes," 139.

67. Conan Doyle, *Hound of the Baskervilles, CSH* 2:684.

68. Conan Doyle, "The Adventure of the Blue Carbuncle," *CSH* 1:257.

69. Conan Doyle, "Adventure of the Cardboard Box," *CSH* 2: 889. Cf. *ASH* 2:194–95.

70. Nonconformity did not win any right to vote for Parliament or take any position under the crown until 1828, and no Nonconformist could enter the universities of Oxford or Cambridge until after 1870. The Free Churches were only just beginning to flex their political muscles in alliance with the Liberal party. Partly as a result of their growing political consciousness, the Liberals swept into office in 1906 with the largest majority the House of Commons had seen to date. Nonconformity was also changing theologically. It had been very conservative at the beginning of the century, but from the middle of the nineteenth century, it moved rapidly in a more liberal direction. In 1903 liberal theologian R. J. Campbell became minister of the influential City Temple in London and became a leader of the "New Theology." Cf. John W. Grant, *Free Churchmanship in England, 1870–1940* (London: Independent Press, n.d.), especially 114–205.

71. G. Lowes Dickenson, *The Greek View of Life*, 23d ed. (London: Methuen, 1957), 33.

72. *Masters of Mystery,* 22.

73. Conan Doyle, *A Study in Scarlet, CSH* 1:21–-22.

74. Conan Doyle, Introduction to "The Yellow Face," *CSH* 1:351.

75. Conan Doyle, "A Scandal in Bohemia," *CSH* 1:161–75.

76. Conan Doyle, "Yellow Face," *CSH* 1:362.

77.   Conan Doyle, "A Scandal in Bohemia" and "Yellow Face," 1:167 and 351, respectively.

78.   Conan Doyle, "The Adventure of the Speckled Band," 1:258.

79.   Conan Doyle, "A Scandal in Bohemia," 1:165.

80.   *Masters of Mystery*, 22.

81.   Cf. William Godwin, *Caleb Williams*, ed. David Mc-Cracken (London, 1794; reprint, New York: W. W. Norton, 1977), vii–viii.

82.   Symons, *Mortal Consequences*, 21.

83.   Ibid.

84.   Wrong's introduction to *Crime and Detection*, in *Art of the Mystery Story*, ed. Haycraft, 18.

85.   Godwin, *Caleb Williams*, 318.

86.   David McCracken, introduction to *Caleb Williams*, xv.

2. The Golden Age

1.   Haycraft, ed., *The Art of the Mystery Story*, 7.

2.   Symons questions Sayers' suggestion in *Mortal Consequences*, 9–10. Cf. Symons' chapter 2 for his discussion of the genre's legacy.

3.   A. A. Milne, *The Red House Mystery* (London: Methuen, 1922), x–xi.

4.   See Ronald A. Knox, "A Detective Story Decalogue," and S. S. Van Dine, "Twenty Rules for Writing Detective Stories," in *Art of the Mystery Story*, ed. Haycraft 194–96 and 189–93, respectively.

5.   Ibid., 189.

6.   Symons, *Mortal Consequences*, 92.

7.   Ibid., 76.

8.   G. K. Chesterton's five series of stories about Father Brown are as follows: *The Innocence of Father Brown* (1910; reprint, Harmondsworth, Eng.: Penguin, 1982), hereafter cited as *The Innocence; The Wisdom of Father Brown* (1914; reprint, Harmondsworth, Eng.: Penguin, 1982), hereafter cited as *The Wisdom; The Incredulity of Father Brown* (1923; reprint, Harmondsworth, Eng.: Penguin, 1982), hereafter cited as *The Incredulity; The Secret of Father Brown* (1927;

reprint, Harmondsworth, Eng.: Penguin, 1982), hereafter cited as *The Secret; The Scandal of Father Brown* (1929; reprint, Harmondsworth, Eng.: Penguin, 1982), hereafter cited as *The Scandal.* See also Melville Davisson Post, *Uncle Abner: Master of Mysteries* (1918; reprint, New York: Dover, 1975) hereafter cited as *UAMM;* and Baroness Orczy, *The Man in the Corner* (1909; reprint, New York: International Polygonics Ltd., 1977).

9. Chesterton, "The Crime of the Communist," *The Scandal,* 118.

10. Chesterton, "The Blue Cross," *The Innocence,* 24–25.

11. E.g., prejudices against Jews, foreigners, Asians, and inhabitants of the Mediterranean countries.

12. *Puritan Pleasures,* 89–116, 240–41.

13. Ibid., 91, includes the first quote. See Chesterton, "The Queer Feet," *The Innocence,* 61, for the second quote.

14. E.g., Chesterton says that Valentin "was one of the great humanitarian French freethinkers; and the only thing wrong with them is that they make mercy even colder than justice." "The Secret Garden," *The Innocence,* 30.

15. Chesterton, "The Blue Cross," *The Innocence,* 24.

16. Ibid., 29.

17. *Puritan Pleasures,* 92–95.

18. Cf. Chesterton's "The Arrow of Heaven," *The Incredulity,* 41 and "The Man with Two Beards," *The Secret,* 53, in which Father Brown tackles wealthy industrialists. And cf. "The Resurrection of Father Brown," *The Incredulity,* in which the priest recognizes the claims of the poor.

19. Chesterton, "The Flying Stars," *The Innocence,* 77.

20. Ibid., 80.

21. *Puritan Pleasures,* 95.

22. Ibid., 113.

23. Ibid., 91.

24. Ibid., 113.

25. Chesterton, "The Secret of Father Brown," *The Secret,* 11.

26. Routley, *Puritan Pleasures,* 93.

27. Ibid., 113.

28. Cf. *Detectionary* by Otto Penzler et al., eds. (1971; reprint, New York: Ballantine Books, 1980), 3.

29. Post, "The Angel of the Lord," *UAMM*, 41.

30. Post, "The Straw Man," *UAMM*, 171.

31. For Abner's thoughts on predestination, see *UAMM*, 63 and 190–92.

32. Post, "The Adopted Daughter," *UAMM*, 236.

33. Post, "The Doomdorf Mystery," *UAMM*, 13–25.

34. Post, "The House of the Dead Man," *UAMM*, 90.

35. Post, "The Tenth Commandment," *UAMM*, 124.

36. Cf. "Doomdorf Mystery," "House of the Dead Man," "The Devil's Tools," and "The Hidden Law," all in Post's *UAMM*.

37. Post, "Tenth Commandment," 125. Cf. Ps. 15.2 and 37.31; also Jer. 31.33.

38. Post, "A Twilight Adventure," *UAMM*, 95–106.

39. "Doomdorf Mystery," 25.

40. Post, "The Wrong Hand," *UAMM*, 31.

41. Abner helps these victims—a slave woman: "Devil's Tools," 131–143; poor immigrants: "Doomdorf Mystery," 13–25 and "An Act of God," 57–68. And Abner renounces possessions in "Wrong Hand," 33–35. All stories are found in *UAMM*.

42. Cf. the use made of the stories of David and Uriah the Hittite (2 Sam. 11.1–12.9) in "Tenth Commandment," 123–130; Naboth and his vineyard (1 Kings 21,1–15) in "Naboth's Vineyard," 239–52; Ruth (Ruth 2) in "The Age of Miracles," 107; Cain (Gen. 4) in "Wrong Hand," 31. Cf. also "An Act of God," 59. Abner's protest against the slaughter of Indians can be found in "Tenth Commandment," 127. All Abner stories are found in *UAMM*.

43. Abner discounts supernatural phenomena in "Angel of the Lord," 49–55. But the possibility of God's intervention through human agents is shown in "Age of Miracles," 107–18.

44. Post, "Straw Man," 179 and 175–76.

45. Post, "The Edge of the Shadow," *UAMM*, 216. (Cf. Ps. 111.10; Prov, 1.7 and 9.10.)

46. Cf. 239–252 in *UAMM*. Cf. 1 Kings 21.1–15. The quotation is found on pages 247–48.

47. For details regarding the publication of "the man in the corner" stories, cf. the introduction by Burke N. Hare to the International Polygonics edition of *Man in the Corner*, cited previously. These stories first appeared in the *Royal Magazine* of London in 1901 but were not produced in book form

until 1909, although a second series of stories, *The Case of Miss Elliott,* was published in England somewhat precipitately in 1905.

48. Hare, introduction to *Man in the Corner,* n.p.

49. The man in the corner remarks on one occasion, "I suppose there is some truth in the saying that Providence watches over bankrupts, kittens, and lawyers." "The De Genneville Peerage," *Man in the Corner,* 270. Providence is spoken of as punitive in "The Motive," 260 of the same work.

50. See "A Night's Adventure," 49, and "The Edinburgh Mystery," 140, in *Man in the Corner.*

51. Orczy, "The Fenchurch Street Mystery," *Man in the Corner,* 3.

52. Orczy, "The Dublin Mystery," *Man in the Corner,* 192.

53. Cf. "Fenchurch Street Mystery," 5–10.

54. Orczy, "The Mysterious Death in Percy Street," *Man in the Corner,* 296–301.

55. Arthur Morrison, "The Lenton Croft Robberies," *Best Martin Hewitt Detective Stories,* ed. by E. F. Bleiler (New York: Dover, 1976) 14.

56. R. Austin Freeman (1862–1943) trained as a pharmacist and then qualified as a surgeon at the Middlesex Hospital Medical College, London, but he had not the necessary capital to put up his plate in General Practice. He therefore joined the British Colonial Service and served on the Gold Coast (Ghana), only to return to England after a few years for health reasons. He continued his medical career in various salaried appointments, and Freeman's training provided the basic material for Dr. Thorndyke's cases. Freeman's scientific bent also gave him the opportunity to test the evidence presented in his stories. Cf. E. F. Bleiler's introduction to *The Best Dr. Thorndyke Detective Stories,* ed. E. F. Bleiler (New York: Dover, 1973), v–ix.

57. Freeman, "The Case of Oscar Brodski," *Best Dr. Thorndyke Detective Stories,* 41.

58. Cf. Michele Slung, ed., *Crime on Her Mind* (New York: Pantheon Books, 1975), 357–77. It has been pointed out that Anna Katharine Green's *Leavenworth Case* appeared almost a decade before Sherlock Holmes, see Slung, ed., *Crime on Her Mind,* 152. And the female sleuth has continued to appear

during the latter part of this century: e.g., Cordelia Gray, Kate Fansler, Sarah Kelling Bittersohn, V. I. Warshawski, and many more.

59.   Ernest Bramah, *Best Max Carrados Detective Stories*, ed. E. F. Bleiler (New York: Dover, 1972).

60.   Bramah, "The Ghost at Massingham Mansions," *Best Max Carrados*, 168–69.

61.   Poking fun at snobberies: "The Last Exploit of Harry the Actor," 196; and awareness of prejudices and problems: "The Knight's Cross Signal Problem," 29, 35–36. Both stories are included in Bramah's *Best Max Carrados*.

62.   Bramah, "Last Exploit of Harry the Actor," 219–20.

63.   Criticism of the sensationalism: "The Vanished Petition Crown," 46–47; criticism of Christian Science: "The Disappearance of Marie Severe," 107–10; and criticism of capital punishment: "The Poisoned Dish of Mushrooms," 130, in Bramah's *Best Max Carrados*.

64.   Bramah, "The Ingenious Mr. Spinola," *Best Max Carrados*, 221–44.

65.   Bramah, "Disappearance of Marie Severe," 96.

66.   "The Holloway Flat Tragedy," *Best Max Carrados*, 89.

3. The Gilded Cage: The English Country-House Murder

1.   J. B. Priestley, *Literature and Western Man* (New York: Harper & Brothers, 1960), 224.

2.   Dorothy L. Sayers, *Murder Must Advertise* (London: Gollancz, 1933), 8–9.

3.   Cf. the figure of Captain George Fentiman in Dorothy L. Sayers, *The Unpleasantness at the Bellona Club* (1928; reprint, New York: Avon Books, 1963).

4.   A *batman* is a personal valet to an officer in the British army and has nothing to do with Marvel comics.

5.   Nicholas Blake, *Thou Shell of Death* (New York: Harper & Brothers, 1936).

6.   Nancy Blue Wynne, ed., *An Agatha Christie Chronology* (New York: Ace Books, 1976), 13, 23.

7.   The play portrays the typical guest house of the early 1950s when it first appeared; G. C. Ramsey pointed out that

detective fiction can be read as social history; cf. chapter 3 "Mystery Writers as Social Historians" in his *Agatha Christie: Mistress of Mystery* (New York: Dodd, Mead & Co., 1967).

8. Agatha Christie, *Ten Little Niggers* (London: Collins, 1939). It was published in America as *Ten Little Indians* and as *And Then There Were None*.

9. Agatha Christie, *Ten Little Niggers*, 189.

10. Ibid., 181.

11. For additional information, see chapter 10.

12. American title, *Murder at Hazelmoor*.

13. Agatha Christie, *Murder at the Vicarage* (1930), reprinted with *Sleeping Murder*, (New York: Dodd, Mead & Co., 1976), 200.

14. Christie, *Murder at the Vicarage*, 364; cf. 372.

15. Ibid., 248.

16. Ibid., 262–63.

17. Ibid., 363.

18. Ibid., 241–42.

19. Ibid., 252.

20. Patricia Wentworth, *Miss Silver Comes to Stay* (1948; reprint, New York: Bantam, 1983), 105.

21. Title in England: *The Crime at Black Dudley* (1929; reprint, New York: Manor Books, 1962).

22. Margery Allingham, *A Cargo of Eagles* (New York: William Morrow, 1968).

23. Margery Allingham, *Mystery Mile* (1930; reprint, New York: Manor Books, 1963).

24. Margery Allingham, *Black Plumes* (1940; reprint, New York: Manor Books, 1975).

25. Catherine Aird, *The Stately Home Murder* (1970; reprint, New York: Bantam, 1980).

26. A. A. Milne, *The Red House Mystery* (1922; reprint, New York: E. P. Dutton, 1928). Alexander Woollcott praised Milne's book and is cited by Raymond Chandler, "The Simple Art of Murder," in *Art of the Mystery Story*, ed. Haycraft, 226.

27. Milne, *Red House Mystery*, 91–92; cf. 20–21, 34, 59.

28. Ibid., 135, 139.

29. E. C. Bentley, *Trent's Last Case* (1913; reprint, London: Penguin, 1937). This comment is taken from *Bookman* [New

York], May 1913, and appears in Haycraft, ed., *Art of the Mystery Story*, 381.

30.   Cf. the articles by Willard Huntington Wright, Dorothy L. Sayers, Lee Wright, John Carter, Harrison R. Steeves, and Philip Van Doren Stern in Haycraft, ed., *Art of the Mystery Story*.

31.   Cf. the articles by Knox, Chandler, and Thomson, in Haycraft, ed., *Art of the Mystery Story*.

32.   E. C. Bentley, *Those Days* (London: Constable, 1940) 254, as cited by Routley, *Puritan Pleasures*, 120, and Symons, *Mortal Consequences*, 93.

33.   Bentley, *Trent's Last Case*, 204–5, 104–5

34.   Ibid., 132–33, 118.

35.   Ibid., 52.

36.   Ibid., 48.

37.   Ibid., 244.

38.   Ibid., 38, 23.

39.   Ibid., 27.

40.   Ibid., 103–4.

41.   In Bentley's *Trent's Last Case*, comments on how industry treated labor: 11, 121; on American lynch laws: 187; on the pride of being an American Indian: 203–4; and considerations on being a billionaire: 47. Cf. Chesterton, "The Flying Stars," *The Innocence*, 93.

42.   Sayers, *Murder Must Advertise*, 186–87.

43.   *Trent's Last Case*, 249.

44.   Dorothy L. Sayers, *Clouds of Witness* (London: Gollancz, 1926.)

45.   Leo Bruce, *Case for Three Detectives* (1936; reprint, Hornchurch, Eng.: Ian Henry Publications Ltd., 1975).

46.   Ibid., 75.

47.   Ibid., 36. The reference was to the Western brothers, a popular cabaret and radio act in which Jack and Claude Hulbert spoofed Britain's "old boy" network.

48.   Ibid., 171, 176.

49.   Ibid., 64.

50.   Ibid., 96, 99.

51.   Ibid., 11, 59.

52.   Ibid., 59.

53. Ibid., 73.

54. Ibid., 81.

55. Ibid., 113–14.

56. Ibid., 114.

57. Ibid., 225.

58. Ibid., 240.

4. Shadows of Change: Dorothy L. Sayers, among Others

1. Janet Hitchman, *Such a Strange Lady: A Biography of Dorothy L. Sayers* (New York: Harper & Row, 1975), 37.

2. Dorothy L. Sayers, *The Whimsical Christian* (1969; reprint, New York: Macmillan, 1978), 36.

3. Ralph E. Hone, *Dorothy L. Sayers: A Literary Biography* (Kent, Ohio: Kent State Univ. Press, 1979), 40.

4. Ibid., 41.

5. Hitchman, *Such a Strange Lady,* 41.

6. Hone, *Sayers,* 42.

7. Dorothy L. Sayers, *The Mind of the Maker* (London: Methuen, 1941), 50.

8. Ibid., 61–62.

9. Ibid., 62.

10. *Murder Must Advertise,* 186–87.

11. *The Nine Tailors* (London: Gollancz, 1934), 10.

12. Gladys Mitchell, *The Saltmarsh Murders* (1932; reprint, London: Hogarth, 1984), 7.

13. Ibid., 125, 117.

14. Ibid., 128.

15. Ibid., 196, 127.

16. Ibid., 154, 185.

17. Ibid., 47.

18. Ibid., 216, 274–75.

19. Romilly and Katherine John, *Death by Request* (1933; reprint, London: Hogarth, 1984).

20. Ibid., 8, 13.

21. Ibid., 51.

22. Ibid., 291.

23. Ibid., 47.

24. Ibid., 6.

5. Acquiring an English Accent: The British Import

1. John Dickson Carr, *The Mad Hatter Mystery* (1933; reprint, New York: Macmillan, 1984).

2. John Dickson Carr, *Dead Man's Knock* (New York: Harper & Brothers, 1958), 213.

3. Erle Stanley Gardner, *The Case of the Waylaid Wolf* (1959; reprint, New York: William Morrow, Pocket Books, 1962), 83.

4. Ibid., 212.

5. Symons, *Mortal Consequences*, 9.

6. Virginia Rich, *The Baked Bean Supper Murders* (New York: E. P. Dutton, Ballantine Books, 1984), 275.

7. Phoebe Atwood Taylor, *Out of Order* (1936; reprint, New York: Pyramid, 1971), 178, 184, 186.

8. Lange Lewis, *The Birthday Murder* (1945; reprint, New York: Perennial Library, 1980).

9. Ibid., 35.

10. Ibid.

11. Ibid., 186–95.

12. Mignon G. Eberhart, *R.S.V.P. Murder* (New York: Random House, 1965).

13. Hilda Lawrence, *Death of a Doll* (1947; reprint, New York: Penguin, 1982).

14. Otto Penzler et al., eds., *Detectionary*, 84.

15. E.g., these locales in Elizabeth Daly's works: Clayborn House in New York City, *Somewhere in the House* (1946; reprint, New York: Bantam, 1984); Stonehill, Vermont, *The Book of the Dead* (1944; reprint, New York: Rinehart, 1960); the Bradlock residence, *The Book of the Lion* (1951; reprint, New York: Bantam, 1985); a Connecticut cottage occupied by the Gamadges, *Evidence of Things Seen* (1943; reprint, New York: Rinehart, 1960); the house of Angela Duncannon, *Murders in Volume 2* (1941; reprint, New York: Rinehart, 1960); the New York City house belonging to John Ashbury, *The Wrong Way Down* (1946; reprint, New York: Bantam, 1983); the Fenway family mansion in New York City, *Arrow Pointing Nowhere* (1944; reprint, New York: Dell, 1972); Johnny Redfield's estate, *Any Shape or Form* (1945; reprint, New York:

Dell, 1981); the Dunbar residence in New York City, *And Dangerous to Know* (1949; reprint, New York: Dell, 1981). Although it does not concentrate on a single residence, *Night Walk* (1967; reprint, New York: Dell, 1982) continues the tradition by centering in the closed and somewhat feudal community in the village of Frazer's Mills.

16. Elizabeth Daly, *Book of the Lion*, book jacket.

17. S. S. Van Dine, *The Scarab Murder Case* (1930; reprint, New York: Scribner's, 1984), 141.

18. Ibid., 3, 13.

19. Ibid., 156. Cf. Vance's comment when he remarks that to send a man to the electric chair just because of a wrong reaction to being accused (due to hormone deficiency) "isn't cricket." S. S. Van Dine, *The Benson Murder Case* (1926; reprint, New York: Scribner's 1983), 124.

20. Van Dine, *Benson Murder Case*, 22.

21. Ibid., 91.

22. S. S. Van Dine, *The Bishop Murder Case* (1926; reprint, New York: Scribner's, 1983), 47.

23. Ibid., 225-38.

6. Creating an American Tradition: The Hard-boiled Maverick

1. Raymond Chandler, "The Simple Art of Murder" (first published in *Atlantic Monthly*, December 1944), revised for Haycraft, ed., *Art of the Mystery Story*, 222–37. The quotation is found on page 222.

2. J. O. Tate, "The Longest Goodbye: Raymond Chandler and the Poetry of Alcohol," *TAD* 18 (Fall 1985): 392–406. Tate pointed out that Chandler himself attended an English public school and was something of an Anglophile: he loved many English things and was addicted to a typically British cocktail, the gimlet (gin and Rose's lime juice). Furthermore, Philip Marlowe, his P.I. hero, "expresses a profound ambivalence between English good manners and an American vernacular."

3. Raymond Chandler, "Simple Art of Murder," 236–37.

4. Sara Paretsky, *Deadlock* (1984; reprint, New York: Ballantine Books, 1985), 112.

5. Nelson, *Your God Is Alive and Well*, 17.

6. Ibid., 17–18.

7.   Ibid., 163.

8.   Chandler, "Simple Art of Murder," 237.

9.   Dashiell Hammett, *The Maltese Falcon* (1929; reprint, New York: Vintage Books, 1972).

10.   Ibid., 29.

11.   Ibid., 39, for Spade's comment on miracles. Later he relieves Joel Cairo of his weaponry on two occasions. See pages 46–47, 71–72.

12.   Ibid., 111.

13.   Ibid., 115.

14.   Ibid., 34.

15.   See Dashiell Hammett, *The Glass Key* (1931; reprint, London: Pan Books, 1975) and *The Continental Op* (1923; reprint, London: Pan Books, 1980).

16.   The Continental Op recognizes the threat represented by Creda Dexter in "The Tenth Clew" and by Elvira in "The House in Turk Street." He also recognizes that Smith ("The Tenth Clew") has been tipped off regarding his profession as detective. See *The Continental Op*, 45.

17.   Ibid., 46–47.

18.   Cf. Ibid., 45.

19.   Raymond Chandler, *The Little Sister* (1949; reprint, London: Pan Books, 1978), 5.

20.   Moose Molloy is described in Raymond Chandler, *Farewell, My Lovely* (1940; reprint, Harmondsworth, Eng.: Penguin, 1982), 7.

21.   Raymond Chandler, *The Big Sleep* (1939; reprint, London: Hamish Hamilton, 1984), 176.

22.   Ibid., 12.

23.   Ibid., 123, 190.

24.   Ibid., 132.

25.   Ibid., 170.

26.   Ibid., 186.

27.   Nelson, *Your God Is Alive and Well*, 170.

28.   John D. MacDonald, *The Scarlet Ruse* (Greenwich, Conn.: Fawcett, 1973), 114–15.

29.   Ibid., 169.

30.   Ibid., 170–71.

31.   John D. MacDonald, *Pale Grey for Guilt* (Philadelphia: Lippincott, 1968), 137–38.

32. Ibid., 170.

33. Ibid., 47, 82.

34. John D. MacDonald, *One More Sunday* (1984; reprint, New York: Fawcett Crest, 1985). The dedication in this book also reveals MacDonald's Puritan roots.

35. Ross Macdonald, *The Goodbye Look* (New York: Knopf, 1969), 127.

36. The name of Christ as an oath: Robert B. Parker *Mortal Stakes* (Boston: Houghton Mifflin, 1975), 6, 11, 34, 43, 49, 100, 122, 128, 129, 138, 140, 145, 166. Christ as a contemporary: "Did you have to look funny to be saved? If Christ were around today He'd probably be wearing a chambray shirt and flared slacks," 161.

37. Ibid., 168–72.

38. Ibid., 170.

39. Ibid., 172.

40. Nelson, *Your God is Alive and Well*, 170.

41. See Symons, *Mortal Consequences*, 10.

42. Richard Hofstadter, *Anti-intellectualism in American Life* (New York: Random House, 1962).

43. Hammett, *Maltese Falcon*, 43, 51, 199.

44. Ibid., 226.

45. Frederick Isaac, "The Changing Face of Evil in the Hard-Boiled Novel," *TAD* 16 (Summer 1983): 241–47.

46. Ibid., 247.

47. Ibid.

7. Change and Decay

1. *Puritan Pleasures*, 223.

2. Ibid., 222.

3. One could cite in support not only the constant reappearance of classical writers like Dorothy L. Sayers and Agatha Christie on the newsstands but also the popularity of detective writers who chose crime settings from periods of history when the religious and theological standards could be assumed, e.g., the medieval settings used by Ellis Peters, or by Umberto Eco in *The Name of the Rose*, and the Victorian settings used by Peter Lovesey and Anne Perry. It is also worth mentioning in this respect, Van Gulik's "Judge Dee" stories set in Imperial China.

4. First published in the 1920s, some of the stories were republished in Arthur Train, *Mr. Tutt at His Best* (New York: Scribner's, 1961). The republication may have been in part inspired by the appropriateness of the Tutts' attitude to American society as it was developing in the 1960s and 1970s. So Samuel Tutt observes to Ephraim Tutt, "I guess you're right, Mr. Tutt. Christianity and the Golden Rule are all right in the upper social circles, but off Fifth Avenue there's the same sort of struggle for existence that goes on in the animal world. A man may be all sweetness and light to his wife and children and go to church on Sundays; he may play pretty fair with his own gang; but, outside of his home and social circle, be a ravening wolf," 32.

5. Written under the pseudonym Cameron McCabe, *The Face on the Cutting-Room Floor* (1937; reprint, Harmondsworth, Eng.: Penguin, 1986).

6. Ibid., 143; cf. 204–5.

7. Ibid., 232–36. Cf. also 195.

8. Ibid., 198, 201.

9. Ibid., 204.

10. Ibid., 213–17. This passage contains a fine discussion of the detective story as illustrative of the human confusion.

11. Ngaio Marsh, *Dead Water* (1963; reprint, New York: Berkeley, 1978), 123–24.

12. Ibid., 152.

13. Ngaio Marsh was a New Zealander, and New Zealand abolished the death penalty in 1941. It was reinstituted in 1950 and abolished again in 1961.

14. Poul Ørum, *Scapegoat* (first published as *The Whipping Boy*), trans. Kenneth Barclay (New York: Pantheon Books, 1975).

15. Pierre Audemars, *Slay Me a Sinner* (New York: Walker & Co., 1980), 168.

16. Ibid., 170.

17. Janwillem Van de Wetering, *Outsider in Amsterdam* (Boston: Houghton Mifflin, 1975).

18. Ibid., 123–24.

19. Ibid., 148–49.

20. Ibid., 245.

21. Friedrich Dürrenmatt, *Die Panne* (Zürich: Arche Ver-

lag, A.G., 1956). English translation by Richard and Clara Winston, *Traps* (New York: Knopf, 1960). Also published in a revised British edition, "A Dangerous Game," in *The Novels of Friedrich Dürrenmatt*, (1960; reprint, London: Picador, 1985), 275–320, hereafter cited as *The Novels*. The quote is from *Traps*, 7. Cf. "A Dangerous Game," 279.

22.   Dürrenmatt, *Traps*, 8. Cf. "A Dangerous Game," 279.

23.   *Traps*, 5.

24.   Ibid., 8.

25.   Ibid., 98. Cf. "A Dangerous Game," 316–18.

26.   *Traps*, 19. Cf. "A Dangerous Game," 285.

27.   *Traps*, 100–101. Cf. "A Dangerous Game," 315–16.

28.   Friedrich Dürrenmatt, *Der Richter und sein Henker* (Zürich: Benziger Verlag, 1952). English translation by Therese Pol, *The Judge and His Hangman* (New York: Harper & Brothers, 1955; Berkeley, 1958). Also published in a revised edition in *The Novels*, 7–81.

29.   Dürrenmatt, *Judge and His Hangman*, Berkeley ed., 37.

30.   Ibid., 77–78.

31.   Ibid., 96. Cf. *The Novels*, 57.

32.   Dürrenmatt, *Judge and His Hangman*, Berkeley ed., 102, 128–43.

33.   Ibid., 143, 83.

34.   Ibid., 74.

35.   Yves Jacquemard and Jean-Michel Sénécal, *The Body Vanishes* (New York: Dodd, Mead & Co., 1980). Originally published as *Le crime de la maison Grün*.

36.   Anthony Gilbert, *The Looking Glass Murder* (New York: Random House, 1966), 15.

37.   Ibid., 7.

38.   Ibid., 122.

39.   P. D. James, *A Taste for Death* (London: Faber & Faber, 1986), 295.

40.   Josephine Tey, *A Shilling for Candles* (1936; reprint, New York: Berkeley Medallion, 1972).

41.   Namely the film industry: Tey, *A Shilling for Candles*, 26–29; and the press: Ibid., 179.

42.   In Tey's *Shilling for Candles*, see criticism of contemporary culture: 87, 232; criticism of influence of the privileged: 83; and recognition of an unjust world: 152.

43. Amanda Cross, *The Theban Mysteries* (New York: Knopf, 1971), 25.

44. Ibid., 73. In Sophocles' *Antigone*, Tiresias is the Theban prophet who was blinded by Juno but given the gift of infallible prophecy. Even though the prophet must be led around by a young boy, his ability to foretell the truth is awesome.

45. Cross, *Theban Mysteries*, 75.

46. Ibid., 96–98.

47. John Buxton Hilton, *Hangman's Tide* (New York: St. Martin's Press, 1975), 62.

48. Hugh Pentecost, *Death after Breakfast* (New York: Dodd, Mead & Co., 1977), 143.

49. Ibid., 145.

50. John R. L. Anderson, *Death in the North Sea* (1975; reprint, New York: Stein & Day, 1976), 188.

51. Ibid., 190–91.

52. Desmond Cory, *The Circe Complex* (Garden City, N. Y.: Doubleday, 1975), 30.

53. Ibid., 38.

54. Ibid., 8.

55. Ibid., 50–51.

56. Ibid., 151.

57. Cf. Desmond Cory, *A Bit of a Shunt up the River* (Garden City, N.Y.: Doubleday, 1974).

8. The Different Faces of Realism

1. See my chapter 6, section I.

2. Robert Barnard [R. B. Martin], *Death in a Cold Climate* (New York: Scribner's, 1980).

3. Ibid., 80–81.

4. Simon Brett, *A Comedian Dies* (New York: Scribner's, 1979), 111–12.

5. Ibid., 89.

6. Elizabeth Foote-Smith, *Never Say Die* (New York: G. P. Putnam, 1977), 30.

7. In Foote-Smith's *Never Say Die*, there are superfluous four-letter words: 34, 68, 79, 80, 111, 122, 123, 124, etc.; see also trendy concepts: 68–70. 73–75, 80, 81, 92–93, 97, 99, 111–12, 119–20, 124–25.

8. Leo Rosten, *King Silky* (New York: Harper & Row, 1980), 361.

9. A. B. Guthrie, *No Second Wind* (Boston: Houghton Mifflin, 1980). This story contains some snide comments about religion and the clergy. Cf. ibid., 189, 193. Quote is from page 149.

10. Kenneth Giles, *A File on Death* (New York: Walker & Co., 1973), 152.

11. Cf. Peter Dickinson, *The Old English Peep Show* (New York: Harper & Row, 1969); *The Green Gene* (New York: Pantheon Books, 1973). Peter Dickinson seems to be intrigued by the relationship of different cultures to each other. Compare his treatment of the New Guinea culture in London: *The Glass-sided Ants' Nest* (New York: Harper & Row, 1968); his confrontation of Saxons and Celts in Britain: *The Green Gene*; his treatment of a Baltic exiled government in London: *The Lively Dead* (New York: Pantheon, 1975).

Cf. Colin Watson, *Lonely Heart 4122* (New York: G. P. Putnam, 1967), which announces the arrival of Miss Lucille Edith Cavell Teatime in the little market town of Flaxborough; *Charity Ends at Home* (New York: Dell, 1968); *Just What the Doctor Ordered* (New York: G. P. Putnam, 1969); *Six Nuns and a Shotgun* (New York: G. P. Putnam, 1974).

12. Robert Barnard, *Blood Brotherhood* (1978; reprint, Harmondsworth, Eng.: Penguin, 1983). Another book that contains no likable characters and goes beyond realism is Robert Barnard's story of an Australian university, *Death of an Old Goat* (1977; reprint, Harmondsworth, Eng.: Penguin, 1983). It turns ultimately not on the deductions of the detectives but on a piece of general knowledge known to any Oxford University freshman.

13. Barnard, *Blood Brotherhood*, 156.

14. Cf. Donald E. Westlake, *The Busy Body* (New York: Charter, 1966); *God Save the Mark* (New York: Random House, 1967); *Who Stole Sassi Manoon?* (New York: Random House, 1968); *The Hot Rock* (New York: Simon & Schuster, 1970); *Bank Shot* (New York: Simon & Schuster, 1972); *Jimmy the Kid* (New York: Evans & Co., 1974); *Brother's Keepers* (New York: Evans & Co., 1975).

15.   Donald E. Westlake, *Enough* (New York: Evans & Co., 1977); *Too Much!* (New York: Evans & Co., 1975).

16.   Lionel Black, *Ransom for a Nude* (New York: Stein & Day, 1972), 190.

17.   Ibid., 60.

18.   Lucille Kallen, *Introducing C. B. Greenfield* (1979; reprint, New York: Ballantine Books, 1980), 74.

19.   Ruth Rendell, *An Unkindness of Ravens* (1985; reprint, London: Arrow Books, 1986), 235.

20.   Ed McBain [Evan Hunter], *Hail, Hail, the Gang's All Here!* in *Three From the 87th* (Garden City, N.Y.: Doubleday, 1971).

21.   Ibid., 7.

22.   Joe Gores, *File #1: The Mayfield Case*, in *Boucher's Choicest*, ed. Bernkopf.

23.   Ibid., 68.

24.   Lesley Egan, *Paper Chase* (New York: Harper & Row, 1972), 135.

25.   Sue Grafton, *"A" Is for Alibi* (1982; reprint, New York: New American Library, 1984), 30.

26.   Chandler, *The Big Sleep*, 170, quoted in chapter 6 of the present work. Cf. Grafton's *"A" Is for Alibi*, 170, 136.

27.   Dell Shannon, *Root of All Evil* (New York: William Morrow, 1964), 223. Ruth Rendell, *An Unkindness of Ravens*, 215.

28.   William McIlvanney, *The Papers of Tony Veitch* (New York: Pantheon, 1983).

29.   Ibid., 243.

30.   Ibid., 37.

31.   Ibid., 51, 162.

32.   Ibid., 207, 238.

33.   Ibid., 243, 137–38.

34.   Ibid., 71, 210, 59.

35.   Ibid., 59. Cf. 193.

36.   Ibid., 161.

37.   Ibid., 37.

38.   Ibid., 37–38.

39.   Ibid., 36.

40.   Ibid., 163.

41. Ibid., 182.

42. Harvey Cox, "Religion in the Secular City; a Symposium," *Christianity and Crisis* (20 Feb. 1984): 35. My italics.

43. As quoted by Janet Hitchman in her introduction to Dorothy L. Sayers, *Striding Folly* (Sevenoaks, Eng.: New English Library, 1985), 28.

44. Upfield, *Death of a Swagman*, 131.

9. Realism Turns to Religion

1. Jane Dentinger, *First Hit of the Season* (New York: Dell, 1984), 73.

2. Ibid., 37, 88.

3. E.g., Ralph McInerny, *Her Death of Cold* (New York: Viking, 1977), 112; Leonard Holton, *Out of the Depths* (New York: Dodd, Mead & Co. 1966).

4. Lawrence Sanders, *The Second Deadly Sin* (New York: G. P. Putnam, 1977), 256–57.

5. Ibid., 11.

6. Ibid., 40–41.

7. Ibid., 66.

8. Ibid., 134.

9. Ibid., 295.

10. Holton, *Out of the Depths*, 23.

11. Ibid., 43–44.

12. James Fraser, *Deadly Nightshade* (New York: Harcourt, Brace & World, 1970), 84–85.

13. Ibid., 185.

14. Cf. William Bradley, "The Ethics of James Bond," 35–46.

15. Peter Dickinson, *The Lively Dead*, 192.

16. Ibid., 88.

17. Ibid., 127–28.

18. Cf. the article by William A. S. Sarjeant, "Obsequies about Oxford: The Investigations and Eccentricities of Gervase Fen," *TAD* 14 (Summer 1981): 196–209.

19. Edmund Crispin, *Frequent Hearses* (1950; reprint, Harmondsworth, Eng.: Penguin, 1982), 48.

20. Sarjeant, "Obsequies about Oxford," 202.

21. Ibid., 204.

22. W. J. Burley, *Wycliffe's Wild Goose Chase* (Garden City, N.Y.: Doubleday, 1982), 12.

23. Elizabeth Lemarchand, *Nothing To Do with the Case* (New York: Walker & Co., 1981), 122.

24. Michael Innes, *Appleby's Other Story* (New York: Dodd, Mead & Co., 1974), 113.

25. Lemarchand, *Nothing to Do with the Case*, 48–49.

26. David L. Lindsey, *Heat from Another Sun* (New York: Harper & Row, 1984).

27. Ibid., 25.

28. David Lindsey in an interview reported in "Works in Progress," *Bookstop Shopper* (an occasional publication of the Bookstop, a bookstore in Austin, Texas), n.d. [1984?].

29. Lindsey, *Heat from Another Sun*, 296.

30. Peter Alding, *Ransom Town* (New York: Walker & Co., 1983), 60.

31. Cory, *The Circe Complex*, 223–26, and *A Bit of a Shunt up the River*.

32. *A Bit of a Shunt Up the River*, 15.

33. Cf. ibid., 117.

34. Ibid., 176.

35. Ibid., 177–78.

36. Cf. ibid., 187.

37. Lord C. P. Snow, quoted from John C. Carr, *The Craft of Crime: Conversations with Crime Writers* (Boston: Houghton Mifflin, 1983), 176. The quote first appeared in *Financial Times* of London, May 1970.

38. Mary Jane Latsis and Martha Henissart, quoted in Carr's *Craft of Crime*, 176–201. See particularly 184–89.

39. Carr, *Craft of Crime*, 176–77.

40. Ibid., 197.

41. Emma Lathen, *Double, Double, Oil and Trouble* (London: Gollancz, 1979), 7.

42. Emma Lathen, *Sweet and Low* (1974; reprint, New York: Pocket Books, 1975), 7–8.

43. Emma Lathen, *Ashes to Ashes* (1971; reprint, New York: Pocket Books, 1972), 97.

44. Ibid.

45. Michael N. Stanton, "Dick Francis: The Worth of Human Love," *TAD* 15 (1982): 137–43.

46. Carr, *Craft of Crime*, 204.

47. Ibid., 205.

48. Stanton, "Dick Francis," 140.

49. Carr, *Craft of Crime*, 204–5.

50. Stanton, "Dick Francis," 139.

51. Dick Francis, *High Stakes* (1975; reprint, New York: Pocket Books, 1977), 99.

52. Dick Francis, *Nerve* (New York: Harper & Row, 1964).

53. Stanton, "Dick Francis," 142.

54. Ibid., 143.

55. John Braine, quoted on the book jacket of James' *Taste for Death*.

56. P. D. James, *The Skull beneath the Skin* (New York: Scribner's, 1982), 86–87.

57. Ibid., 106.

58. P. D. James, *An Unsuitable Job for a Woman* (1972; reprint, New York: Popular Library, n.d.), 13.

59. Ibid., 15.

60. Ibid., 247.

61. P. D. James, *Death of an Expert Witness* (New York: Popular Library, 1977), 251–52.

62. P. D. James, *The Black Tower* (New York: Popular Library, 1976), 97.

63. James, *The Skull*, 110, 46.

64. James, *Black Tower*, 39–40.

65. P. D. James, *Innocent Blood* (New York: Scribner's, 1980), 67.

66. James, *Black Tower*, 45–46.

67. Ibid., 238–39.

68. Ibid., 41.

69. Ibid., 42.

70. *The Skull*, 107.

71. Ibid., 110.

72. *Black Tower*, 263.

73. *Death of an Expert Witness*, 97.

74. *Innocent Blood*, 70.

75. *Black Tower*, 61.

76. *A Taste for Death*, cf. 33, 38.

77. Ibid., 87; cf. 385, 447–48.

78. Ibid., 105–6.

79.   Cf. ibid., 183, 189, 249, 332–33.

80.   Cf. ibid., 267, 275, 284.

81.   Ibid., 295.

82.   Ibid., 335–36.

83.   Ibid., 345.

84.   Ibid., 351.

85.   Ibid., 454.

86.   Ibid., 403.

10. Illustration of the Theme: The Agatha Christie Pilgrimage

1.   As announced in the *Austin American-Statesman*, 28 November 1986. It was still running as of August 1990, after 38 years and more than 15,684 performances.

2.   Dorothy B. Hughes, "The Christie Nobody Knew," in *Agatha Christie: First Lady of Crime*, ed. H. R. F. Keating (New York: Holt, Rinehart and Winston, 1977), 128.

3.   Agatha Christie, quoted by H. R. F. Keating in "Hercule Poirot—a Companion Portrait," in Keating's *Agatha Christie*, 215.

4.   Agatha Christie, *Parker Pyne Investigates* (1934; reprint, Harmondsworth, Eng:, Penguin, 1953), 41.

5.   Joyce Egginton, "Grandma Christie," *News Chronicle* [London], Saturday, 31 October 1953.

6.   See "The Dream," 131–32, 154, and "Problem at Sea," 171–72, 178; in Agatha Christie, *The Regatta Mystery* (New York: Dodd, Mead & Co., 1939).

7.   Cf. "The Girl in the Train," in Agatha Christie, *The Golden Ball and Other Mysteries* (New York: Dodd Mead & Co., 1924).

8.   Christie, "The Dream," 130.

9.   Agatha Christie, *Three Act Tragedy* (London: Collins, 1935), 162 (American title: Murder in Three Acts).

10.   Agatha Christie, *A Pocket Full of Rye* (1953; reprint, London: Fontana Books, 1958), 191.

11.   Cf. Sherlock Holmes' comments in "The Five Orange Pips" and *A Study in Scarlet, CSH*, 1:224–25, 23.

12.   E.g., as in *One, Two, Buckle My Shoe* (American title: *The Patriotic Murders*).

13. E.g., *Nemesis* (New York: Dodd, Mead & Co., 1971) and *A Caribbean Mystery* (New York: Dodd, Mead & Co., 1965), 174.

14. "A Christmas Tragedy," in *The Thirteen Problems* (1932; reprint, London: Pan Books, 1961), 138 (American title: *The Tuesday Club Murders*).

15. The incident comes from *Come, Tell Me How You Live*, one of the few pieces of autobiography by Agatha Christie, in which she described what life was like on one of Sir Max Mallowan's archaeological digs. The book was begun before the war, finished in 1944, published in London by Collins in 1946, and republished in 1975. It describes expeditions that took place in 1935–36 and 1936–37, which were "uneasy years in England, with Hitler and Mussolini strutting before their troops in Europe." Cf. Michael Gilbert, "A Very English Lady," in *Agatha Christie*, ed. Keating, 66–69.

16. Agatha Christie, *The Moving Finger* (1943; reprint, London: Pan Books, 1950), 73.

17. Ibid., 41.

18. Ibid., 50. Mrs. Dane Calthrop reappears in Agatha Christie, *The Pale Horse* (London: Collins, 1961).

19. Christie, *Moving Finger*, 52.

20. Cf. Routley, *Puritan Pleasures*, 134–37.

21. Winks, ed., *Detective Fiction*, 215.

22. Colin Watson, "The Message of Mayhem Parva," in Keating's *Agatha Christie*, 106.

23. Julian Symons, "The Mistress of Complication," in Keating's *Agatha Christie*, 34.

24. Agatha Christie, *The Clocks* (1963; reprint, New York: Pocket Books, 1965), 116–19.

25. Wynne, ed., *An Agatha Christie Chronology*, 177.

26. Cf. Agatha Christie, *Pale Horse*.

27. Cf. Eph. 6.12.

28. Wynne, ed., *An Agatha Christie Chronology*, 135.

29. Agatha Christie, *Postern of Fate* (London: Collins, 1973), 194.

30. Cf. Agatha Christie, *At Bertram's Hotel* (1965; reprint, New York: Pocket Books, 1967), 179–80.

31. Cf. Agatha Christie, *The Third Girl* (London: Collins, 1966).

32. Agatha Christie, *Ordeal by Innocence* (London: Collins, 1958).

33. It is possible that this title came from Georgia Harkness' hymn that begins "Hope of the world, Thou Christ of great compassion." The third verse reads:

> *Hope of the world, afoot on dusty highways,*
> *Showing to wandering souls the path of light;*
> *Walk Thou beside us lest the tempting byways*
> *Lure us away from Thee to endless night.*

34. Agatha Christie, *Endless Night* (1967; reprint, Roslyn, N.Y.: Detective Book Club, 1968), 185.

11. Verdict and Sentence: Sherlock Redivivus?

1. Cf. an interview reported in the *Listener* [London], 11 October 1984, 17.

2. C. H. B. Kitchin, *Death of His Uncle* (1939; reprint, New York: Perennial Library, 1984), 35.

3. Cf. Gilbert, *World of Mystery Fiction: A Guide*, 4. Erik Routley also noted the threatened demise of classical detective fiction and hinted at the reasons behind the skullduggery. But because he ignored the nonconforming school that was critical of society (and which began with Godwin), he was perhaps unduly pessimistic about the mystery of the missing corpse, *The Puritan Pleasures*, 221–23.

4. Arnold J. Toynbee, *A Study of History*, 6 vols. (London: Oxford Univ. Press, 1936–45).

5. Michael Innes, *Appleby Intervenes* (New York: Dodd, Mead & Co., 1965), 238.

6. Dashiell Hammett, *The Dain Curse*, in Dashiell Hammett, *Five Complete Novels* (New York: Avenel Books, 1980), 258.

7. Cf. Geoffrey Barraclough, "Art and Literature in the Contemporary World," in *Introduction to Contemporary History* (1964; reprint, Harmondsworth, Eng.: Penguin, 1967), 233–68.

8. Cf. Karen Haller, "We're off our rocker. It's official: Life has become truly stupid," *Austin American-Statesman*, 2 December 1986.

9. Symons, *Mortal Consequences*, 9.

10. Harry Kemelman, *Monday the Rabbi Took Off* (Greenwich, Conn.: Fawcett, 1973), 191. Cf. 136.

11. Elizabeth Linington, *No Evil Angel* (New York: Harper & Row, 1964), 145.

12. Josephine Tey, *The Franchise Affair* (1948), in *Three by Tey* (New York: Macmillan, 1954).

13. Tey was prophetic in expressing the popular radicalism of Toby Byrne, her mythical Bishop of Larborough, and in his use of a trendy journal, the *Watchman*, to publicize his views. See Tey, *Franchise Affair*, 138–39.

14. Ibid., 139.

15. Cf. Wood, *Passenger from Scotland Yard*, 211.

16. Alan Hunter, *Death on the Heath* (1981; reprint, New York: Dell, 1983), 157–58.

17. Peter Lovesey, "The Extremely Shady Past," in *Murder Ink*, rev. ed., ed. Dilys Winn, 95.

18. Catherine Aird, *Last Respects* (1982; reprint, New York: Bantam, 1984), 137. Cf. 136.

19. E.g., the stories of Brother Cadfael by Ellis Peters and the works of Umberto Eco and Van Gulik, as mentioned earlier in this work in the introduction and corresponding note 25, and chapter 7, note 3.

20. As well as works of Van Gulik, see Lillian de la Torre [Lillian Bueno McCue], *Dr. Sam Johnson, Detector* (New York: Knopf, 1946); the Bow Street Runners: Ragan Butler, *Captain Nash and the Wroth Inheritance* (New York: St. Martin's Press, 1976); the classical period of the 1930s and 1940s: James Anderson, *The Affair of the Bloodstained Egg Cosy* (New York: David McKay and Ives Washburn, 1975) and *The Affair of the Mutilated Mink Coat* (New York: Avon, 1981); Stuart Kaminsky, *Catch a Falling Clown*, (New York: St. Martin's Press, 1981); time of the British Raj in India: H. R. F. Keating, *The Murder of the Maharajah* (Garden City, N.Y.: Doubleday, 1980). Keating developed a later Indian setting for his Inspector Ghote series.

21. Particularly the work of Anne Perry and her character Charlotte Ellison Pitt; Teona Tone and her character Kyra

Keaton; and Anna Clarke with *The Lady in Black* (1978). The emphasis on women detectives may also be traced in Michele Slung, ed., *Crime On Her Mind.*

22. E.g., Peter Lovesey, *Waxwork* (1968; reprint, New York: Pantheon, 1978); *Wobble to Death* (London: Macmillan, 1970); *A Case of Spirits* (London: Macmillan, 1975); *Swing, Swing Together* (London: Macmillan, 1976); *Keystone* (New York: Pantheon, 1983). In *The False Inspector Dew* (New York: Pantheon, 1982), Lovesey shows himself just as adept in evoking the spirit of the early 1920s, during an Atlantic crossing on the *Mauretania* in 1921.

23. See Leo Bruce, *Case for Three Detectives.*

24. Nicholas Meyer, *The Seven-per-cent Solution* (New York: Ballantine Books, 1974).

25. H. Paul Jeffers, *The Adventure of the Stalwart Companions* (New York: Harper & Row, 1978).

26. Samuel Rosenberg, *Naked Is the Best Disguise* (New York: Penguin, 1973).

27. Robert Lee Hall, *Exit Sherlock Holmes: The Great Detective's Final Days* (New York: Scribner's, 1977).

28. Ibid., 83.

29. Led by hints given by Holmes and Moriarty themselves, Watson suspects the two are brothers. See Hall, *Exit Sherlock Holmes,* 6–7, 47. Also, see pages 166–67, where Wiggins suggests that Moriarty is Holmes' creation.

30. Ibid., 15–16.

31. Ibid., 16.

32. Ibid., 71, for questions about Holmes' past.

33. Ibid., 147, 188.

34. Cf. the popularity of Erich von Däniken, *Chariots of the Gods: Unsolved Mysteries of the Past,* trans. Michael Heron (New York: G. P. Putnam, 1970).

35. Margery Allingham, *Dancers in Mourning* (1937) in *Crime and Mr. Campion* (Garden City, N.Y.: Doubleday, 1937), 498.

36. Cf. J. B. Priestley, *Salt Is Leaving* (New York: Harper & Row, 1966), and even more pertinently, *It's an Old Country* (Boston: Little, Brown & Co., 1967).

37.   J. B. Priestley, *Literature and Western Man*, 445.

38.   Ibid., 444.

39.   Charles Dickens, *Martin Chuzzlewit* (1843–44; reprint, London: Penguin, English Library, 1985), 801.

40.   J. B. Priestley, *Literature and Western Man*, 445.

Index

Robert S. Paul was born in Walton-on-Thames, England, and after education at Oxford was ordained to the ministry of the Congregational Church at Leatherhead, in Surrey, where he remained for nine years. Later he spent four years working with the World Council of Churches in Switzerland, then went on to serve in the United States as professor of church history and Christian thought for twenty-nine years—in Hartford, Connecticut; Pittsburgh, Pennsylvania; and finally in Austin, Texas. He returned to retirement in his native Surrey in 1987.